A FORTUNE in your ATTIC

The publishers wish to express their sincere thanks to the following for
their kind help and assistance in the production of this volume:

ANNETTE CURTIS
JANICE MONCRIEFF
NICHOLA FAIRBURN
KAREN DOUGLASS
JOSEPHINE McLAREN
TANYA FAIRBAIRN
FRANK BURRELL
ROBERT NISBET

In appreciation of their thorough knowledge in this field a special thanks to

Paul Sheppard and Gwendoline Edwards
Border Bygones, The Valletts,
Forge Crossing, Lyonshall, Kington,
Herefordshire HR5 3JQ.

We are grateful to them for their involvement and assistance with text and the supply of original
material.

While every care has been taken in the compiling of information
contained in this volume the publishers cannot accept any liability for
loss, financial or otherwise, incurred by reliance placed on the
information herein.

ISBN 0-86248-053-1

Printed and bound by Clark Constable, Edinburgh.

A FORTUNE in your ATTIC

Time was, when it was comparatively easy to tell if an article was valuable, for it was either made of silver, encrusted with ormolu or incorporated Sevres plaques or precious stones — in other words it was fairly obvious to everyone it was worth a few bob.

But now, when a teddy bear sells for over £1,000, a weathervane depicting a leaping horse fetches £24,000 and a golf ball, circa 1840, sells for more than £2,000 it is amply demonstrated that the passing of the years gives many commonplace items not only a nostalgic fascination but in some cases a real monetary value.

It is a world governed by curious rules; rules which allow any and all to participate in the fascinating game of collecting at any chosen level from attractive yet inexpensive home furnishings to big money investment.

Rarity does not always herald instant wealth, for one of the most important rules of the game is supply and demand. The bigger the collecting field — the bigger the market therefore, the greater the chance of a rare item being fully appreciated — and that means money.

If nobody collected milk bottles then the earliest, a 19th century Thatcher Milk Protector, wouldn't be worth £150 and for the same reason a 1955 Dinky Vulcan bomber wouldn't be worth £1,200 and a Doulton jug of Winston Churchill wouldn't be worth £7,000.

The purpose of 'A Fortune in your Attic' is to take a detailed look at just the type of article that has been pushed under the stairs, stuck in the garage or stashed away in the loft, for with a little research and a bit of good luck you really could have A FORTUNE IN YOUR ATTIC.

Tony Curtis

ACKNOWLEDGEMENTS

Alpha Antiques, (J. J. Binns), High Street, Kington, Herefordshire. (Vanity Fair)
Anderson & Garland, Anderson House, Market Street, Newcastle.
The Antique Textile Co., 100 Portland Road, London W11 4LQ. (Costume)
Bearnes, Rainbow, Avenue Road, Torquay, Devon.
Yasha Beresiner, Inter Col, 1a Camden Walk, Islington Green, London. (Playing Cards)
Frank Bingham, The Stagg Inn, Titley, Herefordshire. (Brass)
Bonham's, Montpelier Galleries, Montpelier Street, London.
Brunel Curio's, (P. R. Ware), 29 Catherine Street, Frome, Somerset. (Tools)
Butler & Hatch Waterman, 86 High Street, Hythe, Kent.
Shirley Butler, Oddiquities, 61 Waldram Park Road, Forest Hill, London SE23. (Fire Irons & Fenders)
Capes, Dunn & Co, The Auction Galleries, 38 Charles Street, Manchester.
Carnforth Stamp Centre, (Peter Horrobin), 38 Market Street, Carnforth.
Chelsea Auction Galleries, Lots Road, Chelsea.
Christie's S. Kensington, 85 Old Brompton Road, London.
Christie's, 8 King Street, St. James, London.
Andrew C. Clark, 12 Ing Field, Oakenshaw, Bradford BD12 7EF. (Robots)
S. W. Cottee & Son, The Market, East Street, Wareham, Dorset.
Courts Miscellany, (George Court), 48 Bridge Street, Leominster. (Tins)
Cruso & Wilkin, 2 Northgate, Hunstanton, Norfolk.
Cubitt & West, Millmead, Guildford, Surrey.
Steven Currie, 12 Colebrooke Terrace, Kelvinbridge, Glasgow. (Beer Cans)
Dee & Atkinson, The Exchange, Driffield, Yorks.
Dickinson, Davy & Markham, 10 Wrawby Street, Brigg, S. Humberside.
Dreweatt, Watson & Barton, Donnington Priory, Newbury, Berks.
N. & A. Du Quesne Bird, Bartlett Street Antique Centre, Bath.
Bryn Edwards, 22 Ridgeway, Cardigan, Dyfed. (Beer Mats)
Gwendoline Edwards, Lyonshall. (Buttons)
Chris & Jackie Franklin, Pembridge, Herefordshire.
Christopher Frost, The Enchanted Aviary, 63 Hall Street, Long Melford, Suffolk. (Taxidermy)
Geering & Colyer, Highgate, Hawkhurst, Kent.
Andrew Grant, 59-60 Foregate Street, Worcester.
Ivy Grant, Seas-Gu-Daighean, Lymden Lane, Stonegate, Wadhurst, Sussex. (Miniature Bottles)
Michael C. German, 38B Kensington Church Street, London. (Walking Sticks)
Barry Griffiths, The Queens Head, Kington, Herefordshire. (Sporting)
John Hogbin & Son, 53 High Street, Tenterden, Kent.
Pauline Holliday, The Red Lion Inn, Pembridge, Herefordshire. (Horse Bits)
Kevin Holmes, Trench Enterprises, Three Cow Green, Bacton, Stowmarket, Suffolk. (Jigsaw Puzzles)
Paul Jones, Herefordshire Alternative Arts Centre, Pembridge. (Traps)
Kingsland Auction Services, Kingsland, Leominster.
N. J. Marchant Lane, Salters Cottage, Bramshott, Liphook, Hants. (Fishing Reels)
W. H. Lane & Son, Central Auction Rooms, Penzance, Cornwall.
Lawrence Fine Art, South Street, Crewkerne.
Min Lewis, Antiques, St. Davids Street, Presteigne, Powys. (Prams)
James & Lister Lea, 11 Newhall Street, Birmingham.
R. J. Lucibell, 7 Fontayne Avenue, Rainham, Essex. (Inhalers)
Iris Martin, (Lace & Lacemaking Bobbins)
Janet Maund, Braydon, 391 Innsworth Lane, Churchdown, Glos. (Fans)
Neales, 192 Mansfield Road, Nottingham.
Osmond Tricks, Regent Street Auction Rooms, Clifton, Bristol.
Outhwaite & Litherland, Kingsway Galleries, Fontenoy Street, Liverpool.
Phillips, George Street, Edinburgh.
Phillips, Hepper House, Leeds.
Phillips, The Old House, Station Road, Knowle, Solihull, W. Midlands.
Nicholas J. Pine, Milestone Publications, 62 Murray Road, Horndean, Hants. (Bairnsfatherware)
Presteigne Antiques Centre, (Mike Lewis), High Street, Presteigne, Powys.
Put The Clock Back, (Tim & Shirley Ward), Farm View, Upperfield, Ledbury. (Postcards)
Reeds Rains, 114 Northenden Road, Sale, Cheshire.
Rookery Books, (Mrs. E. Williams), 7 High Street, Presteigne, Powys.
Ian Scott, 18 Winnow Lane, Boston Spa, Yorks. (Uniform Buttons)
Robt. W. Skinner Inc., Bolton Gallery, Route 117, Bolton, Mass.
Mike Smith, Fayre House, 31 Stockleys Lane, Tingewick, Bucks. (Bottles, Oiliana)
H. Spencer & Son Ltd., 20 The Square, Retford, Notts.
Stalker & Boos, 280 North Woodward Avenue, Birmingham, Michigan.
Steamtown Railway Museum, Carnforth, Lancs. (Railwayana)
"Street Jewellery" & "More Street Jewellery" by New Cavendish Books
Street Jewellery Society, 10 Summerhill Terrace, Newcastle upon Tyne NE4 6ER
Dave Sutton, 8 View Close, Biggin Hill, Kent.
Christopher Sykes, Old Parsonage, Woburn, Milton Keynes. (Bottle Openers, Corkscrews)
Theriault, P.O. Box 151, Annapolis, Maryland 21404.
Vidler & Co., Auction Offices, Cinque Ports St., Rye, Sussex.
Wallis & Wallis, Regency House, 1 Albion Street, Lewes, Sussex.
Warren & Wignall, The Mill, Earnshaw Bridge, Leyland, Lancs.
Hilda White, The Castle Hotel, Kington. (Key Rings)
Paul Williams, Antiques, Aberpath, Dyfed.
Jim Wills, Manor Farm, West Woodlands, Frome, Somerset.
Jean Wilson, 24 Haws Avenue, Carnforth, Lancs.
John Wilson, 50 Acre End Street, Eynsham, Oxford. (Autograph Letters & Documents)
Peter Wilson, Nantwich.
Woolley & Wallis, The Castle Auction Mart, Salisbury.
Anita Yarwood, Burghill, Hereford. (Persian Antiques)

CONTENTS

ACTORS & ACTRESSES

The subject of theatre and cinema personalities must be one of the most underrated categories of postcard collecting.

These cards were produced in vast quantities and many high quality photographic examples are still readily available for no more than fifty pence a card.

Some may involve a bit of research in identifying the personality, especially those stars of the early music halls but, this can add rather than detract from their interest and as interest in a collection grows so does knowledge.

Prestigious personalities command the best prices as do cards of the ballet and circus and autographed specimens always go for a bit more.

Jessie Matthews, No. 2 Film Weekly Series, London, real photo, Gaumont/British star. Born March 11th 1907. First noted film 'There Goes The Bride'. £1.25

Loretta Young, born in Salt Lake City, Jan. 6th 1913. Her films include 'Caravan', 'Clive of India' and 'Heroes for Sale'. 20th Century Fox, printed postcard. £2.50

Marlene Dietrich, Paramount Pictures star, first important role was in 'The Blue Angel', other noted films include 'Desire', 'Morocco' and 'Dishonoured'. £3

Mr. Geo. Grossmith, Jnr., Beagles Series No. 538A, 1874-1935. First appeared in 1892 at the Criterion, became famous for his impersonation of the 'Dude' or man about town. 30p

Miss Claire Romaine, Rotary Series No. 1678. Played Mrs. Malton Hoppings in 'The Toreador' which was the last show that the Old Gaiety put on in 1901. 30p

Sarah Bernhardt, prestige performer, Rotary Series No. 228A. Numerous legends exist as to her eccentricities, probably one of the best actresses the world has ever seen. £4

(Paul G. Sheppard)

9

ACTORS & ACTRESSES

Gaynor Rowlands, Philco Series No. 3056B, with facsimile autograph. £1

Millie Legarde, Rotary Series No. 1311, real photo postcard. 40p

Wanda De Boncza, hand-tinted photo, Nadar Series. 60p

Miss Adeline Genee (ballet), prestige performer, Raphael Tuck's Celebrities Series No. T201. £7

Jean Harlow, MGM. Born March 3rd 1911. First success 'Hell's Angels'. Best films 'Dinner at Eight' and 'China Seas'. £1.50

Marcelline, The Hippodrome Clown, prestige performer, Raphael Tuck's Stage Favourites Series No. 506S. £5

Italian artist 'Folanda di Savoia', signed on back and stamped in blue 'Emilo Solustri via principe eugenio 23 Roma 32' with message. £1.50

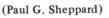

Mr. Edward Compton as David Garrick, presented by public subscription Feb. 7th 1906. A noted family of actors and actresses, Edward 1854-1918 was a good actor whose talents received 'insufficient recognition'. 75p

(Paul G. Sheppard)

Greta Garbo, born in Stockholm. First film was an advertising film about Hats. MGM Pictures star. Best films 'Romance', 'Grand Hotel', and 'Queen Christina'. £3

10

ACTORS & ACTRESSES

Miss Mabel Hirst, Rotary Series No. 1739B, real photo.   30p

Jon Pertwee as 'Worzel Gummage', Southern Television.   50p

Miss Ruby Ray, Davidson Glossy Photo Series No. 1181, posted in 1904.40p

Anna Pavlova (ballet), Rotary Series No. 11836G, prestige performer.   £6

Miss Delia Mason, Rapid Photo Co. Series No. 2258, silverprint series.   40p

Fred Earle, prestige performer, Raphael Tuck's Stage Favourites Series No. 506S, 1904.   £5

Miss Evie Greene, Rotophot Series 7206, Thiele photo. Played at the Gaiety in G. Grossmith Jnr's. 'Havana' as Consuela, best known as 'Nan' in 'A Country Girl' at Daly's.   50p

Mr. Lewis Waller as 'Monsieur Beaucaire', Rotary Series No. 302S, 1860-1915. English actor/manager. Born in Spain of English parents. First appeared in Toole's Theatre in 1883. Went into management at The Haymarket in 1895. Married Florence West. (Paul G. Sheppard) 40p

Eugene Stratton, 1861-1918, Rotary Series No. 135, 1904, An American Negro impersonator who became a well-known music hall star. Noted for singing Leslie Stuart's 'Coon Songs' such as 'Lily of Laguna'. He retired in 1914.   £5

ACTORS & ACTRESSES

Miss Phyllis Rankin,
Rotary Series No. 158.
40p

Mr. George Miller, in female
attire, Rotary photo No.
1284A. £2

Miss Mabel Love, real
photo postcard, Rotary
Series No. 1554. 40p

Marie Studholme, Rotary
photo No. 222L. Once a
chorus girl at The Gaiety,
later became an acclaimed
artiste. 35p

Miss Muriel Mellerup as 'Lady
Godiva' in Coventry Hospital
Pageant 29th June 1929, real
photo. £1.50

Maurice Chevalier, No. 2 Film
Weekly Series, London, real
photo. Came from a poor
family in Paris. First film
'Innocents Abroad'. £3

Madame Sarah Bernhardt,
1845-1923, Rotary Series.
One of the best-known
French actresses, appeared
in her own plays and was
also an accomplished poet
and sculptress. £5

Elizabeth Allan, No. 2 Film
Weekly Series, 112 Strand, London,
real photo. Born in Skegness, started
with Shakespeare at the Old Vic.
(age 17). First film was 'Alibi' 1931.
First Hollywood film 'service' won
an £8,000 year contract from MGM
in 1933. £1

Lilian Harvey, No. 2 Film
Weekly Series, London,
real photo. First dancer on
the Berlin stage noted for
'Congness Dances' perfor-
mance which brought her
to front rank in cinema
career. £1.25

(Paul G. Sheppard)

ACTORS & ACTRESSES

Mr. Edmund Waller,
Rotary Series No.
4257B.   40p

Ruth Vincent, Wrench
Series No. 10451, real
photo postcard. 45p

Myriam Clements, Rotary
Series No. 1510, complete
with harp.   £1

Miss Normah Whalley,
Davidson's Glossy
Photo Series No. 1189,
real photo postcard.
                    40p

Miss Fyfe Alexander in
'Little Mary', Raphael
Tuck's Celebrities of the
Stage Series No. 5138.
                    60p

Norma Shearer, No. 2 Film
Weekly Series, London,
real photo. MGM star chosen
to play Juliet in 'Romeo &
Juliet'.   £1.25

Mr. Seymour Hicks (1871-1949),
in 'The Catch of the Season',
Beagles photo. This English actor/
manager/dramatist, wrote a number of plays 'The Gay Gordons' &
'Sleeping Partners'. In 1931 he received the French Legion of Honour and was knighted in 1935.
He married Ellaline Terriss. 60p

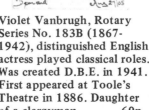
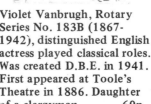

Violet Vanbrugh, Rotary
Series No. 183B (1867-
1942), distinguished English
actress played classical roles.
Was created D.B.E. in 1941.
First appeared at Toole's
Theatre in 1886. Daughter
of a clergyman.   60p

(Paul G. Sheppard)

Dan Leno, Rotary Series, 1860-
1904, real name George Galvin,
'The epitome of Cockney hum-
our'. Was known as the 'King's
Jester' when commanded to
Sandringham in 1901 by Edward
VII. Toward the end of his life
he became ill due to overwork.
                    £6.50

13

ACTORS & ACTRESSES

Marie George, Philco
Series No. 3006.   35p

Mr. C. Hayden Coffin, Rotary
Series No. 109D.   35p

Adeline Genee, Philco
Series No. 3068A.
£6.50

Miss Adrienne Augarde,
Rotary Series No. 1697E.
50p

Miss Mab Paul, Raphael
Tuck's Celebrities of the
Stage Series No. 682. 50p

Miss Camille Clifford, the
original Gibson Girl,
Beagles photo 1904. 60p

James Stuart, film star,
real photo in colour.
£1.50

Miss Kitty Gordon with
car, B.B. Series, London.
75p

Starsky & Hutch, facsimile
signatures on reverse. Tam-
kin Series.   70p

(Paul G. Sheppard)

14

ACTORS & ACTRESSES

Miss Eleanor Souray,
Bassano Ltd. photo.
40p

Bobby Darin, large size
card in colour.   £1.50

Maude Aston, Philco
Series No. 3068E. 30p

Miss Adeline Genee (ballet),
prestige performer Tuck's
Celebrity Series No. T203.
£7

Jack Buchanan, No. 2 Film
Weekly Series, London, real
photo. First appeared on stage
in 1912. First major film for
B. & D. 'Good Night Vienna'.
£1

Miss Gladys M. Marsh, Daily
Mirror Beauty 2nd Prize
winner. Rotary Series M313,
1920.   £1.50

Mrs. Patrick Campbell and
Mdme. Sarah Bernhardt,
Rotary Series No. 359F.
£3

Miss Roberta Williams, real
photo postcard by Alfred
Ellis & Walery.   30p

Mr. Farren Soutar,
Beagles Series No.
1249.   30p

(Paul G. Sheppard)

Peggy Morgan (Miss),
Rotary photo.   30p

'Asteria', the flying lady
in sepia tone.   £2

Miss Nina Sevening, C.W.F.'
& Co., Faulkner Series.40p

Janet Alexander, Rotary
Series No. 1519A, 1904.
                40p

Mr. Cyril Maude
Philco, Series No.
3008.   40p

Miss Ella Snyder, Schofield
& Co., real photo card with
applied glitter.   70p

Mr. Fred Terry, P.H.R. Series
No. 9198, (1863-1933).
Handsome, romantic actor,
first appeared on stage at the
Haymarket in 1880, married
Julia Emilie Neilson. Mainly
remembered for his performances as Sir Percy Blakeney
in 'The Scarlet Pimpernel'.35p

Olga Nethersole, 1863-1951,
Rotary Series No. 168F,
English actress/manager. First
appeared at Theatre Royal,
Brighton 1887, later at the
'Garrick' in London. Managed
the Adelphi & the Shaftesbury
Theatres. Famous for her roles
as 'fallen women' which in
America shocked puritans. £1

Lillie Langtry, 'The Jersey
Lillie', prestige performer,
Rotary Series No. 152D.
Daughter of the Dean of
Jersey, intimate friend of
Edward VII when he was
'Prince of Wales'. Married
twice, first a wealthy Irish-
man Edward Langtry, then
later Sir Hugo de Bathe. £8

(Paul G. Sheppard)

Mr. Rutland Barrington.
25p

Mae West, Paramount
Pictures No. 10. £3.50

G. P. Huntley, Rotary
Series No. 1578B. 30p

Mr. James Blakley as T.
Bedford in 'The Schoolgirl'
Davidson Series.   60p

Miss Maude Allan as
'Salome', Rotary photo
No. 4946F.   50p

Anna Pavlova (ballet),
PPH Series No. 6065.
£6

Mr. Bransby Williams, Rotary
Series No. 1191, 1904, (1870-
1961). Top-line Music Hall
performer specialising in characters from Dickens and im-
personations of famous actors.
Played before Edward VII in
1904 at Sandringham. Toward
the end of his life he became a
success on television.   80p

Mr. Martin Harvey as 'Sir Dagoney'
Rotary Series No. 115F, 1863-
1944, English actor/manager,
knighted in 1921 for his services
to the theatre. First appeared on
stage in 1881 and in 1882 joined
Irvings Co. at the Lyceum. His
death broke the last link with the
Victorian stage. Also received an
Honours Degree from Glasgow
University.   £1
(Paul G. Sheppard)

Sir Charles Wyndham, Rotary
Series No. 102D. Trained as
a Dr., qualified as a surgeon
but gave it up to become one
of the finest of English actor/
managers. He was knighted in
1902, his greatest role was
that of David Garrick in Tom
Robertson's play.   £3

J. Leicester Jackson in 'The Greatest Domestic Drama of the Present Day' at the Theatre Royal, Wednesbury, called 'Her One Great Sin'. £3.50

Mr. A. B. Mackay as General Borushi in 'A Woman Worth Winning' at the Theatre Royal, Wolverhampton. £3

Miss Julie Kennard as Lady Isobel in 'East Lynne'. 'Do come and see me May 25th 1908, Grand Theatre, Wolverhampton'. Give-away postcard printed by White & Farrell, Hull. £4.50

Rollo Balmain as the Marquis of Quex from 'The Gay Lord Quex', at the Grand Theatre, Wolverhampton, printed by Senior & Co., Bristol, unposted. £3.50

Sinclair Lewis, Nobel Prize Winner 1930, author of 'Sam Dodsworth'. £1

Edith Day, Theatre Advertising postcard 'Brilliant Holiday Programme' at the Alhambra, Leicester Square, WC2, posted 16th May 1934. £5

(Paul G. Sheppard)

ADVERTISING CARDS

Of all the categories in the broad spectrum of postcard collecting Advertising cards have to be one of the most interesting.

This area covers everything from the sale of Tonic Wines to the inauguration of a monument in commemoration of the foundation of the Universal Postal Union in 1909.

Original postcards of poster reproductions and other visually attractive material commands the highest prices and early Art Deco and Art Nouveau cards are very popular. At the lower end of the market inserts and give-away view cards are still available for only a few pence each.

Claymore Whisky 'Defenders of the Empire', drawn by Harry Payne, published by Raphael Tuck 1924. £8

Victorian lettercard, postally used March 14th 1895, hooded circle postmark, internally overprinted to advertise Gents clothing.   £8

Bamforth 'comic' series No. 1830 'Guinness' stout.   £1.50

Flowers of the riverside repro. of 1920, London Transport poster by Camden Graphics.
25p

Dalkeith picture postcard overprinted on reverse to advertise two new sets of 'poster reproduction postcards'.   50p

Venetian hotel advertising postcard pensione 'Da Cici'.   75p

(Paul G. Sheppard)

ADVERTISING CARDS

Postcard advertising the San Francisco Portola Festival 1909.   £3.50

1920's order request postcard from tobacconist in Firenze.   £2

John Thridgould postcard advertising 'Comic Postcards', comic card on reverse.   £2.50

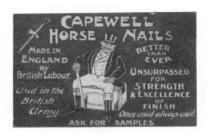

Capewell Horse Nails, a patriotic John Bull extols their virtues, circa 1908.   £7

Camden Graphics Series No. PC 448 'Benson & Hedges'.   25p

Readers Digest 'promotional' postcard for lucky numbers in the £12,500 prize draw, no date or postmark.   £2

Fry's Cocoa, designed by Maud Fabian, published by Hancock & Corfield Ltd., London, circa 1910.   £20

Pure Indian Tea , view of leaf weighing on reverse, 'Britain's best beverage', postage 'paid' in advance, red cancellation 23 April 1912.   £2

(Paul G. Sheppard)

20

'The Burlington Proofs', Fine Arts Publishing Co. Ltd. card advertising 'send today for the charming Fine Arts Mezzogravure catalogue showing the full series in minia-ture'. 75p

Inauguration of the monument commemor-ating the foundation of the Universal postal union in 1909, Swiss card. £3

Ever-Ready advert postcard 'send for full particulars of our new Motor Car Accessories', posted July 24th 1907, 'Try the Ever-Ready Tyre Jack'. £4

Sample novelty greeting card for the baking industry, lift the brown flap to reveal a couple kissing and verse, by Angus Thomas Ltd. £3.50

Petter's Famous 'Handy-Man' oil engines, giving details of cost and models available, circa 1910. £18

Gladiator Cycles, modern card by Athena. 25p

Numbered Minster Development 'lucky' give away card for land plots on the Isle of Sheppey, Kent, viewing every Monday by steamboat. £2.50

American Hotel Advertising postcard, 'Home baked rolls and muffins, all meals cooked by women', Breakfasts 15c to 50c on reverse. £1.50

(Paul G. Sheppard)

ADVERTISING CARDS

Sing Fat Co. Inc., the famous Oriental bazaar in Chinatown, Los Angeles.   £4

Cicely Courtneidge and Jack Hulbert world premier of new comedy 'Under your Hat' at the Prince of Wales Theatre.   £5

Bipex Postcard No. 4, 'season ticket' postcard 1982 'Scout'.   £1

Filey — for the family, modern repro. card by Camden Graphics. 25p

German advertising card with alcohol interest. 75p

Ford — the greatest thrill in motoring, modern repro. card by Camden Graphics.   25p

'Bubbles' Pears Soap advert by Sir John Millais, plain back — 75p; advert back £2.

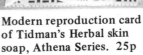

Modern reproduction card of Tidman's Herbal skin soap, Athena Series. 25p

Cook's Lightning Soap poster type advert with verse.   £12

(Paul G Sheppard)

1908 German Festival card (official No. 2), Turnfest posted in Frankfurt 23.7.08, Art Nouveau type illustration on reverse.   £5

Vibrona Tonic Wine, By Appointment to H.M. The King of Spain.   £4

Festival of Empire official card overprinted in red for Pageant of London Crystal Palace and Imperial Exhibition 1911.   £3

Bipex official season ticket postcard, British International Postcard Exhibition, Bipex post-card No. 5 14—17 Sept. 1983.   75p

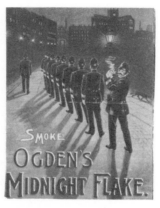

'Smoke Ogden's Midnight Flake', modern reproduc-tion card by Athena. 25p

Gary Player advertising 'In our house breakfast means Jungle Oats'. £4

Greek Theatre/Festival advert/commemorative card.   £4

'Heller' confectionery ad-vertising postcard with descriptive postcard back.
                    £1

Benger's Food Ltd. 'Happy Children' Series No. 10, photographic postcard.   £3

(Paul G. Sheppard)

'The shape of travel to come', British Rail advanced passenger train, 1982.   75p

Buckley's beer novelty advertising postcard/beermat showing map of areas where Buckley's can be found, 'Cardyn Post' on reverse.   £1

Holdfast Boots, published by James Walker & Co., Dublin, circa 1908.   £18

'Groaten', The Eight Minute Porridge, published by Chamberlain, Pole & Co. Ltd., Bristol.   £15

'St. Julien Tobacco', modern reproduction card by Athena.   25p

'None for the Road', insurance for total abstainers by The Ansvar Insurance Co. Ltd., 1960.   75p

Wheeler & Wilson, 'High Class Sewing Machines are the best', circa 1905.   £18

'Main' gas cooker, 'Meals are always ready to time', circa 1930.   £6

'Silvox' Beef Extract, published by C.W.S. Ltd. £15

(Paul G. Sheppard)

ADVERTISING GIVE-AWAYS

Over the years, manufacturers have advertised and promoted their products by means of 'free gifts'. Based on the premise that it is always nice to be given something for nothing, especially an object that is either useful or decorative, they have stamped their name on a variety of goods ranging from the sublime to the ridiculous.

Goods range from a motor car to a very cheap and nasty key ring with a fascinating selection of interesting items somewhere in between.

Some of the best examples have come to us via the early exhibitions such as The British Empire Exhibition held in 1924/25 at Wembley, and a more modest range from the tradition upheld by door to door salesmen of giving away to customers the tiny sample tins of polish or little gadgets like needle threaders or bottle openers.

China mug from Rolls Royce. £4

Ogden's 'St. Julien' tobacco advertising weather gauge. £20

Pot lid for Burgess's genuine Anchovy Paste, 3½in. diam. £6

Deckers 'Scurf Pomade' beaker, 1930's. £10

Four Robertson's Golly musicians, 3in. high. £15

Horlicks Malted Milk beaker, 4½in. high. £3.50

(Paul G. Sheppard)

Hudson's Soap handbag mirror, 5cm. diam.   £6

A pomade mug made of Staffordshire pottery advertising Butler's Medical Hall, Dublin, circa 1830, 5in. high. (Christopher Sykes) $£135

Sunlight Soap advertising rubber, ¾in. wide.   £2

'Palethorpes Sausages' give-away pencil complete with case. £2.50

1967 desk calendar given away by the Electric Maintenance & Repair Co. Ltd.   £1

Brass pipe stomper 'The Bacca Stopper', probably a give-away.   £6

Pot for Holloway's Ointment for Gout and Rheumatism, 1½in. tall.   £7

Bouquet perfume counter display.   £3

Pot lid for Woods Areca Nut Tooth Paste, Plymouth, 2in. diam.   £7

(Paul G. Sheppard)

ANGLING BOOKS

With a following in Britain reported to be in the millions, and a worldwide interest of equal enthusiasm, it is little wonder that anything connected with the noble art of fishing will find a ready market. Angling books are no exception, especially if they have an association with the father of the sport Izaak Walton.

Born in Stafford on 9th August 1593 he led an unremarkable life as an ironmonger until his retirement in 1644, when he set about to produce what is regarded as a masterpiece, 'The Complete Angler', published in 1653, 'a discourse on rivers, fishponds, fish and fishing'. Such is the interest that a copy of this work made £415 at auction as long ago as 1896. It has since had numerous editions, the earlier the better.

Hardy Brothers 'Angling Specialities' catalogue, 1906. £150

Hardy Brothers Ltd. 'The Anglers' Guide & Catalogue', 1915. £100

Hardy's Anglers' Guide, 1952. £10

Hardy Brothers Ltd. 'Hardy's Anglers' Guide', 1927. £35

Hardy's Anglers' Guide 'Coronation Number', 1937. £20

Hardy Brothers Ltd. 'Hardy's Angler's Guide', 1925. £35

(N. J. Marchant Lane)

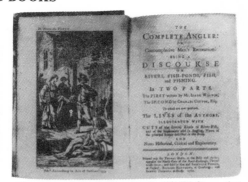

A Companion to Ronald's Fly Fisher's Entomology, a canvas-covered wallet with printed extracts from the work on pages opposite the relevant fly pockets, circa 1930, 6 x 3½in.
£30

The Complete Angler by Izaak Walton, 1st John Hawkins Edition, 8th Edition, 1760.
£125

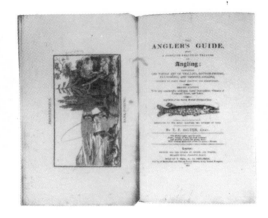

The Life of Izaak Walton by T. Zouch with numerous engravings, 1826. £60

The Angler's Guide, by T. F. Salter, 2nd Edition, full calf binding, 1815. £85

Art of Angling by Thomas Best, contemporary half calf binding, 10th Edition, 1814.
£55

The Art of Angling by Charles Bowlker, in fly wallet form with flies, 1829. £120

(N. J. Marchant Lane)

ANIMAL TRAPS

This is precisely the sort of apparatus one is likely to find accumulating dust in the murky depths of an old tool chest. It is always worth the effort involved in identifying this miscellaneous 'junk' for much of it has some value and, there is at present, a growing enthusiasm for all the old tools and mechanical devices of another age.

Animal traps fall into three categories; the type which captures the creature alive and unharmed; the trap which kills outright and the type designed to trap the animal by a limb and restrain it until the hunter arrives.

Thankfully, the use of most of these traps is now illegal in this country. The gin trap has been banned for over thirty years, and the round trap, or pole trap, with smooth teeth or 'jaws' designed to be set aloft on a pole, trapping unsuspecting birds, has been outlawed since 1906.

An old plate and spring mouse trap. £2

A circular pole trap with no teeth on the jaws. £5

The Little Nipper mousetrap. 35p

Selfset spring action metal rat trap. £1

Rabbit trap with spring type safety device. £2

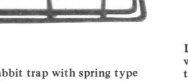

Late Victorian mole trap which springs shut when the mole puts its head in the hole. £7

(Paul Jones)

ANIMAL TRAPS

Rodent trap for putting in the run.   £5

Tump type mole trap designed to spear the mole when the lever plate is pushed, circa 1880. £11

Wire rat trap.   £6

Calliper action fox or badger trap.   £8

20th century wire bird trap.   £6

Circular pole trap with pin and plate action.   £4

Mole trap in which jaws close when ring is activated.   £7

Large late Victorian gin trap designed to snap shut when animal treads on the baseplate.   £10

Gamekeeper's gin trap complete with chain and groundspike, circa 1900.   £6

(Paul Jones)

30

ASHTRAYS

Over the years, many thousands of different types of ashtrays have been produced in just about every conceivable material and form. One may find everything from stylised aeroplanes to armchairs in materials ranging from bronze to bakelite.

A popular specialist area is in collecting advertising ashtrays. Clubs, pubs, hotels, large companies and organisations have nearly all, at one time or another, issued a special ashtray decorated with their name and sometimes an illustration of their premises and location. Souvenir ashtrays, produced for the turn of the century holidaymakers, also make an interesting collection. These are quite plentiful and generally inexpensive. There are however, one or two exceptions — and this makes the search that bit more interesting. While most are priced at around two or three pounds, sometimes less, anything from the Goss factory is worth considerably more. Some fine examples fetch upwards of £20.

Schweppes Table Waters ashtray of painted aluminium. £2

White enamel ashtray with canted corners. £2

John Smith's Bitter ashtray by Wade, England. £4

Black china 'Superkings' ashtray. £1.50

Burns ashtray by W. H. Goss. £20

'Guinness is good for you' ashtray. £8

'Inter Continental' London, manufactured by Schonwald, Germany. £2

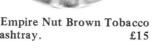

Empire Nut Brown Tobacco ashtray. £15

American souvenir ashtray 'The Big Apple', New York City. £4

(Paul G. Sheppard)

31

ASHTRAYS

'Double Diamond Works Wonders', bakelite ash-tray. £2.50

Victorian horn ashtray on plated feet. £4

'The Westbury', London W1, manufactured by Wade, England. £2

Circular ashtray by W. H. Goss with ribbed edge. £12.50

20th century Indian brass ashtray inlaid with semi precious stones. £8

Ashtray to commemorate 'Melville College Memorial Pavilion 1956', manufactured by Bron pottery, Peebles. £2

Brass ashtray advertising 'Richards Mineral Waters', made by C. E. Wilkins. £5

Evan Evans Bevan Ltd. 'Vale of Neath Ales' by Empire Porcelain Co. £3.50

1930's brass ashtray 'The More We Are Together, The Merrier We Will Be'. £7

(Paul G. Sheppard)

ASHTRAYS

Edward VIII commemorative ashtray.   £22.50

Commemorative pewter ashtray for 'University College of Wales', Aberystwyth.   £7

'Scribe' Paris, 'Lotti' Paris and 'Carlton', Cannes, triple hotel ashtray of red earthenware.   £2

'Players Please' metal ashtray.   £1.50

China armchair ashtray by B. G. R. in the 1930's style.   £2

Ind Coope Allsopp ashtray by Mintons, England. £4.50

Wills's Capstan china ashtray, Made in England.   £4

'Winston Churchill' ashtray by Hammersley & Co., Stoke on Trent.   £5

Souvenir china ashtray from Llandudno.   £3

(Paul G. Sheppard)

ASHTRAYS

The Achievements of Arthur
Wellesley ashtray.   £2.50

Italian souvenir ashtray
from Rapallo.   £3

Carlsberg Lager ashtray.
£3

'Player's Please' brass ashtray.   £2

Combined brass ashtray
and cigarette lighter, made
in Switzerland.   £6

1930's wooden barrel
type ashtray.   £4

Souvenir ashtray 'A
present from Swansea'.
£2.50

Castrol Oil glass ashtray.£4

(Paul G. Sheppard)

Italian china comic ash-
tray.   £1

AUTOGRAPH LETTERS & DOCUMENTS

Original letters and documents written or signed by the famous names of history in all fields, from great authors to naval and military leaders, Kings and Queens, scientists, artists and musicians, provide a fascinating field for the private collector, as well as the raw material for historical and literary research. The collector will find himself in competition with the research libraries of the world, but will also have the reward of working alongside historians with a common aim. There is a particular demand for literary letters and for royal documents, but any piece of paper or parchment bearing a famous name is likely to be of some value. The signatures of many of our popular entertainers and recent sportsmen are of little worth, but there is always the chance that they may gain interest in the future.

The value of any letter or document will depend on many factors, most importantly the identity of the writer and the scarcity of the signature. In addition, the contents and condition are significant and must always be taken into account. There are numerous facsimile reproductions, not only of important letters but of routine notes like the acknowledgements sent out by Churchill in response to messages of greetings, and forgery has long been a popular pastime. It is sensible to buy from a reputable dealer who will guarantee the authenticity of everything he sells.

Although most of the examples illustrated are indicative of the upper end of the market there is still a wealth of material from lesser personalities which can be bought at prices well within the reach of most collectors.

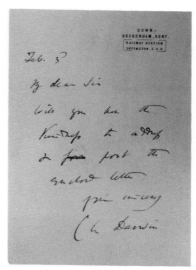

Charles Darwin: Brief autograph letter signed, 1 page 8vo, 3 February n.y. £750

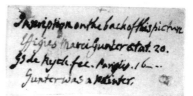

Horace Walpole, 4th Earl of Oxford: Autograph inscription, 4 lines on a small card, ca. 6½ x 3¼mm., unsigned, n.d. £35

Robert Browning: Cabinet photograph of Browning, signed and dated 5 May 1886. £450

(John Wilson)

35

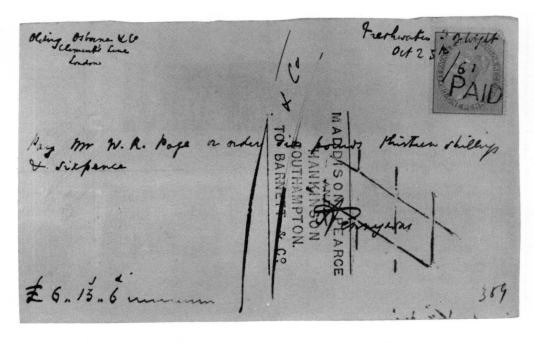

Alfred, Lord Tennyson: Autograph cheque signed, on notepaper. £65

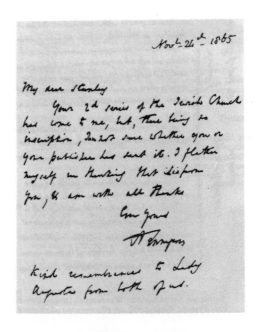

Baron Alfred Tennyson: Autograph letter, signed, 1 page 8vo, Farringford, 24 November 1865.   £125

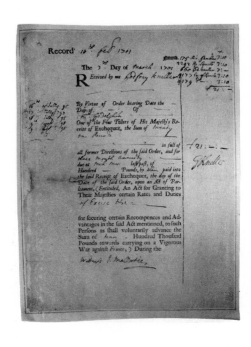

Sir Godfrey Kneller: Document signed, 1 page folio, 7 March 1701.   £150

(John Wilson)

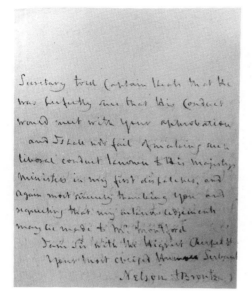

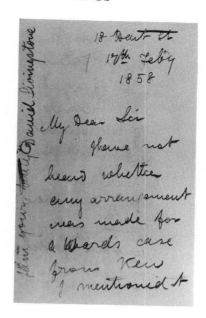

Horatio Nelson: Autograph letter signed 'Nelson & Bronte', 2 pages 4to, 16 January 1805, (last page). £1,250

David Livingstone: Autograph letter signed, about the Zambesi, 2 pages 8vo, 17 February 1858, (first page). £350

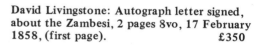

Charles II: Document signed, 1 page folio with embossed paper seal, 28 July 1669. £250

Field-Marshal Montgomery: Photograph with Eisenhower, signed. £55

(John Wilson)

Charles Dickens: Cheque drawn on Messrs. Coutts, completed and signed,
12 May 1868.   £180

Sir Thomas Wentworth, 1st Earl of Strafford: Autograph letter, signed ('Wentworth'), 1 page folio, Wentworth, 11 September 1636.   £250

Florence Nightingale: Fine series of forty Autograph letters signed, in all 151 pages 8vo and 16 sides on card, 27 September 1884 to 6 July 1888.   £2,500

(John Wilson)

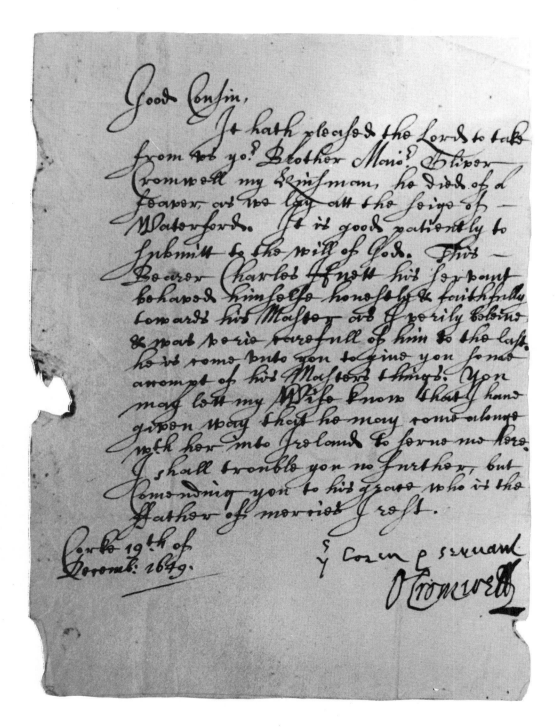

Oliver Cromwell: Fine letter signed to his cousin, 1 page folio, 19 December
1649.   £1,500

(John Wilson)

Charles Dickens: Autograph letter, signed to his publisher (Edward) Chapman, 1 page 8vo, Broadstairs, 4 August, 1848. £250

Robert Browning: Autograph receipt, signed, 1 page 16mo; Florence, 17 July 1854. £125

George III: Autograph letter (unsigned) to the prime minister, 1 page 4to, Windsor, 29 June 1783. £135

Henry VIII: Document signed, 1 page folio (oblong) on vellum, 1 May 1545. £5,000

(John Wilson)

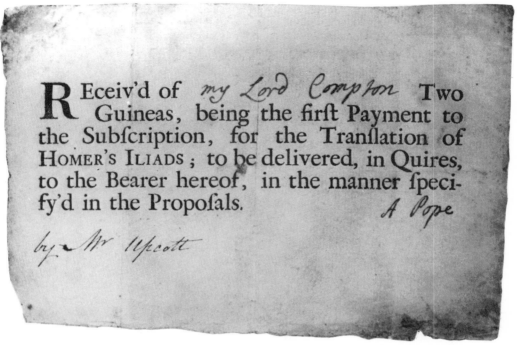

REceiv'd of *my Lord Compton* Two Guineas, being the firſt Payment to the Subſcription, for the Tranſlation of HOMER'S ILIADS; to be delivered, in Quires, to the Bearer hereof, in the manner ſpecify'd in the Propoſals. *A Pope*

by Mr Upcott

Alexander Pope: Printed receipt signed, 1 page 16mo; n.d. £220

James Scott, Duke of Monmouth: Letter signed to Sir Thomas Chicheley, 1 page 8vo with address-leaf, Whitehall, 6 May n.y. £225

Wilfred Rhodes: Photograph of Rhodes in well-worn Yorkshire blazer, signed 165 x 210mm., n.d.; together with a signed photograph of George H. Hirst, 1871-1954 (badly torn) £35

(John Wilson)

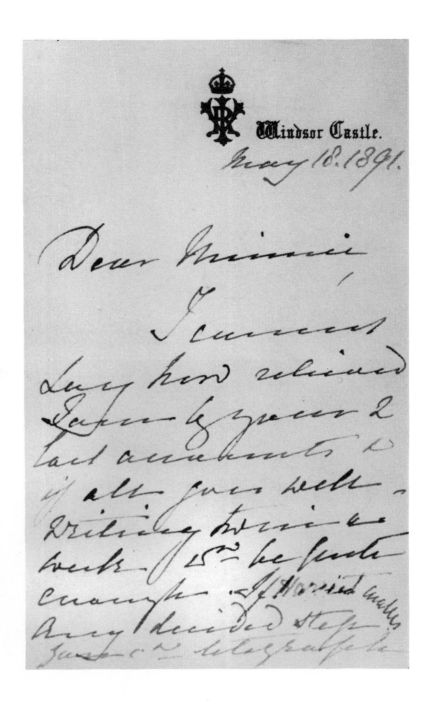

Queen Victoria: Autograph letter signed ('V.R.I.'), 2-½ pages 8vo, 18 May 1891, (first page).   £150

(John Wilson)

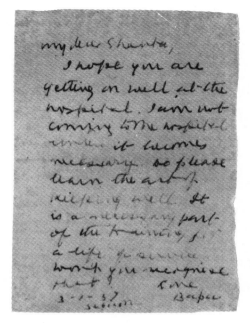

M. K. Gandhi: Fine series of sixteen Autograph letters signed ('Bapu'), 21 pages 8vo, June 1936 to December 1939.   £3,850

Bruce Bairnsfather: Autograph caricature of Old Bill, in pencil, signed, 194 x 165mm., on a sheet of salmon-coloured paper, removed from an album.   £28

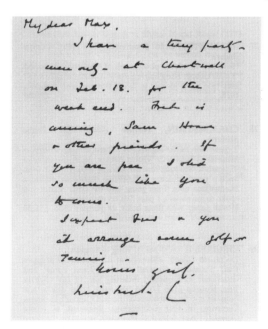

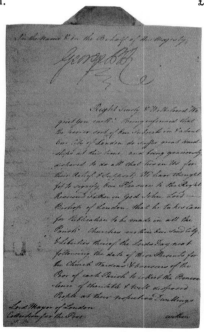

Sir Winston Spencer Churchill: Autograph letter, signed ('Winston S.C.'), 1 page 8vo, Treasury Chambers, Whitehall, 1 February 1926.   £320

George IV: Document signed 'George P.R.' as Prince Regent, 2 pages folio, 4 March 1811 (first page).   £110

(John Wilson)

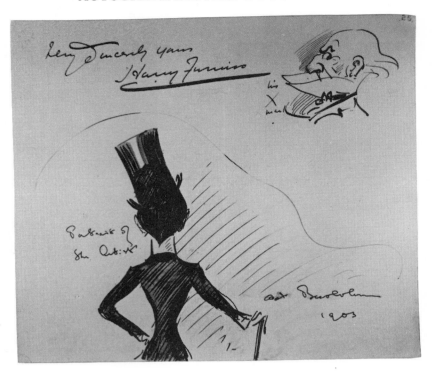

Sir Max Beerbohm: Self-caricature signed, on a large album leaf, 1903.
£525

Hans Christian Andersen: Autograph manuscript signed, 1 page 8vo (oblong), Dresden 1 November 1860. **£850**

(John Wilson)

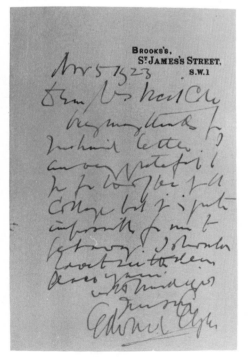

Florence Nightingale: Autograph letter signed, 3 pages 8vo with envelope, 29 November 1869, (last page). £350

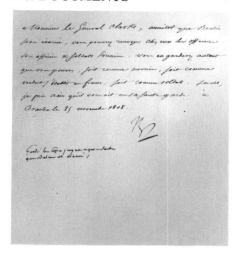

Napoleon I: Letter signed ('Np') to Clarke, ½ page 4to, 28 November 1808. £450

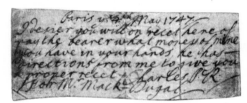

Charles Edward Stuart: Autograph document, signed ('Charles P.R.'), 50 x 126mm., Paris 4 May 1747. £650

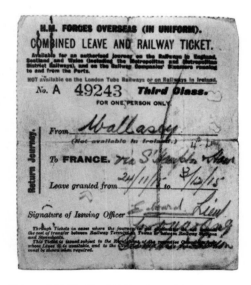

Edward VIII: World War I combined leave & railway ticket, signed 'Edward', 25 November 1915. £85

Sir Edward Elgar: Autograph letter signed, 1 page 8vo, 5 November 1923. £110

(John Wilson)

Louis Pasteur: Autograph statement signed,
1 page 4to, 23 September 1888.   £600

Duke of Wellington: Autograph letter signed,
1 page 8vo, London, 18 March 1846.   £65

Franz Liszt: Autograph letter signed, 2 pages
8vo with envelope, 'Lundi' n.d. (last page).
£385

Edward Jenner: Autograph letter signed, 2
pages 4to, with address, 30 December 1821,
(last page).   £850

(John Wilson)

AUTOMATONS

Developed by the Swiss Jacquet-Droz family, and later by the French, mechanical toys grew in complexity until the mid-Victorian era, by which time most occupations had been interpreted with mechanical ingenuity to make delightful adult playthings.

Many automata employ casts of thousands. A modest example is in the form of a 19th century Power Pageant. As the musical part plays three tunes, a fully rigged three masted ship sails across its paper sea, a tall funnelled railway train crosses the bridge in the background and, as if that were not enough, the water wheel also revolves.

This is however, only small beer compared with some of the commercial constructions, up to four feet wide, which are designed to coax pennies from Victorian pockets in seaside arcades. Some of these contain enormous battling armies, while other delights include complete circus performances, all turns being performed skilfully, if rather jerkily to appropriate background music.

A bisque headed automaton with Armand Marseille head, probably German, circa 1900, 14½in. high.
£187

A sailor's hornpipe automaton, English, circa 1880, 14 x 16in. £748

A bisque-headed Marotte doll, impressed 3/0, German, circa 1890, 12½in. high. £264

Late 19th century German hamster powered automaton, 32in. high. £352

A picture automaton, the timepiece in the church facade activates the clockwork mechanism, probably French, 35in. long. £770

Late 19th century German Boy on Swing automaton, 44in. high. £605

19th century wooden and papier-mache automaton, 36in. high. (Theriault's) £664

Early 20th century enamel singing bird automaton, 3¼in. high. (Robt. W. Skinner Inc.) £762

An automaton handcart with two Armand Marseille bisque headed dolls, 19½in. long, German, circa 1910. £880

An advertising display automaton on oak base, circa 1930, 25in. wide. £880

French bisque automaton, probably Farkas, circa 1920, 12in. high. (Theriault's) £533

French bisque automaton by Emile Jumeau, circa 1890, 19in. high overall. (Theriault's) £2,137

A musical automaton of a conjuror, probably by L. Lambert, French, circa 1880, 16in. high. £1,430

A singing bird automaton, the domed brass cage with hinged door, French, circa 1900, 21½in. high. £880

A musical automaton of a dancing couple by Vichy, French, circa 1860, 13½in. high. £1,320

AUTOMATONS

French musical automaton of a piano player, circa 1915. £1,100

Late 19th century French landscape automaton on ebonised base, 22in. high. £440

A 19th century bisque-headed Magicienne automaton. (Phillips) £5,500

French bisque automaton by Leopold Lambert, circa 1900, 20in. high. (Theriault's) £1,595

German bisque automaton, dolls by Armand Marseille, circa 1890, 12in. high. (Theriault's) £635

French-type bisque automaton, 18in. high, circa 1890. (Theriault's) £955

A bisque headed automaton, the German head impressed 5/0, probably French, circa 1900, 18in. high. £462

A 19th century European singing bird automaton, 22in. high. (Robt. W. Skinner Inc.) £1,115

French musical automaton of a girl seated, smelling flowers, by Leopold Lambert, circa 1880, 19¾in. high. £1,650

AVIATION CARDS

This is both a popular and highly specialised field with cards ranging from a modest fifty or sixty pence to the all time British auction record of £1,675 achieved for a postcard dropped from a balloon in 1902. This rare example, celebrating a postal delivery by air from Manchester to Haslingden demonstrates the ever present problem of categorising a collection. An exacting collector might insist that this card belongs to the category of Postal history and not in Aviation.

Postally unused balloon and airship cards will generally sell for between £10-£25 and there are still many good photographic examples of cards depicting civil aviation, military aviation, and commercial airlines available on the market for no more than a few pounds.

Cards issued to mark the occasion of early Aviation Meetings are well worth collecting at prices ranging from £4-£20. It was a tradition to issue a composite picture card to celebrate early meetings such as Blackpool 1909, Betheny Airfield 1909 and Lanark 1910. These cards were generally produced in advance of the event and were traditionally composed of a superimposed photograph of a named pilot placed in one corner, and sometimes featured a superimposed photograph of an aeroplane. These photo montage cards are worth between £3-£7.

All subject material relating to the early events and other important highlights in the history of aviation are keenly sought after by collectors. Key points:

The English Channel first crossed by balloon in 1785. Louis Bleriot crossed by aeroplane in 1909 winning the Daily Mail prize of £1,000 on August 27th. In the same year at Rheims, Farman carried two passengers in his plane for over six hours. These events of 1909 mark the real beginnings of aerial navigation.

Daily Mail Aeroplane Tour 1914, Monsieur Salmet and his Bleriot monoplane.   £6

Military 'Hawker Hurricanes' flying in line, real photo printed on union flag by Valentines.   £1

The S6 at Calshot, winner of the Schneider Trophy, later developed into the Hurricane fighter.   £15

The 'de Havilland' two-seater biplane, real photograph by The Aircraft Manufacturing Co. Ltd., circa 1920.   £4

(Paul G. Sheppard)

AVIATION CARDS

Short 'Singapore III' flying boat, real photograph published by Valentine & Sons Ltd. £2

General Joffre inspecting a German albatross 'just downed', postcard sold in aid of blinded soldiers children's fund, numbered. £3.50

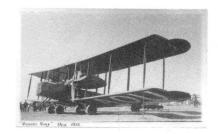

Channel Air Ferries, real photo, posted from Isles of Scilly 4.7.38. £5

Vickers Vimy aeroplane, March 1920, real photo. £4.50

Real photograph of a 'flying bomb' on display in Holland after the War, published in Amsterdam. £6

(Paul G. Sheppard)

AVIATION CARDS

Valentine Aircraft recognition card, 'The Messerschmitt', German single-seat fighter. 60p

The Daily Mail Aeroplane Tour 1914, Mr. Raynham and his Avro waterplane. £6

Real photograph of an Italian Seaplane at Calshot. £15

Real photograph of the 'Miles Mohawk' by Valentine & Sons Ltd., circa 1937. £2

The arrival of Louis Bleriot by aeroplane, having flown from Calais to Dover, 25th July 1909. £5

(Tim Ward)

BADGES

For the enthusiast, a collection of badges offers unlimited variety and all the potential of an extremely attractive visual display.

The current trend is to collect by theme with motor cycle badges topping the popularity poll. Other well liked subjects include military, transport, masonic, pop music, sport and commemorative badges.

Early cloth and card badges in good condition are quite rare for, over the years, natural deterioration has reduced their value. Early tin type, pin back badges are now becoming much more collectible.

Probably the most attractive badges of all are the enamelled chrome and silver type but, because of their general appeal, they have been reproduced quite extensively. Be selective.

Fire Watcher, crescent back enamel badge. £1.50

Worcester Diocese, Sunday School Teacher enamel badge, by Thomas Fattorini, pin back. £2.50

H.F.W.I. Pageant, Oct. 1925, enamel badge, by W. O. Lewis, Birmingham, pin back. £4

Midland Railway Service badge by Thos. Fattorini, Bolton, crescent back. £8

'Birch Grove' train badge, pin back, modern. 60p

Modern 'Thruxton' souvenir badge, pin back. 50p

Lea & Lea Castle Nurses Training School silver badge by W. H. D. 1968. £4

Shropshire & West Midlands Agricultural Show badge 1958, card. 60p

'The Countryside' silver gilt enamel badge, 1905. £4

(Paul G. Sheppard)

BADGES

Modern enamel badge 'HMS Victory', pin back.　50p

British Motor Racing Fund, Birmingham Medal and Badge Co. Ltd., pin back.　£12

I.W.A. National Waterways Rally 1982.　35p

Custodio de Mello (Brazilian Officers Training Warship) badge.　£2

Aberystwyth enamelled souvenir badge.　50p

Gilt brass souvenir badge, Blackpool, pin back.　£1

'I. & I. Survive' badge. 35p

Birmingham Dental Hospital badge by Marples & Beasley, Birmingham, pin back.　£2

British Red Cross Society enamelled badge, prong back.　£1.50

R.S.P.C.A. Junior Division badge, pin back.　75p

'Crown and Anchor' enamel badge, pin back.£1.50

'Pure Pink Paraffin' badge.　20p

(Paul G. Sheppard)

54

BADGES

N.U.G.C., T.G. enamelled badge by Fattorini, Birmingham, pin back.   £3.50

John Thompson Works badge for long service, by the Birmingham Medal & Badge Co. Ltd.   £1.50

'Giving for Living', Royal Manchester Children's Hospital.   35p

Castle badge No. 3155, by Fattorini & Co., Birmingham.   £2

Royal Masonic Institution for Girls by G. Hennings & Son, London.   £10

Ever Ready 'Power to the People', plastic safety pin badge.   25p

Alexandra Day Fund, 1976.   50p

Ford 'Main Dealer' enamel badge by F. T. Davis Ltd., prong back.   £3

'Beacon Radio 303', pin back badge.   25p

Lamb and Staff religious badge, pin back.   75p

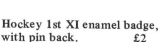

Hockey 1st XI enamel badge, with pin back.   £2

Nickel silver Girl Guide's badge by Collins, London, pin back.   75p

(Paul G. Sheppard)

BADGES

E.E. Engineering Society enamel badge by Fattorini, Birmingham, crescent back.   £2.50

British Legion badge by Birmingham Medal & Badge Co. Ltd., crescent back.   £2.50

Armstrong Siddeley Cycling Club badge, silver plated and enamel, pin back.   £9

1970's Volvo enamel badge, pin back.   £2

A G.P.O. badge No. 143.   £12

Hereford County Youth Service badge by H. W. Milner, pin back.   £2

A rare Gaumont Cinema Club Committee badge, pin back.   £7.50

'Fox Firkin' tin badge. 50p

Kington Town enamel 'Supporters Club' badge by W. O. Lewis, Birmingham, crescent back.   £3.50

Hallmarked silver Swastika badge by A.J.S., pin back.   £3

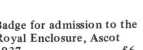
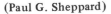

Badge for admission to the Royal Enclosure, Ascot 1937.   £6

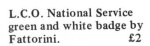

L.C.O. National Service green and white badge by Fattorini.   £2

(Paul G. Sheppard)

56

BAIRNSFATHERWARE

Bruce Bairnsfather was the war artist who created the famous cartoon character 'Old Bill'. The long-suffering, archetypal 'Tommy' of World War I. During and after the war, a vast range of 'Bairnsfather-ware was produced.

These wares fall into 7 main categories:

Original paintings, drawings, sketches and letters by Bairnsfather.

Pottery items bearing 'Fragments from France' cartoons and models of Old Bill's head.

Bystander Products. Original 'Fragments from France' cartoons, postcards, (there are 56 available in a complete set) jig-saws and prints.

Metal Ware. Car Mascots of Old Bill, ash trays, etc.

Theatre and Cinema ephemera including posters, advertising post-cards, magazines and photographs of the various plays and films made about Old Bill or by Bairnsfather.

Books and Magazines about or by Bairnsfather.

Miscellaneous: Dolls, hankies, badges, glass slides.

The market is still in its infancy and these wares are currently largely overlooked and inexpensive. A boost to the market is assured, however, by publication of the first priced and illustrated catalogue to Bairnsfather-ware 'In Search of the Better 'Ole'' (Milestone Publications, 62 Murray Road, Horndean, Hampshire PO8 9JL).

Once a collectors market is established the demand for 'Old Bill' products is self generating the more the interest grows, which indicates good prospects for a healthy investment.

'Old Bill', doll in fair condition. £40

A.D. Nineteen Fifty 'I see the war babies battalion is a coming out'. £1.50

Grimwade, dish with transfers of 'Old Bill'. £40

The Fatalist 'I'm sure they'll 'ear this damn thing squeakin'. £1.50

Metal car mascot of 'Old Bill'. £100

(Nicholas J. Pine)

57

BAIRNSFATHERWARE

Carlton shrapnel Villa 'Tommies dugout somewhere in France'.   £30

Grimwade pottery plate 'Well if you knows of a better 'ole go to it'.   £35

Grimwade mug 'Well if you know of a better 'ole go to it'.   £35

Happy memories of the zoo 'What time do they feed the sealions Alf?'   £1.50

Grimwade bowl with transfers of 'Old Bill'.   £30

That sword 'How he thought he was going to use it — And how he did use it'.   £1.50

Carlton 'Old Bill' British Empire Exhibition.   £50

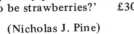

Grimwade pottery plate 'When the 'ell is it goin' to be strawberries?'   £30

'Old Bill' pottery head, white. £35

(Nicholas J. Pine)

Grimwade bowl 'What time do they feed the sealions Alf?' £30

Grimwade pottery plate 'Gott Strafe This Barbed Wire'. £30

Carlton 'Old Bill' with coloured balaclava 'Yours to a cinder Old Bill'. £75

Situation shortly vacant 'In an old fashioned house in France an opening will shortly occur for a young man, with good prospects of getting a rise'. £1.50

'Old Bill' coloured pottery head. £40

So obvious. The young and talkative one 'Who made that 'ole?' The fed-up one 'Mice'. £1.50

Grimwade shaving mug with transfers of 'Old Bill' and Arms of Margate. £40

A small metal car mascot of 'Old Bill' £100

Grimwade pottery plate 'With a loaf of bread beneath the bough'. £30

(Nicholas J. Pine)

A 'Temporary Gentleman' in France, by
Bruce Bairnsfather.   £15

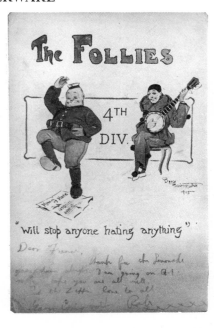

The Follies 'Will stop anyone hating anything',
Bruce Bairnsfather 1915.   £20

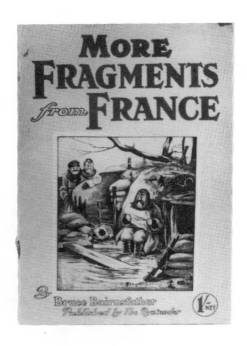

'More Fragments from France', World War I
magazine by Bruce Bairnsfather.   £5

Postcard for the Surrey Red Cross 'Old Bills
made like new'.   £2

(Nicholas J. Pine)

BAKELITE

The synthetic resin known by the tradename 'Bakelite' was invented in 1909 and named after its inventor L.H. Baekeland.

Originally developed to cope with a function within the ignition systems of aeroplane engines it was found to be the ideal material for a million and one other purposes. It was quickly taken up by commercial manufacturers and put to use in the production of everything from heavy domestic appliances to tiny decorative objects.

Hailed as the 'new wonder material' it was moulded with all the skill and artistic flair of the day and because of its popularity throughout the Art Deco period many quite sophisticated pieces in this style survive today.

The most inexpensive and practical material available, it remained popular right up until the 60's when it was superseded by modern plastics.

1930's bakelite finger sponge.   £1.50

Bakelite cigarette case.   £1

1930's bakelite bowl by Seaforth.   £1.50

Bakelite office desk jotter with pencil attached.   £8

Saville 'Mischief' perfume in bakelite top-hat case, 2in. high.   £5

A bakelite three-piece suite of doll's furniture.   £15

Bakelite teapot stand with cork insert.   £2

'The Home Tote' by L. Adams Ltd., in a bakelite case.   £30

(Paul G. Sheppard)

BAROMETERS

Torricelli, as every schoolboy knows, invented a method of producing the vacuum. In 1660, Robert Boyle adapted Torricelli's technique to the production of a weather glass. Naturally enough, it was not long before the device attracted the attentions of many a notable horologist and instrument maker. Among these was Daniel Quare, Thomas Tompion, John Patrick, Henry Jones and Charles Orme, any of whose works attracts enormous sums of money. As can be seen however, not all barometers are equally expensive.

By midway through the 18th century, rococo scrolls were often incorporated in the design of barometer cases which, by the final quarter of the century had evolved into the ever-popular wheel (or banjo) shape. Most have mahogany, or occasionally satinwood, frames with delicate boxwood stringing on the edges and silvered dials enclosed by convex glass. Good examples incorporate in their designs such extras as thermometers, hygrometers, spirit-levels and even clocks — each device adds a bit to the value.

A 19th century Adie's Sympiesometer by Crichton, London, in mahogany case. (Dreweatt Watson & Barton) £660

A George III stick barometer by Josh. Somalvico, London, in mahogany case. (Dreweatt Watson & Barton) £350

Rare inlaid walnut double tube angle barometer by C. Orme, 1741, 40½in. high. £2,640

A 19th century mahogany cased banjo barometer by Jones. (W. H. Lane & Son) £170

A Georgian inlaid mahogany wheel barometer. (Warren & Wignall) £320

An early 18th century oyster veneered stick barometer, circa 1705. (Dreweatt Watson & Barton) £2,900

A 20th century classical Revival gilt carved barometer, Italy, 38in. long. (Robt. W. Skinner Inc.) £270

Victorian oak cased Admiral Fitzroy barometer with weather glass, the thermometer, 46in. long. (Reeds Rains) £200

BARREL TAPS

Although barrel taps are most commonly made of wood, some fine examples were produced in brass or silver plate. Others were chrome or nickel plated.

To discourage pilfering, the early taps made for ale, wine or cider barrels were often fitted with a key and locking device. Later versions were fitted with a thumbturn tap on top which occasionally featured a locking lever and padlock.

An average barrel tap, or spigot, in fair condition, will sell for around £5 a piece. When cleaned up, a grouping of the different types will make an attractive and interesting display — and this is just the sort of material likely to be found tucked away in a long forgotten suitcase at the back of the garage. You may even be lucky enough to find a tap stamped with both the brewery and the maker's name.

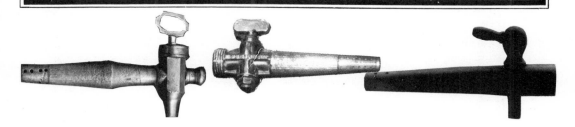

An early 19th century brass barrel tap with detachable key. £8

A fine brass barrel tap. £4

Wooden barrel tap, 7in. long, circa 1880. £3

Victorian brass barrel tap with integral key and hammering pin. £6

19th century brass barrel tap, 3in. high. £2

'In line' brass barrel tap. £3

20th century wooden barrel tap. £3

Brass barrel tap with swivel lever and locking plate. £6

A fine brass barrel tap by Ansells. £5

(Paul G. Sheppard)

BEDCOVERS

Bedcovers and quilts, many of very humble origin indeed, are now most enthusiastically collected in all parts of the Western world.

They are treasured for their intricate designs, colourful patterns and, perhaps more important still, the skill demonstrated in the fine hand stitching. Some examples are considered to be so rare and valuable that they hang, framed and under special glass to prevent fading.

The original concept was a simple one — to make use of odd scraps of fabric in producing a bedcovering with a practical function. As many more women became proficient in the art, traditional patterns developed, but even these formal designs show much individual style.

In setting out the pattern for a quilt, a paper pattern was cut, often from whatever bits and pieces were to hand; letters, household accounts and other documents were used. The paper pieces were sometimes stitched into the backing of the quilt and may provide a clue in dating a piece.

Finely woven bedcover 'The Dog's Card Game', 6ft. x 4ft. £15

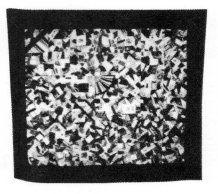

A Victorian silk crazy quilt made by Rowene and Sarah Bowen of Newport, Rhode Island, approx. 8ft.2in. x 7ft.5in. (Robt. W. Skinner Inc.) £538

An applique quilt signed and dated 'Sarah Ann Wilson - 1854', consisting of thirty appliqued squares of floral and animal design, 7ft.1in. x 8ft.4in. (Robt. W. Skinner Inc.) £22,222

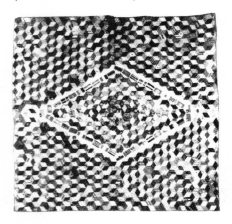

A Centennial patchwork calico block pattern quilt, American, 1876, approx. 84 x 84in. (Robt. W. Skinner Inc.) £466

A wool and cotton jacquard coverlet, Pennsylvania or Ohio, 1830-50, 82 x 70in. (Christie's) £623

An American patchwork and applique quilt, 'Stars and Stripes', 87 x 80in. (Christie's) £380

American 19th century cotton applique quilt, 88 x 86in. (Christie's) £953

Early 20th century American pieced and quilted coverlet with sixteen blazing stars, 97 x 95in. (Christie's) £353

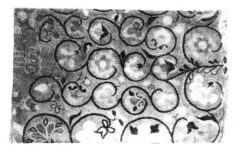

Victorian crazy quilt and two pillow shams, American, circa 1870, 61 x 61in. (Robt. W. Skinner Inc.) £308

A bed rug with reddish tan background, inscribed 'HH-1770', American, 4ft.6in. x 6ft.10in. (Robt. W. Skinner Inc.)£2,692

BEER CANS

Beer cans were first produced in 1935. The earlier examples featuring a cone shaped top were superseded in the late 1950's by a flat topped can which required the use of an opener. By the 1960's the ring pull had taken over. It is interesting to note that collectors prefer ringpull cans to be intact and so empty the contents from the bottom of the can.

The size of cans in the U.K. is 15½ fl.oz. (440ml), 9.2/3 fl.oz. (275ml.) and party cans in 4, 7 and, until recently, 5 pint cans. 11.2/3 fl.oz. cans are made for the export market, this being about the most popular size worldwide.

Over 25,000 different cans have been made and many collectors specialise in a particular country, size, brewery or theme. Rarity and design determine the desirability of a can — cone top or flat top cans generally being the hardest to find. Condition is important — a badly rusted or dented can is of little interest although restoration can be very rewarding.

Newcastle Brown Ale, Golden Jubilee, 1977. 30p

Tennent's Lager, Lager Lovelies — Linda, 1969, 15½fl.oz.   £15

Tennent's Lager, English Series — Young Lady in Trafalgar Square, 1962.   £20

Guinness, 15½fl.oz., 1975.   £2.50

Tennent's Lager — Shirley, 1971. £12

McEwan's Pale Ale, 15½fl.oz., 1960.   £8

Tennent's Lager, Housewives' Choice — Thelma (Herring Fritters) 1964. £20

Tennent's Lager, Scottish Series, 2nd, — Sailing down the Clyde at Rothesay, 1961.   £15

(Steven Currie)

66

Harp Lager, 1967, 9.2/3fl.oz.   £6

Worthington India Pale Ale, 1969, 9.2/3fl.oz.   £4

Hull Brewery Anchor Export Beer, 1969, 9.2/3fl.oz.   £12

Felinfoel Prince's Ale, 1969, 9.2/3fl. oz.   £20

Piper Export — A Pipe Major of the Royal Scots, 1966.   £6

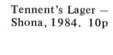

Tennent's Lager — Shona, 1984. 10p

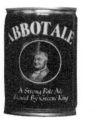

Greene King Abbot Ale, 1978, 9.2/3fl.oz.   15p

Marks & Spencers Bitter, 1976, 9.2/3fl.oz.   £2

Tennent's Lager, poster offer, paper label 1980.   50p

Heineken Lager, misprint, no black ink, 1978.   50p

Tollemache Cobbold Pinlet Draught Bitter, 1960, 7 pint.   £20

(Steven Currie)

BEER CANS

Hall & Woodhouse Gold. Medal Brock Lager, 1972, 11. 2/dfl.oz. £6

Tennent's Lager — Penny — at the end of the day, 1976, 11.2/3fl.oz. 75p

Tennent's Lager, temporary can 1975, 11.2/3fl.oz. £20

A large 4 pint beer can of Ruddles Bitter, the Rutland Brewery, 1981. 40p

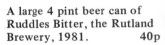

Barclay's Export Pilsner Lager, cone top 1955, 12fl.oz. £20

Tennent's Sweetheart Stout, 1985. 5p

Farrimond's F.B., cone top, 1937, 12fl.oz. £5

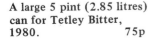

A large 5 pint (2.85 litres) can for Tetley Bitter, 1980. 75p

Younger's Sweet Stout, 1969. £5

Aitken's Export, 1958. £20

Guinness, £1 voucher offer, 1980. 15p

(Steven Currie)

BEER MATS

Many beer mat collectors, (or, as they are known in the trade, Tegestologists), would readily acknowledge that it was an interest in the seemingly infinite variety of mats rather than an eye for any possible monetary value that launched them into this particular field. Changes in a growing market however, now reflect a current value on some mats of up to several pounds and, since most collections are fairly large, this could represent a considerable sum of money.

Apart from the very early pre-war advertising cork mats, which are quite rare, early beer mats made of thick card and issued by the breweries and tobacco companies to advertise their products are the most desirable examples. Artist drawn sketches and the modern puzzle or competition specimens also create a lot of interest.

Guinness for you.
50p

Pick a Red Rose stout.
10p

Long John Scotch Whisky.
60p

Wicked Lady cocktail.
50p

Stella Artois, Mexico Olympics.
£1.75

United Clubs draught beer.
£3

Mackeson, taste the goodness.
40p

Mimosa when you feel like a Snowball. 25p

Trumans for fans of good beer. £2.50

A Girl's Survival Guide, Babycham.
10p

Vaux, Brewed in the North.
£2

Cameron's Strongarm.
£3.50

Roman Bronnen Sources.
£2

Tuborg covers the world.
£3.75

'Beer at its Best', Tetley.
50p

Mackeson Stout 'Try that unique rounded flavour'.
£7

(Bryn Edwards)

BEER MATS

Ponderosa Western
Saloon.   £1

Bitter's On The Move
To Watneys.   £1.50

Heineken Bier. 75p

Keg Trumans
Brown.   £3

Vale of Neath Ales.
70p

Cornhill London Dry
Gin.   50p

Safir De Gheest.£2

Tom Thumb cigars.
£1

Britvic fruit juices.
£1.25

Make it a Buckley's.
£1.50

Merry Xmas, Happy
New Year, Guinness.
30p

Ansells King-Pin
mild 'the better keg
beer'.   £2

Lamot, its most desir-
able.   20p

Ansells Ind Coope,
Wales 1969.   £2

Captain Morgan
Jamaica Rum. £4

'Magnet for me',
John Smiths, Tad-
caster.   30p

Cherapear for a cham-
pagne glass.   £4

Escort filter tipped
'Big in quality'. £2

Booth's London Dry
Gin.   £1

For a Hot Tip see
over.   £9

(Bryn Edwards)

BEER MATS

Nelson Tipped Cig-
arettes.   £4

Seven-Up Mixer. 20p

Have a mild brown
Cigarella.   60p

Jubilee Stout. £1.50

Hancocks Five Five,
A Great Bottled Beer.
          £3

Fall in Love with
Cherapear. £3.50

Bass, Blue Triangle.
          75p

Evan Evans Bevan
Ltd., Vale of Neath
Ales.   £2

McEwan's Export, the
best buy in beer. 50p

To be sure say . . .
Gordon's for me. £1.50

Bass Naturally. 75p

Alpine lager. 80p

Hancocks is great
beer.   £3

Blue Mountain Rum.
          £4

Newcastle Strong
Brown Ale.   40p

Younger's Tartan
Keg Bitter.   50p

Stones Ales, decidedly
good.   £1

Wills's Woodbines
Smoked by Millions.
          £4

Senior Service 'The
Best Cigarette'. £8

Wills's Capstan Cig-
arettes.   £4

(Bryn Edwards)

71

Park your Guinness here.   £1

Piper Extra Strong, Extra export.   £3

Johnnie Walker Scotch Whisky. 40p

Coates Somerset cider 'comes up from Somerset'.   20p

Breaker Malt Liquor.   60p

Buckleys 1767-1967, Anniversary beer mat.   £1.50

Royal Crown, Real American Cola. 80p

Try a cool Picon Soda   60p

Lambert & Butler King Size.   10p

Trumans for disco-verers of good beer.   75p

Hancocks Barley-brite, A Great Keg Bitter.   £1.50

Mild Van Dyck Cigars 'have the mildness you like'.   £1.25

Domingo 'A really mild cigar for a really mild price'.   £1

Tuborg Delicious Danish Lager. £2

Stone's Original Green Ginger Wine.   £1.50

Rhymney 'Welsh Brown' the best round here.   £1

M. & B. 'Sam Brown its marvellous beer'.   80p

Brains, Cardiff, Est. 1713. 40p

Chipmunk Crisps, Go on treat your-self.   60p

M. & B. Marvellous Beer (blue glass sil-houette).   40p

(Bryn Edwards)

BELLS

While bells come in many shapes and sizes there are basically only two types.
One is the open 'church' bell shape with a clapper suspended on the inside and the other the 'rumbler' which is closed with a loose clapper moving freely within the bell.
From the giant Russian bell Kolokol to the miniature bells for dressing dolls, there are bell ringers' hand bells, assembly bells for chapel and school, and an immense number of decorative and serving bells.
One of the most common examples found on the market today is the 'cluckett' often used as a sheep bell and easily recognisable by its flat appearance.
Occasionally, one may come across a good example of a punch bell — strike it with your hand and it rings. You may even be lucky enough to find a medieval 'crotal' such as those used by falconers, priests and jesters, but beware of reproductions.

Victorian wooden handled bronze hand bell. £12

A French table bell 10.2cm. high, maker's mark J.D., Paris, 1761, 138gr. £3,604

Spanish 17th century table bell with baluster handle, 9oz. 14dwt.(Christie's) £432

Mid 17th century Dutch bronze bell, 13in. high. £1,760

Welsh brass souvenir bell with lion handle. £3

Victorian cranberry glass bell, 12in. high. £85

20th century brass souvenir table bell of a lady in a crinolin dress, 4in. tall. £3

A 19th century cloisonne bell of waisted 'U' shape, 12½in. £572

(Paul G. Sheppard)

BLOW LAMPS

An appreciation of the craftsmanship that went into the making of fine old tools has lifted the market to record levels and extended the interest to encompass all sorts of pieces of equipment.

It is not at all uncommon today, to find a highly polished old brass blow lamp occupying pride of place on the most fashionable of mantlepieces.

The blow lamp, invented towards the end of the nineteenth century, was usually fuelled by paraffin or kerosene and operated on a pressurised pump action. The most prominent makes were Primus, Monitor and Sievert.

A large Primus blow lamp with metal handle.   £6

A Swedish Sievert brass blow lamp with composition handle.   £11

A Monitor No. 26 brass paraffin blow lamp.   £8.50

Swedish brass blow lamp by Sievert with metal handle.   £9

All metal British made blow lamp.   £4

All metal blow lamp by F. T. Paris.   £7.50

(Paul G. Sheppard)

BOTTLE OPENERS

Small and useful objects like bottle openers were, and still are, considered to be the ideal material for advertising purposes.

Usually marked with the company name, a date and perhaps a few words announcing a new product they were generally inexpensive to manufacture and could be given to customers as a token of goodwill.

Some examples produced to commemorate a special event were sold as souvenirs.
Items of 'local' interest as well as novelty pieces will always attract a higher premium.

An English silver Crown cork bottle opener of Art Deco design, date letter 'D' for 1939 and initials WW, 3½in. long. **£35**

A heavy pewter paperweight and bottle opener, stamped on base 'Ducky' by Kirby & Beard of Paris, circa 1930. **£68**

A Crown cork opener in iron and sheet metal, advertising 'Guinness'. **£3**

A tin opener and Crown cork opener and corkscrew, 'Oasis Rd No. 888293. Hy Squire & Sons Ltd.', 4¾in. long. **£9**

A novelty golf ball Crown cork bottle opener, stamped 'Made in England', 3½in. long. **£12**

A Crown cork bottle opener and all steel pocket corkscrew, maker's name 'Made & Pat'd. in USA Vaughan Chicago', 3in. long. **£23**

(Christopher Sykes)

75

A Crown cork opener in cast iron and sheet metal with double sided 'Crown Opener Rd. 702661' and 'Made in England'.   £3

Skyline Bottle Boy, all chrome helical corkscrew with two Crown cork openers, 5in. long.   £7

A Crown cork opener, advertising 'MacFarlane's Rd 702661' and 'Aerated Waters'.   £3

A Scandinavian Crown cap opener, circa 1860, 6in. long.   £17

An advertising pocket Crown cap bottle opener, on one side the Johnnie Walker gentleman and on reverse is 'Born 1820 Still Going Strong', 1½in. long.   £45

A Crown cork bottle opener in the form of a miniature beer bottle, 3½in. long.   £5

A Crown cork opener in cast iron and sheet metal, advertising 'Mackeson I. Rd 811274'.   £3

A novelty Crown cork bottle opener, the turned wooden bottle forms the handle, the opener is stamped 'An Tsin Tir Adheanta', 5¾in. long.   £18

A Crown cork opener with single sided 'Great Stuff This Bass'.   £3

(Christopher Sykes)

BOTTLE OPENERS

All metal rachet top bottle opener. £3

Chromium plated bottle opener and bottle top with screw fitting. 50p

Crown opener, Patent No. 811274. £1

Combined can and bottle opener with wooden handle. £2

Brass and nickel 'Bell' bottle opener, Indian, circa 1950. £4

Combined screwdriver, bottle opener and spanner. £2

Fisholow all metal bottle opener. 40p

Key-shaped combined bottle opener and cork-screw. £5

Smiths 'The Beer to Enjoy' bottle opener. 50p

(Paul G. Sheppard)

BOTTLES

Bottles most popular with British collectors fall into four categories:-

1. Mineral water, beer and other beverage bottles.
2. Quack medicine and 'Cure All' bottles.
3. Glass and stone ink bottles.
4. Poison bottles.

Most collections start with a mineral water bottle, the most popular being Hiram Codd's marble-stoppered lemonade bottle, and the transfer-printed stone ginger beer bottle. Especially sought after are coloured varieties of the Codd bottle. A few years ago they could be bought for under £10, but today, the dark green and amber varieties change hands at about £75 and the cobalt blues well over £100.

The patent medicine 'quack cure' category also shows an indication of some staggering increases in value. Not long ago a Warners Safe Cure Bottle, green in colour could be bought for less than £15. Today you may be lucky enough to pick one up for £50.

The variety of both stone and glass ink bottles to be found is vast, ranging from a simple eight-sided variety to the most sought after of all, the cottage ink, so called because it was moulded in the form of a small cottage with doors and windows. Until recently these were considered to be worth between £10 and £15. Now, because of demand, they average around £40 and certain very rare examples go to overseas collectors at around the £250 mark.

Poison bottles too are becoming a very specialised category with the cobalt blue varieties the most valued. Of particular interest would be a blue poison bottle shaped rather like a submarine or in the figural form of a skull and crossbones which are considered so rare that the price would be negotiable between buyer and seller

A. J. Smith & Co. pictorial whisky flagon, £20, non-pictorial £10.

Eclipse patent wasp waist cobalt blue bottle, 8in. high. £175

Cobalt blue castor oil bottle, 6¼in. high. £4

Hart & Co. ginger beer bottle with blue top and print, 6¾in. high. £150

Prices Patent Candle Co. bottle of cobalt blue, 7¼in. high. £30

A rare ginger beer by W. A. Scott, Montrose, with swing stopper. £200

(Mike Smith)

Glass bottle with embossed Madonna and Child, containing holy water, 5in. tall. £12

A sealed wine bottle of 'bladder' form, inscribed 'C. Coke 1727', 20cm. £165

Schweppes stoneware ginger beer bottle. £4

A small Prattware 'Shakespeare' cream pot. £22

Small blue glass perfume bottle with crown stopper, 3in. high. £7

A pot for Boots 'Confection of Senna', 3in. tall. £8

Edwardian hair lotion by G. Thomas, 'Extract of Honey and Flowers'. £3

An unusual glass 'Cottage' inkwell. £30

Pettifer's Ewe Draught for safe lambing, 6in. high. £1

'Caviare' pot by Jacksons of Piccadilly, 3¼in. high. £5

Martin poison bottle with shaped neck, 4½in. long. £40

James Keiller & Sons stone-ware marmalade pot, 1.3/8in. high. £30

Radam's Microbe Killer bottle, heavily embossed, 10¼in. high. £45

Rare ginger beer bottles, Pallett & Springwell, 6¾in. high, £100; Spa, 4in. tall, £100; Tuddenham, 2¼in. high, £85; Bourne Denby, ¾in. high, £40.

W. & J. Ratcliff slab seal stout bottle, 10¾in. tall. £60

Wallich's 'Improved Inhaler' of unusual jug shape complete with handle, distributed by Burroughs, Wellcome & Co. £30

A mid blue crescent shape poison 'Not To Be Taken', 5in. high. £5

Bolesworth's cream pot, 5½in. high. £150

(Mike Smith)

Field's non-corrosive ink bottle, 2¼in. high. £15

Amber glass Hamilton bottle, 8¾in. long, £70, agua glass.£4

Stranraer sepia printed cream pot, 4in. tall. £6

Aqua glass Codd's bottle, 8½in. high. £2

'Dewars' Peace whisky flask by Royal Doulton, 7in. high. £100

Heavily embossed Hop Bitters by Taylors of Manchester, 11½in. high. £6

'Rock Blue' ginger beer bottle by W. R. Hatton & Sons, 7½in. high. £35

Sir Robert Peel stoneware reform flask, 9¼in. tall. £175

Coventry ginger beer bottle with transfer printed Bicycle emblem, 6¾in. high. £40

(Mike Smith)

Virol bone marrow pot, 9in. tall, £12; 4½in. tall, £2.

Warners Safe Cure bottles, amber glass 6¾in. high, £10; Green Diabettes Cure 8¾in. high, £45.

Parrett & Axe Vales cream pot, 4¼in. high.   £10

Dockhead black glass flask by Wm. Jackson, 7¾in. long.   £150

An early Bellarmine stone-ware bottle, 8¼in. high.   £250

Zara Seal bottle, 10¼in. high. £12 (smaller examples 4in. high, £20.)

Fishers Seaweed Extract bottle with bulbous neck, 5in. high.   £25

An early wine bottle of dark-green metal, circa 1670, 19.5cm. high.   £440

Transfer printed Brunswick Blacking pot, 5in. high, £7; non-transfer-printed. £1

(Mike Smith)

BOTTLES

Taylors Mustard bottle of amber glass, 4in. high. £5

Harwood's Superior black writing ink bottle, 3½in. wide. £50

A cobalt blue Blackwood & Co. Patent Syphon Ink bottle, 4¾in. high. £75

An emerald green Harrogate Wells Spa Water bottle, 8¼in. high. £5

A fine pair of sealed case gin bottles, 11¼in. high, £40; 4.3/8in. high, £80.

'Lynaris' Niagara Patent amber glass bottle, 8½in. high. £75

Ginger beer bottle by Job Wragg, 6¾in. high. £3

Taddy & Co. snuff bottle, 2½in. high. £100

An early Dutch 'onion' bottle, 7in. high. £35

(Mike Smith)

Prices Patent Candle Co. cough medicine in a cobalt blue bottle. £40

19th century octagonal glass ink bottle. £4

Victorian black glass whisky bottle with embossed lettering. £25

A rare cobalt blue Hiram Codd's marble stoppered bottle. £120

Exide glass battery case, 8½in. tall. £2

'Warners Safe Cure' bottle with embossed lettering. £55

Cobalt blue poison bottle 'Not to be taken'. £6

G. & A. Kendall, Wine & Spirit Merchant, stoneware wine jar. £8

Stoneware ginger beer by Govancroft, Glasgow. £2

BOXES

It is hardly surprising that the development of the steam train, steam ship and other relatively comfortable means of transport made trips on horseback virtually obsolete and encouraged Victorians to travel as the people of no other age before them had done. A hangover of the Victorian travel bug is the vast quantity of carrying boxes designed to cater for an almost limitless number of nineteenth century needs.

From surgeons' boxes, complete with blood chilling arrays of saws, scalpels and probes to apothecaries' boxes with their phials and philtres; from barbers' boxes equipped with razors, strops and scissors to simple hat boxes — the Victorians had them all.

Quite apart from these carrying boxes, there were others too, including, picnic boxes, writing boxes, needlework boxes and vanity boxes.

The widely varying quality of all of these examples is reflected in the prices they fetch today.

A Continental brass mounted rosewood jewel casket in Art Deco style, 10in. (Lawrence Fine Art) £187

Late 15th century Tyrolean leather covered casket, 6¼ x 15¾in. £2,420

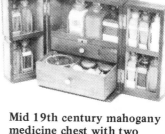

Mid 19th century mahogany medicine chest with two doors at the front, English, 8¾in. wide. £462

A Federal mahogany lap desk with semi-circular roll-top, 18in. wide. (Christie's) £510

Double sided sailor's valentine, octagonal mahogany cases filled with pastel coloured shells and seeds, circa 1850, 20½in. wide. (Robt. W. Skinner Inc.) £492

An early 19th century walnut ballot box on ball feet, 10½in. long. £121

A late 18th century mahogany and walnut collar box, 6½in. diam. £132

19th century European small rectangular chip carved box, 7¾in. wide. (Robt. W. Skinner Inc.) £140

Gillette safety razor in metallic box. £2.50

A papier-mache writing box richly inlaid in mother-of-pearl, circa 1850, 1ft.3in. wide. £550

Needlework toilet box, worked during the reign of Charles II, 11½in. wide. (Phillips) £660

A Victorian painted coal box with cast foliate scroll handles, 15 x 17½in. high. (Lawrence Fine Art) £275

Late 19th century rosewood dressing box with hinged top fitted with mirror, 12in. wide. (Robt. W. Skinner Inc.) £183

An 18th century squirrel cage, 23 x 19in. £187

19th century burl mahogany travelling vanity case. (Stalker & Boos) £416

An 18th century oak ballot box with brass loop handle, 7 x 8in. £198

A William IV rosewood combined work and collector's cabinet, inlaid with mother-of-pearl, circa 1835, 1ft.1¾in. wide. £253

A Sheraton period mahogany serpentine slope-top cutlery box, Sheffield plate fittings, circa 1790, 12½in. high. (Neales) £210

A rosewood stationery casket of wedge form with sloping lid, 6½in. wide. £99

Regency penwork games box of octagonal form, on gilt metal feet, circa 1805, 8¼in. wide. £220

An 18th century mahogany salt box, 10¼in. wide. £308

American 18th century pine pipe box, 16½in. high. (Robt. W. Skinner Inc.) £500

18th century Indian hardwood table top cabinet inlaid in ivory and having side handles, 16in. wide. (Geering & Colyer) £460

An 18th century figured mahogany and inlaid cutlery box, 15in. high. (W. H. Lane & Son) £200

A walnut cased medicine chest with brass carrying handle, English, circa 1840, 12in. wide. £418

French kingwood parquetry and ormolu mounted encrier, circa 1890, 1ft.2½in. wide. £451

An early 19th century rosewood and brass decorated humidor and cigar dispenser, 12in. high. £176

BRICKS

'Bricks?'

'Yes, bricks!'.

There were many small brickworks in full time production throughout the Victorian era and for some, the market was so localised you would be unlikely to find examples of their work outside of a radius of ten miles or so.

There is a wide variety of shapes, size, composition and usage. Early bricks were often stamped with a maker's name or a seal denoting authentication and these add interest for the collector.

Most bricks have only a nominal value but the very best quality of all, the engineering blue bricks, command a high reclamation value.

Now that there is something of a vogue in exposed interior brickwork, collectors are having to compete with interior designers in scavenging the country for good examples.

19th century brick marked 'Lilco' with glazed face.   75p

1970's vent brick with 14 apertures. 50p

19th century brick stamped Rufford Stour-bridge.   £1

1970's vent brick with 5 apertures.   50p

An early red house brick.   50p

Victorian enamel faced brick. 50p

19th century brick stamped Hamptonpark, Hereford.   £1

19th century brick marked B.B. 75p

(Paul G. Sheppard)

BRIDLE BITS

The horse bit is basically a training device designed to curb or restrain the animal. There are as many different types of bit as there are functions for the horse to cope with and each has been specifically constructed to cope with a particular job. This piece of equipment is commonly made of steel and the more decorative version, worn on dress occasions, is often nickel plated.

A dray horse would have a large plain bit and a show horse a more elaborate, ornamental bit. The stallion bit, which consists of a steel ring placed around the lower jaw and attached to strapping over the animal's head, acts to prevent the horse from rearing and is also referred to as a 'chatter bit'. The bridle bit for a pack horse would have the addition of 'rumbler bells' devised to keep the team on the move.

There are all sorts of variations and special attachments which will add highlights to a collection.

Mid 19th century iron jointed Pelham bit. £10

Mid Victorian iron mouthing bit.   £10

Early 19th century iron jointed Pelham.   £8

A fine and large 19th century nickel plated bit. £15

An elaborate polished steel fixed cheek curb.   £14

Mid 19th century iron fixed cheek curb.   £7

(Pauline Holliday)

BRUSHES

If it wasn't for man's innate desire to be orderly and clean, the necessity for the brush would be obviated.

Most of those designed for domestic cleaning duties are of a purely functional nature and generally command little collecting interest, although specialist brushes do have their following, in particular sweep's brushes, those for dusting bottles or even the ubiquitous lavatory brush.

It is those connected with personal hygiene which are more desirable for they are generally of a far better quality, either simply veneered or with Tunbridgeware decoration and even made of silver, tortoiseshell and enamel. Of particular interest are those for shaving, brushing hair and teeth or even those for clothes, shoes and moustaches.

1950's dog's brush with bristle, and wire reverse. 50p

Victorian Tunbridgeware clothes brush. £15

Late 19th century veneered wood clothes brush. £3.50

Late Victorian sweep's brush and sticks. £22

Victorian silver backed hair brush. £15

Omar Ramsden silver dressing table set of two hairbrushes and a hand mirror, 1923, 32.5cm. high. £250

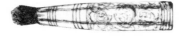
Victorian travelling shaving brush made by T. W., London, 1850. £75

A silver handled toothbrush by Joseph Taylor, Birmingham, 1802, 11cm. long. £85

A boxwood and bone traveller's moustache brush, 7in. long extended, circa 1850. (Christopher Sykes) £67

(Paul G. Sheppard)

90

BUCKLES

Buckles have been worn on shoes, garters, waistbelts and, as a purely decorative feature on all sorts of clothing. Although the original function was simply to hold two edges or strappings together in a fastened condition, they presented such an endless scope for whatever decorative talents were available they quickly assumed the importance of a piece of jewellery.

Examples range from the large 18th century shoe buckles with steel tongue grips, and silver rims of intricately crafted design, to the moulded bakelite floral buckles of the forties, with a dazzling array of patterns in between.

They were made from every possible material and reflect the changing fashions of the times.

The beautiful silver buckles with the flowing designs of the Art Nouveau period are the most popular with collectors today.

A French soft metal Zodiac belt buckle.   £1

Sterling silver belt buckle by Shreve, Crump & Low, Boston, circa 1900, 3 troy oz., 5½in. long. (Robert W. Skinner Inc.)   £95

1930's dress buckle. £1.50

An old large brass harness buckle.   £5

18th century iron buckle with fern leaf motifs, 3½in. long.   £9

A Faberge silver gilt and enamel buckle, 1899-1903.
£721

A Russian silver gilt shaped buckle with a dagger clasp. (Christie's S. Kensington)
£85

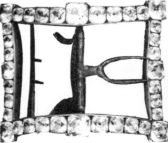

A fine late 18th century shoe buckle of polished steel decorated with crystal stones set in silver.   £38

1930's brass butterfly belt buckle.   £5

(Paul G. Sheppard)

91

BUTTONS

It is known that buttons date from as early as the 6th century A.D. in the Middle East and from the mid fourteenth century in Great Britain. Can you imagine the quantities of buttons produced in the intervening centuries?

Attention focuses mainly on the buttons known to be worth money. The 18th century sets of silver buttons, the beautiful silver and enamel buttons in the Art Nouveau style and the colourfully decorated cloisonne buttons, all have their devotees — at a price, but apart from these, and a few other types of fine quality buttons, antiques dealers tend to neglect the subject, mainly through lack of available information on pricing.

And that is where the collector comes in. Most people just 'keep' buttons, then realise they have a collection. There is still an enormous variety of buttons to choose from, often by the tinful, and most are very reasonably priced. As soon as some sort of 'going rate' has been established, the price is sure to rise.

Pair of mother-of pearl buttons with gilded rims. 50p

Set of twelve French silver buttons. £35

Set of five Islamic silver coin buttons. £10

Civil Defence button by J. R. Gaunt & Son, London. 50p

Card of eight pink buttons by Jason. 50p

Eight decorative pearl buttons. £1

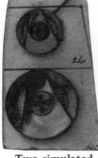

Two simulated mother-of-pearl buttons. £1

Set of eight British Red Cross Society buttons of ebonised wood. £12

Set of ten decorative brass buttons by Jennens & Co., London. £4

Set of eight blue glass dress buttons. £2

Set of four alloy heraldic buttons. £2.50

(Gwendoline Edwards)

CAR PARTS

The advent of the Autojumble is a good indication of the ever increasing enthusiasm for the long established practise of collecting and trading in old car parts. The quantity and variety of marketable goods endorses the theory that there is no part of a motor vehicle which cannot be salvaged and put to some useful purpose.

Quite apart from objects with a utilisable value in restoration, there is a thriving trade in parts which have chiefly a decorative appeal. This category generally includes headlamps, clocks and hub caps. (Up until 1930, hub caps were nickel plated to a fairly dull finish and some were plated in brass. These early examples are now quite valuable).

The glittering prize in ornamentation has to be the car mascot. The earliest date from around 1905 and some are rare and precious objects indeed. The most famous of these must be the 'Spirit of Ecstasy' designed by Charles Sykes R.A. for Rolls Royce in 1911 and, amongst the most beautiful examples are the glass sculptures of Rene Lalique.

An all-brass boa constrictor motoring horn, 6ft. long. (Onslows) £700

Austin A35 bonnet emblem. £3

One of a pair of Austin A35 wing lights. £4

A plated, Fiat lorry hubcap. £2

A cast silver radiator mascot by Omar Ramsden, 1935, 12.8cm., 21.5oz. (Lawrence Fine Art) £935

R.A.C. alloy and plastic car badge. £1

Watch type car voltmeter with contrast lead. £4.50

Glass motor car figurehead by Rene Lalique entitled 'Spirit of the Wind'. (S. W. Cottee & Son) £2,600

Silver plated 'cherub' car mascot, circa 1905. £30

(Paul G. Sheppard)

93

1960 Volvo P1800 rev counter. £20

An early A.A. motor car badge. £7

1968 Ford Corsair hub cap. £2

A 'Spirit of Ecstacy' car mascot. £95

Austin A35 radiator grille. £6

1930's car clock, 3in. diam. £20

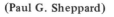

'The Order of the Road' enamelled car badge. £12

A pre 1940 Wilmot Breeden Calormeter for affixing to a card radiator. £22

An R.A.F. motor car display badge. £5

(Paul G. Sheppard)

CARTE DE VISITE

The earliest recorded mention of the Carte de Visite in La Lumiere, 1854, credits two Frenchmen with — 'an original idea for the use of small portraits'.

The Carte de Visite consisted of a portrait, usually full length and measuring approximately 2½ x 3½ins., mounted on a slightly larger card designed as a calling card, which often carried reference to the photographer on the reverse side. The cost might have been anything up to a shilling.

The idea was promoted by one, Disderi, who, having captured the interest of the people, then applied for a patent.

By 1862, 'cartemania' was sweeping society and Disderi is reputed to have earned as much as £50,000 annually from his studio work.

The bestselling Carte de Visite of all time was W. Downey's portrait of the Princess of Wales (1867), which achieved a sale of 300,000 copies.

One of the most notable of all Carte de Visite photographers was C. Silvy who, having moved from France to London, set up studio in 1859 and established a sophisticated clientele. Examples of his work are probably the most desired by collectors.

King Edward.   £10

General Von Moltke. (The London Stereoscopic & Photographic Co.)   £11

Musicians. (Ayling).   £6

Cavour. (Mayer & Pearson).   £8

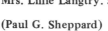

Mrs. Lillie Langtry. £20

(Paul G. Sheppard)

Duchess of Wellington. (C. Silvy).   £13

Philip of Spain. (Elliott & Fry) £11

Prince & Princess Louis of Hesse & Princess Victoria. (Hills & Saunders). £14

Councillor J. W. Consterdine-Chadwick, 1883. £4

Wallet, Queen's Jester. (Henry Spink). £12

Lord Roberts — Court size card, Souvenir of South Africa 1899-1900. (Elliott & Fry). £11

Midget. (J. Groom, Shrews-bury). £6

The Crown Prince of Prussia. (The London Stereoscopic & Photographic Co.) £11

Miss Ellen Terry. £6

(Paul G. Sheppard)

Millais. (Elliott & Fry). £11

CARTE DE VISITE

Duke of Wellington.
(Clarkington & Co.) £13

Mr. Barrington & Miss
Jessie Bond in 'Ruddigore'.
£6

Tennyson. (Elliott & Fry).
£14

The Royal Family. (G. I.
Spalding & Co.)   £12

Queen Victoria — Court size
card. (Hughes & Mullins).
£8

Example of early 'tin
type' photograph. £40

The Railway Worker.
(Saml. Kirk, Nottingham).
£3

Mr. W. Terris & Miss
Millward in 'The Harbour
Lights'. (Theatrical) £6

Miss Anderson.   £9

(Paul G. Sheppard)

Duke of Rutland. (C. Silvy).
£9

Prince Holstein, Augusten-
bourg. (C. Silvy).   £6

Lord Palmerston. (Mayer
& Pierson).   £11

Prince Gorbehekoff, Russian
Prime Minister. (Bergamasco).
£12

Unidentified. (J. R. Dow-
dall).   50p

Mr. Herbert Gladstone, M.P.
£9

Le Sultan. (Abdullah
Freres).   £12

Princess Beatrice, Victoria's
youngest daughter. (W. G.
Lacy).   £6

(Paul G. Sheppard)

Duke of Argyll. (Caldest
Blandford & Co.).   £8

Marquis de Azzeler. (C. Silvy). £5

Victor Emmanuel. (Disderi & Cie). £9

Newcastle. (Caldesi Blanford & Co.). £6

H.S.H. Prince Christian of Schleswig Holstein. (Hills & Saunders). £12

T.H.R. The Crown Prince & Princess of Prussia with their children. (Hills & Saunders). £14

Unidentified. (J. Burton). 50p

Duke of Buccleuch. (Caldesi Blanford & Co.) £6

Princess of Prussia. (W. & D. Downey). £10

Macauley. (Maull & Polyblank). £9

(Paul G. Sheppard)

CARTE DE VISITE

Rev. B. Winthrop, Vicar of Wolverton. (Alexander Bassano). £4

Example of early 'tin type' photograph. £40

Mrs. Winthrop. (Alexander Bassano). £4

Queen Victoria. £12

George Blaiklook. (Robt. Everest). £2

Duke of Albani. £4.50

Unidentified 'Remember Me'. (Mons. Williams). £1

Duchess of Albani. £4.50

Mr. Field of Bragg's Farm. (Bullock, Brothers). £2

(Paul G. Sheppard)

CAT POSTCARDS

Postcards depicting cats is another very popularly subscribed area of collecting.

One of the most famous 'cat' artists must surely be Louis Wain whose work is most highly prized. His series published by Tucks is particularly favoured and a good example will fetch as much as £16 per card.

Early vignettes by this artist fall into the £8-£20 price range. (It is worth noting that when the front of the cards have been written on they are worth less than those in mint condition.)

Other notable artists in this field are Arthur Thiele, Dorothy Travers Pope and for cats in comic situations we can look to the work of Donald McGill and Lawson Wood.

PFB Series No. 7072/A embossed chromo litho study of cats, artist drawn.   £6

AFKH Series deckle edge colour postcard 50's/60's, real photo 'The kitten and the goldfish'.   50p

'Brown Tabby and Persian' cat study by Ernest H. Mills, Salmon Series P.C. No. 4587.   £1.50

Cat study by Louis Wain, published by J. Salmon Sevenoaks (middle period).   £12

Art Photo Series brithday greeting card with cat and flowers, hand-tinted photo.   25p

PFB Series No. 7072/D embossed chromo litho study of cat with bell.   £6

(Paul G. Sheppard)

CAT POSTCARDS

OGZL Series, 'Kittens At Play', art type postcard No. 638.   £1.50

ABM Series No. 53 'Cats At Tea', undivided back chromo litho postcard vignette.   £4

TSN Series No. 1603, art study of cat by T. Sperlich.   £2

'Faulkner' Series art type postcard 'Cats In The Sewing Basket' by A. Talboys. £1.75

OGZL Series 'Mother And Kittens At Play', art type postcard No. 637.   £1.50

Melissa 'Klasik Kards', 'Cats At The Dentist'.   25p

ABM Series No. 79, 'Cats Tea Party', undivided back chromo litho postcard vignette.£4

Embossed chromo litho Easter card, American, 'Cats And Chicks'.   £3

(Paul G. Sheppard)

CHAIRS

Over the years, as rooms have been changed and modernised, many a good chair has been relegated to the attic. It was probably thought at the time that while it was too good to be thrown away it was not worthwhile trying to sell it.

At first glance, an old rickety chair may not strike one as the perfect object for the sitting room but, once restored a transformation can take place.

The Victorian cabriole leg dining chair is probably the nicest chair to have been produced during the Victorian period, dating from about 1850 to the end of the century.

With their full balloon backs and French influenced cabriole legs these chairs achieved a degree of elegance soon to be lost as the popular taste turned towards more ponderous styles. The better made examples of this style were those produced at the beginning of their period of popularity and were usually of rosewood, walnut or mahogany, often with fine floral carving on the backs and knees and the most beautifully carved scroll feet; later chairs were often of beech or oak construction and not so well made or finely carved.

Throughout the late Victorian era, dining chairs tended to be heavy and ponderously respectable in style, drawing room chairs being somewhat lighter and bedroom chairs were often positively frivolous. The super-abundance of down to earth kitchen chairs in the Windsor style is due to the fact that almost every joinery shop in the country found them easy to produce from whatever wood was to hand. They were produced from about 1830 until the end of the Victorian era and were particularly popular in working class homes and in country districts.

Remember, a pair of chairs is worth more than two singles and a set of four is worth a lot more than two pairs, and so on.

A Chippendale style upholstered wing armchair on claw and ball feet. (Cruso Wilkin) £210

A Gordon Russell oak armchair, lacking drop-in seat, 1930's. £99

An oak chair designed by W. Cave, with drop-in seat, circa 1900. £385

Gustav Stickley spindle Morris chair, circa 1907, with sling seat, 32½in. wide. (Robt. W. Skinner Inc.) £1,635

Mid 19th century walnut salon chair with moulded and pierced rail, and serpentine padded seat. £660

Late Victorian mahogany framed armchair with turned legs and arm supports. (John Hogbin & Son) £120

Lady's Victorian mahogany armchair. (Reeds Rains) £300

A small modern mahogany window stick-back chair with square tapered legs. (P. Wilson & Co.) £70

One of a pair of Victorian side chairs with floral needlepoint upholstered seats. (Stalker & Boos) £80

A Thonet bentwood rocking chair (paper label under seat). (Reeds Rains) £45

A George III fruitwood child's high chair. (Cubitt & West) £390

Renaissance Revival walnut armchair, in the style of George Hunzinger, circa 1865. (Robt. W. Skinner Inc.) £273

Charles I oak armchair with gouge and floret carved top-rail. (Reeds Rains) £380

A late George II mahogany open armchair with front cabriole legs. (Lawrence Fine Art) £4,400

A satinwood carver chair, the back having a lattice rail and an oval pierced panel. (Vidler & Co.) £220

One of a set of four Victorian walnut caned side chairs. (Stalker & Boos) £333

Early 19th century mahogany club armchair, probably by Gillows of Lancaster. (Reeds Rains) £350

One of a set of four walnut and mahogany dining chairs. (Butler & Hatch Waterman) £250

A 19th century mahogany framed caneback elbow chair with plush upholstered seat. (Dee & Atkinson) £600

One of a pair of cantilever Modernist armchairs, 1930's. £572

One of a pair of rush-backed wing armchairs. (Bonham's) £420

One of a pair of 19th century Chinese armchairs, inlaid with mother-of-pearl. (H. Spencer & Sons Ltd.) £580

A Georgian period Provincial child's rocking armchair. (Woolley & Wallis) £370

A tub armchair, with slats to floor, 1890's. £71

Victorian carved mahogany rocking chair with padded arms. (Stalker & Boos) £93

One of a set of six Victorian oak balloon back dining chairs. (Reeds Rains) £455

A rosewood library chair dating from the reign of William IV. (Christie's S. Kensington) £600

Elizabethan Revival mahogany platform rocker, by G. Hunzinger, New. York, circa 1882, 39in. high. (Robt. W. Skinner Inc.) £366

Victorian mahogany armchair with spoon-back, in need of restoration. (Butler & Hatch Waterman) £340

Charles II walnut, child's high chair with original adjustable footrest and retaining bar. (James & Lister Lea) £1,000

A Finmar Ltd. plywood armchair, designed by Alvar Aalto. £93

An oak tub chair with open slatted back, circa 1900. £308

A Victorian mahogany framed horseshoe-back armchair with cabriole front legs. (W. H. Lane & Son) £180

CHARITY BOXES

Since the mid nineteenth century many of our charitable organisations have promoted a cause and collected for funds through the use of charity boxes. Early boxes were often attached to the end of a long pole so that people deep in a crowd could be canvassed.

In the 1880's the Church Missionary Societies were among the first to use such a box when soliciting contributions for the poor and needy thus giving rise to the popular nickname 'The Poor Box'.

The real boom in the manufacture of charity boxes came in the early twentieth century with fund raising activities on behalf of the various war relief funds reaching a peak.

Boxes are made in a variety of materials and in all shapes and sizes; some in the image of popular characters such as Sooty, Noddy, Basil Brush and other well loved creatures. The well known 'Life boat sliding down the ramp when a penny is inserted in the slot' is a good example of those incorporating a mechanical function.

Collecting box for the Society for The Propagation of the Gospel, circa 1880. £12

'The Spastics Society' charity box of plastic, 13in. high. £4

'Help the dogs who guide the blind' charity box. £7

Composition Sooty 'Help the Blind' charity box, 12in. high. £9

A large cast-iron charity box in the form of a seated lion, 3ft. high overall with stand. £400

'Please Help the Blind', Basil Brush charity box, 3ft.6in. high. £30

(Paul G. Sheppard)

107

CHARITY BOXES

An R.S.P.C.A. papier mache 'Puppy' charity box.   £25

Automaton charity box in aid of St. Christopher's Railway Children's Home, in which the pistons are operated by a coin in the slot.   £350

R.S.P.C.A. pottery charity box, 8in. wide.   £25

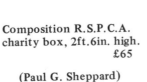

The Spastics Society 'Tumbling Coin' charity box, modern plastic.   £4

Composition R.S.P.C.A. charity box, 2ft.6in. high.   £65

Composition 'Polio' charity box, 3ft. high.   £50

(Paul G. Sheppard)

CHEESE DISHES

It is not often realised that throughout the 19th century people were well used to expecting fresh milk, butter and cheese, for cows were actually kept in the centre of large towns for this purpose right up until the First World War.

Most large houses of the period actually had their own dairy set in the coolest part of the house, usually facing north, where they regularly made butter, curds and whey and cheese. It became fashionable in the 19th century to partake of cheese after dinner and this custom saw the production of vast numbers of decorative china cheese dishes able to grace the diningroom as opposed to the rather plain functional dishes which rarely left the kitchen. Unfortunately some of the larger Stilton cheese dishes have became somewhat redundant for it would cost a king's ransom to fill one.

Wilkinson Ltd. 'bizarre' cheese dish and cover, 1930. £65

Staffordshire blue and white wedge-shaped cheese dish, circa 1890. £15

Crown Devon pottery cheese cover with floral decoration. £12

Staffordshire pottery cheese dish with floral decoration. £12

A tall Stilton cheese dish and cover with moulded basket weave designs, 12in. high. (Dickinson, Davy & Markham) £65

Booth's blue and white wedge-shaped cheese dish. £20

Early 19th century Chamberlain's Worcester dish. £462

Large hand-painted Stilton cheese dish decorated with a country scene. £100

Late 19th century majolica cheese dish with domed cover, 10in. diam. (Robt. W. Skinner Inc.) £250

CIGARETTE CASES

Some indication of the widespread popularity of the smoking habit can be seen in the abundance of delightful cigarette cases on the market today. This is a popular subject for collectors, mainly because they are plentiful, attractive and, although they were designed to house only the smaller cigarettes, in use they re-create the elegance of times past.

Cigarette cases were made from gold, silver, tortoiseshell, papier mache and enamel ware. The box lid was usually a feature of the decoration and here the variety is infinite. They may be inset with precious stones, engraved, painted or inlaid with contrasting materials. The earliest examples are of formal design, demonstrating the skills of the silversmith and engraver, but after it became fashionable for women to smoke, the designs take on the bold and colourful patterns of the modernist era.

A 9ct. gold engine-turned cigarette case by Dunhill, hallmarked London 1926. £250

1930's 'Ivellon' plated cigarette case with contemporary cigarettes. £8

A French enamelled cigarette case by Eugene Grasset, circa 1900. £308

An Imperial two-colour gold and jewelled presentation cigarette case by Bok, St. Petersburg, 1899-1908, 9.7cm. £2,277

A French silver, black lacquer and crushed eggshell cigarette case and a cigar piercer, London 1925, 11cm. wide. £242

A German .935 standard cigarette case, signed Reznicek. (Andrew Grant) £620

CIGARETTE LIGHTERS

Most of the old cigarette lighters on the market today date from around 1900, and there are still many interesting and unusual examples available at a very modest price.

This is a good area for investment. Particularly in the early experimental types and patented examples which demonstrate a skilful facility in combining ideas to good effect. There is a combined battery operated torch and petrol lighter, an evening purse cum dance card lighter and a lighter skilfully disguised to conceal a cosmetic compact.

Some of the most interesting lighters date from the period of the first World War when they were handmade from shell cases and other sundry equipment.

Zetron 'Dunhill' style plated lighter.   £1

Silver cased petrol cigarette lighter by Tiffany & Co., New York.   £55

Beney super petrol cigarette lighter, No. 373.   £3

An unusual early 'Penny' petrol lighter.   £8

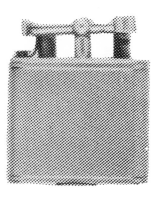
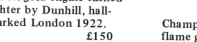

A 9ct. gold engine-turned lighter by Dunhill, hall-marked London 1922.   £150

Champ petrol lighter with flame guard.   £2

(Paul G. Sheppard)

CIGARETTE LIGHTERS

Ronson 'Cadet' petrol lighter, No. 621570. £2

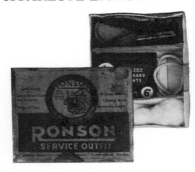

Ronson lighter service kit, 'World's Greatest Lighter'. £4

Omega 'Super' petrol lighter. £3

Polo petrol cigarette lighter, circa 1920. £4

Late 19th century spelter table lighter. £28

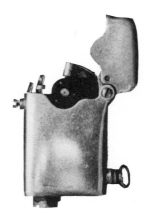

Rare Thorens patent automatic petrol lighter. £12

Osmond alloy petrol lighter in the Dunhill style. £2

An 18ct. gold lighter watch, with the 'Dunhill Unique' lighter mechanism, London 1926. £1,430

World War I initialled petrol lighter made by Frank Stanley. £7

(Paul G. Sheppard)

CLOCKS

One may wonder what would be the result of a generally-taken decision to abolish time-pieces and all they stand for. Would there be a state of anarchic chaos, under whose influence man would degenerate into a savage, feckless brute — or would a calm, tickless hush settle over the world, promoting a general feeling of sublime freedom and goodwill? Whatever the widespread result, one certain thing is that the antiques trade would be very much the poorer, for the centuries have left a legacy of clocks of superb design.

It would take at least fifty chapters the length of this one to discuss fuller the merits of different makers and movements so, with limited space, we have illustrated examples representative of a widely expansive price range.

Before you discount the 'Ebosa' travel alarm made in 1960 and priced at £7 completely out of hand, remember that only ten or fifteen years ago, the Victorian black marble mantelclock was spurned by many at an asking price of less than ten pounds.

A 19th century Masonic bracket clock, marked Swinden & Sons, Birmingham, in castellated mahogany case, 14½in. high. (W. H. Lane & Son)   £140

Goldscheider pottery clock with oxidised metal circular dial, 20in. high. (Reeds Rains)   £250

A small quarter-striking alarm carriage clock, dial signed Breguet, 4½in. high, and a leather travelling case.   £805

'Ebosa' Swiss travel alarm clock, circa 1960.   £7

Ansonia porcelain mantel clock with Roman numerals. (Stalker & Boos)   £183

Early 60's Equity made alarm clock with luminous hands and central optical moving design.   £6

Metamec electric clock with 'tick' and 'silent' control, early 60's.   £4

'Looping' Swiss travel alarm clock in red leatherette case.   £7

A brass carriage clock, by T. Hyde, Sleaford, in ornate case. (Butler & Hatch Waterman)   £130

'Darling' Swiss travel alarm clock, circa 1960.   £7

Late 19th century work's timeclock with punch mechanism.   £60

Jgeha money box clock by Buerer Spar, in enamelled case.   £100

A French Empire gilt bronze mounted black marble mantel clock, 16in. (Lawrence Fine Art)   £209

A Restoration ormolu 'Troubadour' mantel clock with silk-suspended pendulum, 35cm. high. (Christie's)   £813

Lady's travelling handbag clock, Swiss made.   £12

Switana alarm clock with paper dial. £2.50

Art Nouveau porcelain mantel clock, elongated 'A' shape with green glaze and eight-day time and strike movement. (Robt. W. Skinner Inc.) £140

Shavallo battery advertising clock 'Saves Time'. £5

French calendar mantel clock by A. Redier, in a rectangular ebonised wood case, circa 1880, 13¼in. high. (Robt. W. Skinner Inc.) £333

A Restoration ormolu mantel clock with silk-suspended pendulum, 40cm. high. (Christie's) £428

Veglia travelling alarm clock, made in Italy, 1950's. £3

A hammered brass and chromed metal mantel clock, probably Wiener Werkstatte, circa 1905/10, 26.5cm. £693

Smith's alarm clock in chromium plated case. £2

A Doulton Lambeth clock case of rectangular section inset with a circular dial, 14in. high. (Christie's S. Kensington) £500

CLOTHES PEGS

Because a great deal of the paraphernalia of the Victorian kitchen and laundry was thrown away, some of the most basic equipment now has some rarity and curiosity value.

None of it was ever considered to be of any value and, since equipment was constantly changed and modernised it was usually felt that the only way to dispose of it was to throw it away. The humble clothes peg didn't stand a chance.

The clothes peg started off as a split wooden peg with steel banding and progressed to a large hand turned 'dolly' peg; from a smaller 'dolly' peg, to a spring clip wooden peg and eventually to spring clip plastic pegs.

The name 'dolly' derived from the Victorian pastime of decorating and dressing the turned wooden pegs as dolls. Some of these early pegs are quite nicely painted and certainly collectible.

Tanda Toys clothes peg in yellow plastic. 5p

Set of Lilliput miniature pegs in plastic case. 50p

Pair of double ended plastic clip-type pegs. 10p

Set of four wooden clip-type pegs. 20p

Set of eight small dolly pegs. £2

Set of four large dolly pegs. £3

Four coloured plastic clip-type pegs. 20p

Set of six early split wood pegs with steel bands. £3.50

(Paul G. Sheppard)

COATHANGERS

Yes, people really do collect coathangers. And, when you think about it, it's not a bad idea to introduce an element of interest and character to what is, otherwise, a very ordinary and practical function.

The most elaborate hangers are padded and dressed with silks, satins or other attractive period fabrics. Some are filled with dried lavender and others are trimmed and edged with fine old lace.

Even basic wooden hangers have some individuality in their design. They come in a wide variety of shapes and the more interesting examples are stamped or printed with a name and the source of origin. Outfitters & Costumiers, theatre companies, clubs, restaurants, ocean liners, hotels (Raffles, Singapore is a prize) — all may feature in a collection which could span the countries of the world.

'Ritz Cleaners Ltd.' serpentine shape wooden coathanger with wire support.   50p

1960's pine coathanger with wire support.
50p

An Edwardian spring-action velvet lined coathanger.   £1

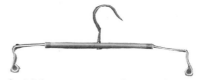

Early 20th century metal expanding coathanger.   75p

An Edwardian beechwood coathanger with wire support.   50p

Oriental hardwood coathanger from the Singapore Inter-Continental.   £1.25

1930's bentwood hanger with wire support.
25p

Beechwood hanger from A. Hukin Costumier, Sheffield.   40p

(Paul G. Sheppard)

COMBS

We have here, two quite different types of comb. One for grooming hair and the other worn purely as an ornament.

In ancient times the grooming comb was used only by the so-called 'civilised' members of society and the teeth were cut to precision by a fine saw. Roman combs may be single or double sided and made of wood, antler, ivory or bone. During the Renaissance period the comb reached its present shape but with teeth of a uniform size. Any variance in the length of teeth would suggest a comb produced from around the 1880's and onwards.

Ornamental combs have either fixed or hinged mounts and are made in all sorts of materials in a wide variety of designs. They can be as large as a tiara and as small and subtle as the delicate Art Nouveau pieces. Large Spanish combs made of tortoiseshell came to the height of popularity with the 1875 production of Bizet's Carmen.

Pacific North-West coast wood comb, possibly Salish, 15cm. high.
£1,000

Japanese blonde tortoise-shell hair ornament and pin, inlaid with gold, silver and mother-of-pearl.
£250

Mid Victorian tortoisehsell comb decorated with metal lover's knots.
£15

A 9ct. gold engine-turned comb by Dunhill, hall-marked Birmingham 1922.
£75

Victorian horn comb decorated with ivy leaves in blue and green enamel.
£20

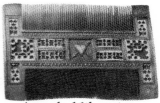

An early 16th century boxwood double-sided comb, 6¾ x 4¾in.
£990

A late Gothic period ivory comb of French or North Italian manufacture.
£4,500

Art Nouveau style tortoise-shell hair comb.
£25

A rare hair comb of tor-toiseshell surmounted by French jet, circa 1830.
£1,250

COMPACTS

The dazzling beauties of the 'B' Movies of the 30's and 40's did much to promote the use of the powder compact. Fashionable and bold, they thought nothing of producing a compact in public and getting on with 'emergency repairs'.

Because they were designed to be carried on the person and used in company, the compact, as much as any piece of jewellery, was chosen to compliment the persona of the user and the vast array of styles reflects the changing fashions of the times.

Compacts range in price from a few pounds to many hundreds of pounds depending on the quality of the piece. We have examples made from precious metals and inset with gemstones, fine quality hallmarked silver, and the beautifully enamelled, sometimes signed compacts of the Art Deco period.

The modestly priced range of compacts made by the firm of Stratton are usually gold plated and many are decorated with tortoiseshell or painted designs.

Victorian silver compact with enamelled lid featuring a kitten. £125

Silver framed powder compact with patented open/shut action, dated 1930. £22

Art Deco silver powder compact, the textured lid slashed with red and black enamel. £100

Revlon 'New York' gold plated compact. £5

Victorian oval silver compact with enamel lid. £100

Stratton floral design compact. £6

1949 silver hallmarked compact by T. & S. £12

An Art Deco enamelled silver compact signed and dated 1937. £88

1930's Stratton 'gaming machine' enamelled compact. £8

(Paul G. Sheppard)

119

COOKERY BOOKS

Part of the fascination of collecting old cookery books is to notice how taste and ingredients are very much from the period in which the books were written.

Although a few exist from the 17th and 18th centuries they are very expensive for it was not until the latter part of the 19th century when there was something akin to a revolution in the kitchen, that a wide variety were produced, notably by Mrs. Beeton and Fannie Farmer.

Of particular interest are those books which still contain colour plates depicting the culinary delights of the period together with hints on how to manage a large household. These often list the uses of all the equipment and pots and pans in the Victorian kitchen which is particularly fascinating.

Occasionally a personal cookery book comes onto the market with hand written recipes and reminders of festivals and important events.

Goodwin's 'Tested Recipes'.
75p

'Cooking En Casserole' by
Mrs. C. S. Peel, OBE. 50p

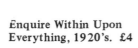

Enquire Within Upon
Everything, 1920's. £4

Good Housekeeping Home-
Made Wines, Pickles and
Chutneys.   50p

'The Aga Recipe Book',
first edition 1956.   £4

'Look and Cook', Glouces-
tershire Training College
1963.   £1.50

(Paul G. Sheppard)

120

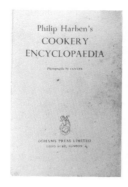 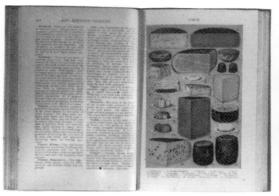 

Philip Harben's Cookery Encyclopedia, first edition, 1955.   £4

Mrs. Beeton's 'All About Cookery' by Ward Lock.
£5

McDougall's Cookery Book, 23rd edition. 75p

Stag Cooking Salt booklet.   25p

Cassell's Household Guide 'A Complete Encyclopaedia of Domestic and Social Economy'.   £15

Midland Counties Milk Recipes.   25p

The 'Belling' Cookery Book, 3rd edition, 1956.
£2

Atora Suet Recipes. 50p

Journey of Discovery, All Round Our House, 1857.
£7

(Paul G. Sheppard)

COOKERY BOOKS

Odhams Electrical Cookery
Book, 1939.   £3

120 Ways of Using Bread.
                    £1.50

French Cooking for
Everywoman, first edition,
1930.   £3

Consult Me 'For all you
want to know', 1896. £6

Mrs. Beeton's Cookery
Book, 1906.   £8

Burcomix Recipe and
Instruction Book. 10p

Presto pressure cooker
recipe book.   75p

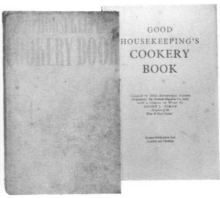

Good Housekeeping Cookery
Book, first edition, 1948. £3

Distil Coffee Recipes with
that delightful coffee flavour.   £2

(Paul G. Sheppard)

CORKSCREWS

Most of the corkscrews, or bottle screws, we see around today, date from the middle of the 19th century. Earlier examples do exist, some going back to the 17th century, but these are extremely rare.

The earliest examples were made of steel and consisted of a simple spiral fixed to a wooden handle. It was only later that more complex designs were introduced with handles made of engraved brass, silver, steel, bone, horn and ivory. The handles were often styled in the shape of animals, birds or some more unusual novelty theme.

The Victorian penchant for new inventions ran riot during the 19th century and hundreds of different corkscrew based devices, in all shapes and sizes, were made; many of them patented. Other devices, such as a bottle dusting brush or any number of other small tools, are often incorporated into the handle. Any corkscrew combined with a gadget will be of interest to a collector and this will be reflected in the selling price.

At one time, the corkscrew was one of the essential tools of day to day living. Even miniature scent bottles were sealed with a cork and the ladies often carried small, intricately designed silver versions for this purpose. Sometimes a Victorian housekeeper would attach a small corkscrew, fitted with a hanging loop to her chatelaine, alongside all the other necessary bits and pieces. (The chatelaine being an ornamental bunch of short chains bearing keys, pencil, scissors etc., which is then attached to the belt at the waist. A similar version, in miniature, could be attached to a gentleman's watch chain and, again, a miniature corkscrew was a popular item.)

There was, at one time, a very pleasing custom for a house guest, upon writing to thank his host, to include the gift of a corkscrew, perhaps with some words of praise engraved on the handle.

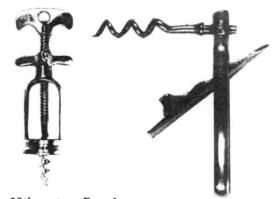

Waiter's Friend stamped 'Hebel' and Made in Germany, 4½in. long. £14

A corkscrew with turned oak crossbar, steel shank and helical worm, circa 1870, 4¼in. long. £5

Combination pocket penknife and corkscrew by John Watts of Sheffield, 3½in. long. £28

A plated champagne tap with integral pointed end above which are the holes for drawing the champagne through, tap 5in. long. £58

Early 20th century French polished steel corkscrew, the open barrel with perfect bladed worm with point, 6in. overall length. £58

A pocket corkscrew made of steel, stamped Universal Pat. June 27,05 (1905), 5½in. long open. £175

(Christopher Sykes)

123

An advertising corkscrew, the turned wood crossbar in the shape of a cork is burnt with 'Sanderson's Vat 69', 4¾in. long. £37

A corkscrew with imitation stag horn crossbar, stamped 'Made in Germany', and helical worm, 3½in. long. £9

An unusual beechwood ribbed handle grip corkscrew, stamped 'DRP27775 German', with long bladed worm, 6¾in. long. £35

A nickel plated bar corkscrew 'Original Safety', manufactured by Gaskell & Chambers, 10in. high. £125

An unusual Monopol type corkscrew with rubber washer to protect top of bottle, stamped Germany. £37

A tinned iron example of a lever corkscrew of the Magic Lever type with perfect 'steep pitched' or 'speed' worm, 8in. long. £38

An all brass two lever corkscrew with perfect bladed worm, butterfly handle at the top, circa 1880, 6in. long. £38

A corkscrew with dusting brush and suspension ring, the baluster turned brass stem terminating in a small Henshall type brass button, circa 1810, 6in. high. £68

A narrow rack King's Screw corkscrew by Thos. Lund, with perfect turned rosewood crossbar complete with dusting brush inner thread, 7¼in. long closed. £484

(Christopher Sykes)

CORKSCREWS

A boxwood pocket two-piece corkscrew with helical worm handle painted on both sides with the word 'Bistro', circa 1960, 3¼in. long.   £7

An all-steel concertina type corkscrew stamped 'Ideal Perfect' and 'Brevete & Depose', length 9¾ x 4¼in. closed.   £125

A polished armour bright all-steel Cellarman's four finger pull corkscrew, 5½in. long.   £9

A 19th century corkscrew/Codd bottle opener with plain steel shank and turned ashwood handle, circa 1875, 4½in. long.   £75

A brass handled corkscrew cast in the form of the door knocker on Durham Cathedral of a mythical beast's head, circa 1930, 7¼in. long.   £25

Pocket folding bow corkscrew in steel, circa 1880, 3in. long closed.   £18

A cast brass souvenir corkscrew, showing gothic-style building named 'John O' Groat's House', circa 1925, 6in. long.   £19

An American Clough single wire corkscrew advertising 'Hennessy's Three Star Brandy', 4in. long.   £26

A corkscrew with turned rosewood crossbar, steel shank and perfect helical worm, 4½in. long.   £18

(Christopher Sykes)

An Art Deco engraved steel corkscrew, stamped 'Stainless Steel', 4¼in. long. £18

A rare flat back brass figural of a clown corkscrew, perfect helical worm, length 7in. circa 1900. £37

A turned 'double cone' shaped ashwood handled corkscrew stamped with maker's name 'W. Marples & Sons. Sheffield', 5in. long. £28

A double action corkscrew of the Thomason's 1802 type with brass barrel, turned bone handle and dusting brush, 9in. long extended. £245

An all steel 'A1 Double Lever' corkscrew, stamped 'James Heeley & Sons Patent 6006 Double Lever', 6½in. long. £78

A corkscrew with wood barrel-shaped grip, round shank and perfect helical worm, circa 1820, 6in. long. £48

A corkscrew with sycamore grip, plain brass ends, square shank with a helical worm, circa 1900, 4½in. high. £9

Monopol type in cast steel bladed worm stamped Foreign, 5in. long. £16

An Art Deco corkscrew, the marbled sea-green composition handle shaped for two finger grip, circa 1930, 2¾in. high. £14

(Christopher Sykes)

Clough's American twisted wire type corkscrew, 1876 patent, grip with advert 'Spiers and Pond', twisted stem and helical worm. £24

A copper/bronze finish corkscrew, the eyebrow top with cast words 'The Lever Signet', with perfect helical worm, 4¾in. long.   £26

Holborn type of finger ring corkscrew with ashwood turned grip, nickel plated shank with bladed perfect worm, circa 1870, 6in. long.   £48

A German open frame steel corkscrew, black ebonised grip and plain bladed worm, circa 1880, 6in. long.   £9

An all steel pocket penknife, with corkscrew etc., stamped at base of knife blade 'Wheatley Brothers Sheffield', circa 1900, length of case 3½in.   £38

A corkscrew with turned 'cigar' shaped applewood crossbar complete with dusting brush, circa 1860, 6in. long.   £37

A turned ashwood English corkscrew combined Codd bottle opener with perfect helical worm with 'flat' steel shank, overall height, 5½in.   £38

A polished armour bright example of the Lazy Tongs corkscrew, stamped Heeley & Sons Makers', length when extended 14½ x 5½in.   £68

A steel corkscrew, the crossbar of turned cherrywood and barrel shaped, circa 1840, 5½in. long.   £45

(Christopher Sykes)

An ivory tusk corkscrew, on one end is a bottle opener, with tulip stem and bladed worm, handle length 6½in. £75

An all-brass figural corkscrew of a terrier with perfect steel helical worm, 3in. long. £19

A genuine horn handled corkscrew by G. B. Wilson Ltd., Pitlochry, with bladed chrome worm, handle length 4¼in. £12

Armstrong patent lazy tongs, with bladed worm, 10in. long extended. £87

Clough type of pocket corkscrew with wooden sheath printed with advertisement for Cowbroughs Nourishing Ale for Invalids, made in U.S., 4in. long. £28

Waiter's friend corkscrew with fluted worm and blade inscribed 'John Watts, Sheffield', 3¼in. long. £28

An American novelty corkscrew in the form of a bottle 2¾in. high, made of brass plated steel. £49

Unusual Perille type corkscrew, stamped J.B. on shaped top, bladed worm, 6½in. long. £56

A nickel plated bar corkscrew that clamps on to the top surface of the bar, manufactured by Gaskell & Chambers, 10in. high. £168

(Christopher Sykes)

COSTUME

An appreciation of fine period costume is fairly widespread and no-one is really surprised when, for example, an open robe and petticoat of yellow silk with vertical green and pink stripes, circa 1760, sells at a leading auction house for thousands of pounds.

The current trend however, shows some astonishing prices paid for clothes from as recent a period as the 1950's.

It all started back in the 60's, when a reaction against formal dress resulted in a fashion for wearing a kind of fancy dress costume. The resulting demand brought a wealth of old clothes onto the market. Once the fashion was established, buyers and collectors became more discriminating in their choice, discarding shabby or perished articles and quite prepared to pay for good examples.

Dresses, coats, shoes, hats, bags, shawls, even underclothes are now keenly collected at steadily rising prices.

Royal Regiment of Artillery silk scarf. £3

Gentleman's waistcoat of cotton woven with striped design, added embellishments of minute sequins outlining pockets, hem, front fastening and collar, British, circa 1785-90. £35

Stomacher, English, circa 1750, floral embroidery on a couched-thread 'vermicelli' ground, trim of gold braid and sequins, 14 x 6in. £360

1930's Hungarian style embroidered blouse, Made in England. £10

A Dragon robe, the black gauze ground embroidered with coiling dragons. (Reeds Rains) £620

Boned and laced corset in pink cotton with lace trim, French, 1880's. £45

A lady's festive jacket with open sleeves, lined with cotton, the couched silver and gold thread embroidery on a red velvet ground, gold braid trim, Albania, mid 19th century. £275

A 1920's flamingo pink ostrich feather cape and fan, fan 110cm. wide, 70cm. tall. (Chelsea Auction Galleries) £180

Mid 19th century black silk brocade two-piece woven with bunches of flowers. (Phillips) £340

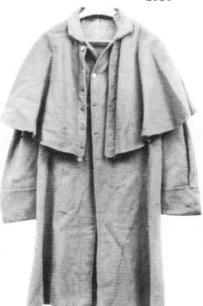

Shawl of silk and wool with pattern woven in orange, red, yellow, green and brown on cream ground, Norwich, circa 1840's, 4ft.6in. x 4ft.9in. £120

Militia great coat with attached cape, coarse blue wool, Massa., circa 1855. (Robt. W. Skinner Inc.) £530

Fold-over shawl with black silk centre, borders woven in fine wool and silk and sewn on by hand, Paisley or Norwich, 1830's, 4ft.6in. x 4ft.8in. £130

(The Antique Textile Co.)

A lady's dress of printed
cotton with ruffled
sleeves, circa 1845,
British.   £140

Large shawl woven in wool on loom
with jacquard attachment, red, orange,
yellow and green on black ground,
British or French, circa 1860, 11ft. x
5ft.2½in.   £140

A green sleeveless
waistcoat (tsiguni)
of felted wool with
heavy embroidery,
late 19th century.
                         £65

A gentleman's coat of cut
velvet woven with patter-
ned pockets, cuffs, collar
and trim to front fasten-
ing, Italy or France, circa
1760.   £260

A Japanese cotton indigo-dyed
double-ikat kimono, 20th
century.   £55

English open robe of striped
silk with ruched trim to
cuffs and skirt front, circa
1770 (back view).   £365

(The Antique Textile Co.)

Shawl woven in fine wool, block-printed in red, green, pink, blue and brown on cream ground, British, circa 1840, 4ft.10in. sq.
£60

Shawl woven in wool on loom with jacquard attachment, red, orange, yellow and green, on black ground, British or French, circa 1860, 6ft.2½in. x 6ft.½in.   £100

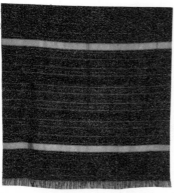

Silk shawl woven on loom with jacquard attachment by Clabburn, Sons & Crisp of Norwich, circa 1850-70. Predominantly pink with stripes of plain white, blue and pink, 11ft.2in. x 5ft.6in.   £180

Central medallion (detail) from a Paisley shawl of circa 1845, woven in wool and silk in red, pink, brown, black and yellow. Size 10ft.3in. x 5ft.7½in.   £135

Good Kashmir shawl hand-woven in twill-tapestry technique in wool, red, pink, blue, green and yellow with black centre. The fringed ends are embroidered, circa 1850, 6ft.6in. sq.   £400

Shawl woven in wool and silk with blue, green, yellow, orange and red, on a cream ground. British or French circa 1840's, 5ft.7½in. x 5ft.9in.   £140

(The Antique Textile Co.)

CURTAINS

To the untrained eye, a bundle of old curtains in a corner of the attic is precisely that, and no more. If you are having a clear out, and have established that they are the wrong size for the sitting room, wouldn't fit in the back bedroom, then for goodness sake, if they look a bit speculative don't throw them out. Old textiles can be worth money.

A length of fabric designed by, for example, Morris & Co., would be quite a rare find. In 1861, William Morris, along with other well-known painters, an architect and an engineer, set up this company whose aims were, to produce decorative articles of the very finest quality, for 'the people'. His designs, taken from plant and animal forms, are extremely attractive and still very popular today.

The company provided, in today's terms, a complete house furnishing service, supplying everything that could possibly be required within a household, from a stained glass window to a set of teaspoons.

A Morris & Co. printed cotton double-sided curtain, selvedge with printed Oxford St. mark, 1891, 181.5cm. wide.　£352

William Morris designed textile in 'peacock and dragon' pattern, circa 1878, 89 x 63in. (Robt. W. Skinner Inc.) £400

One of a pair of Morris & Co. printed cotton curtains, selvedge with printed Queen Square mark, circa 1876/7, 90cm. wide.　　£462

One of a pair of printed plush curtains, 1890's, 130cm. wide.　£385

One of a set of four Jacobean crewel-work bed hangings, embroidered in coloured wools, 3ft.1in. wide. (Lawrence Fine Art)　　£2,420

A Morris & Co. wool curtain, 'peacock and dragon' pattern, 163cm. wide, late 1870's.　　£297

DENTAL INSTRUMENTS

The first statutory law relating to dentistry was an Act passed in 1579 which, although forbidding barbers to act as surgeons, did allow them to continue to draw teeth!

These were tough times. The travelling 'dentist' trudged around from town to town lugging a bag of very primitive implements and performing dentistry, of a sort, on patients anaesthetised by gin. It was not unknown for the dentist to anaesthetise himself from time to time.

Times change however, and with the development of effective and hygienic dentistry came an improved technology applied to instruments and equipment.

Everything from a simple probe to a massive cast iron, adjustable dentist's chair will be included in this fascinating category and most of the equipment collected today is precision made and of the finest quality.

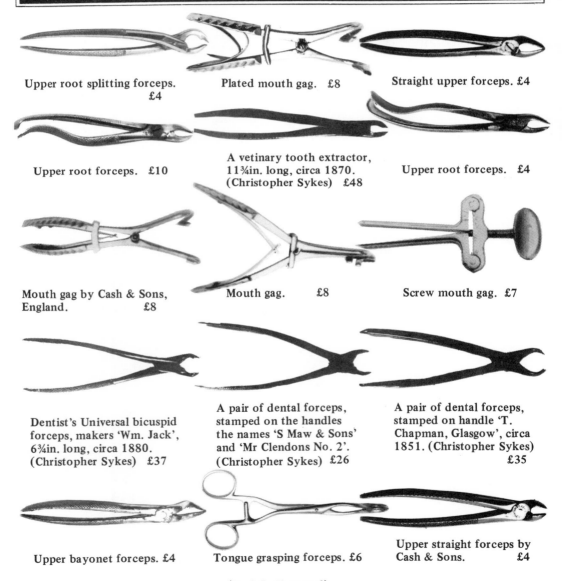

Upper root splitting forceps. £4

Plated mouth gag. £8

Straight upper forceps. £4

Upper root forceps. £10

A vetinary tooth extractor, 11¾in. long, circa 1870. (Christopher Sykes) £48

Upper root forceps. £4

Mouth gag by Cash & Sons, England. £8

Mouth gag. £8

Screw mouth gag. £7

Dentist's Universal bicuspid forceps, makers 'Wm. Jack', 6¾in. long, circa 1880. (Christopher Sykes) £37

A pair of dental forceps, stamped on the handles the names 'S Maw & Sons' and 'Mr Clendons No. 2'. (Christopher Sykes) £26

A pair of dental forceps, stamped on handle 'T. Chapman, Glasgow', circa 1851. (Christopher Sykes) £35

Upper bayonet forceps. £4

Tongue grasping forceps. £6

Upper straight forceps by Cash & Sons. £4

(Paul G. Sheppard)

134

DOMESTIC EQUIPMENT

One of the best fields for investment is the early mechanical devices put onto the market as labour savers. As improvements were made, the old ones were almost invariably thrown away with the result that, nowadays they have considerable rarity and curiosity value.

After a while, it was realised that many of the old gadgets still actually worked. And worked well. Many will swear that their old Victorian coffee mill grinds coffee far better than the brand new electric jobs, that the heavy iron or copper saucepans are far better than their modern counterparts, that bean slicers, apple peelers and cherry stoners add interest to the most mundane of preparatory tasks in the kitchen.

In saying this, I am referring to Victorian appliances, however, it must be said that it is well worth looking out for the now outdated gadgets of the 30's, 40's and 50's. This is a market still in its early stages and with many intriguing contraptions still modestly priced.

Pair of 1950's hair clippers by Burman, England.   £1

Pair of late 19th century boot stretchers.   £7

Late 19th century cast iron scales up to 20 stone, with retractable mirror.   £50

Late Victorian brass shoe horn.   £2

Late 50's high speed rug-making kit complete with instructions.   £5

Battery operated vacuum clothes brush complete with box, 1950's.   £3

(Paul G. Sheppard)

135

A galvanised tin poultry feeder. £2

1930's studio phonograph in a polished wood cabinet, complete with horn and accessories. £300

1930's EPNS cocktail shaker with end cap and inner filter. £15

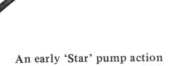

A child's bedpan, made in Lambeth stoneware, circa 1900, diam. 7½in., length of handle 5in. (Christopher Sykes) £68

1950's metal gas fire. £4

An early 'Star' pump action vacuum cleaner. £30

Valor paraffin heater with brass and alloy fittings.£5

19th century adjustable woolwinder. £25

Late 19th century stoneware chicken feeder. £10

(Paul G. Sheppard)

DOULTON

So prolific and varied was the output of the Doulton factory in the late 19th century that most households could boast an example of their work, be it a utilitarian piece of stoneware in the bathroom or a fine pair of vases well able to grace any mantelpiece.

Of particular interest, and value, are the works of Hannah Barlow and her sister Florence whose forte was drawing animals and birds freehand onto the wet clay on a wide variety of wares. Musicians and chessmen in the form of mice and frog cricketers by George Tinworth are also well worth looking for.

The most interest recently however has centred on the Doulton character jugs produced from the 30's to the present day. Find one depicting Sir Francis Drake without a hat and we're talking £3,000 plus, a clown with red triangles on his cheeks is near to £2,000, but the real jewel in the crown is a jug featuring Winston Churchill. Uncoloured, apart from two black handles, this little gem, produced in 1940 and withdrawn because Sir Winston didn't approve of the design, is now worth £7,000 plus.

Royal Doulton figure, 'Mendicant', 20cm. high. (Lawrence Fine Art)£104

A Doulton Lambeth waisted jug with brown-glazed borders, 8½in. high. (Christie's S. Kensington)   £120

A Royal Doulton figure of 'Angela', date code for 1929, 7¼in. high.   £330

Royal Doulton figure, 'The Potter', 18cm. high. (Lawrence Fine Art)   £93

Royal Doulton mask head Toby jug of Lord Nelson, 7¾in. high. (Outhwaite & Litherland)   £180

Royal Doulton figure of a North American Indian, 'Calumet'. (Lawrence Fine Art)   £253

A Royal Doulton Queen
Victoria commemorative
jug. (W. H. Lane & Son)
£90

Royal Doulton pottery jardiniere cobalt blue glazed,
9in. diam. (Stalker & Boos)
£75

A Royal Doulton jug modelled as the Rt. Hon. J. C.
Smuts, circa 1946, 6¾in.
£495

Royal Doulton Toby jug,
'Gladiator', 1960, 7¾in.
high. (Robt. W. Skinner
Inc.)   £289

A pair of Doulton Lambeth
stoneware vases by Florence
E. Barlow, circa 1906.
(Andrew Grant)   £250

A Royal Doulton commem-
orative plate, 'Aero', 1909.
(Christie's)   £95

A Royal Doulton commem-
orative tobacco jar and cover,
6¼in. high. (Christie's S.
Kensington)   £60

Royal Doulton china figure
of a hare wearing tails, 7in.
high. (Reeds Rains) £145

A Royal Doulton mask head
jug, 'The Clown', 6½in. high.
(Outhwaite & Litherland)
£1,700

EGG TIMERS

The majority of egg timers found today take the form of the traditional sand filled hour glass housed in a variety of frames. Many are simple utilitarian frames of turned wood but fortunately the souvenir trade recognised their potential early on, leaving a legacy of delightful little egg timers which, at the very least, can be put to useful purpose.

Generally ignored by the silversmiths, after all it was below stairs, occasionally a little gem will turn up designed to be worn on a housekeeper's chatelaine, for they conducted their duties with the precision of a sergeant-major where precise timing was imperative in a well run establishment.

Mechanical timers have tried to edge in on the market as have silicon chips but the traditional form is one of those inventions which was right first time and can't be bettered.

1930's china novelty egg timer. £5

1930's egg timer in turned wood stand. £1.50

Smith's timer on a bakelite stand. £3

Wooden framed egg timer. £1.50

Brass framed egg timer. £6

1950's mechanical timer with plastic control. £2

Late 19th century housekeeper's plated egg timer designed to hang from a chatelaine. £10

Black Forest souvenir egg timer. £2

(Paul G. Sheppard)

139

ELECTRICAL APPLIANCES

Objects of a manageable size are keenly collected and have a rare advantage over some other categories in that they have the potential to earn their own keep — Prop's buyers for T.V. and film companies often hire period appliances from collectors.

The very earliest examples date from the 19th century and therefore qualify under the '100 years minimum' rule, as legitimate antiques.

The first electric bell, New York 1831, first electric iron, patented 1882, first British electric fan, 1888, first electric kettle, 1891, first electric toaster, 1893, first electric radiator, U.S.A., 1889 — England, 1894, first electric cooker, U.S.A., 1891 — England, 1893 and the first Hoover vacuum cleaner, 1907.

Some television sets also have a rarity value and these include the Baird Mirror Drum, 1933, the Griffin, 1933 and any model by Plew T.V. Co.

1950's electric heater with chrome patterned top, switchable blower and three heat settings.   £14

Premier Patent No. 2652 electric kettle with wooden handle.   £15

An electric kettle, designed by Peter Behrens for AEG, circa 1910, 21cm.   £242

Swan Brand electric toaster with bakelite knobs.   £6

Hoover Model 262 upright vacuum cleaner with built-in light.   £12

Electric fire made by British National, Lanarkshire.   £2

(Paul G. Sheppard)

ELECTRICAL APPLIANCES

Phillips radio in bakelite case.   £12

1950's electric toasting machine.   £20

1950's Grundig radio with push-button control.   £5

1950's Burco electric boiler.   £3

Pye All-Wave Superhet Receiver, together with handbook.   £10

Pair of 1950's electric shoe warmers with original wire.   £4

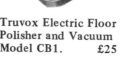

'Xcel' electric fire made in Liverpool.   £2

Truvox Electric Floor Polisher and Vacuum Model CB1.   £25

Marconi radio, Model No. T18DA.   £5

(Paul G. Sheppard)

EYEBATHS

Although eyebaths would not, at first sight, seem to offer a very inspiring field for collecting, most bottle collectors always seem to have a few among their collections.

There are three basic shapes, the stem type, the angle side drenching type and the occluder shape.

Made since the late 18th century, often as part of a toilet service, the most common are made of green, blue, or amber glass. More expensive examples are made of silver, cloisonne, enamel or even gold with embossed or incised decoration. Later eye glasses were often given away with optical products, such as Optrex, and these are generally made of plain glass, plastic, ceramics or bakelite.

Highly prized are these on which the base of the eye glass doubles as an egg-cup or salt cellar.

Cobalt blue glass eyebath, made in England. £3.50

'Optrex Safeguards Sight', blue glass eyebath. £2

Cobalt blue stem type eyebath, made in England. £4

Green glass eyebath, made in England. £2.50

Clear glass stem type eyebath. £2

An 'Undene' glass eye cleanser, 3in. tall. £4

Clear glass eyebath on stand. £2

Blue glass eyebath on stand. £4.50

(Paul G. Sheppard)

142

FANS

It is known that Elizabeth I had an interesting collection of fans, as did the richest and most sophisticated ladies of that day, but it was not until the eighteenth century that they became more fashionable, less expensive and more plentiful.

The fashion really took off throughout the 19th century when the fan was considered not only the indispensable fashion accessory for ladies in society, but also as an appropriate gift to be bestowed upon children and servant girls.

Eighteenth century fan sticks were often very decorative and were made of a variety of materials including ivory, tortoiseshell, mother-of-pearl, carved, gilded and painted to suit the classical scenes depicted on the leaf.

After the turn of the century, fans became smaller to complement the narrower style in dress, but then became progressively larger as time went on until the flamboyant appearance of la belle epoque fans with the Art Nouveau influence so clearly demonstrated in the shape of the leaves and sticks.

The dance fans of the 1920's were designed on a smaller scale to enable the user to juggle with fan, dance card and evening purse and finally, when women began to smoke in public places, the whole business of carrying a fan became impractical.

Of the many types of fan well worth collecting you may consider advertising fans, which are interesting and fun to collect, brise fans, which are all sticks and no leaf, lace fans, feather fans, and handscreen fans. Japanese fans of the 19th century can still be bought quite cheaply and the diligent collector may even be rewarded with an 18th century 'find'.

Late Victorian fan with embroidered satin leaf and gilded and painted black-wood sticks, circa 1880. £30

A small Edwardian child's fan of pierced and shaped celluloid sticks. £4

Mid 19th century Maltese silk lace fan with mother-of-pearl sticks. £60

Tortoiseshell fan with unusual brise sticks, circa 1910. £30

Victorian fan having white silk leaf with lace inserts and sequin decoration, circa 1870. £38

(Janet Maund)

143

FANS

An interesting fan of painted feathers with carved ivory sticks, made in Macao for the export market, circa 1850. £60

A fine 'dancing' fan with white gilded ivorine sticks and gauze leaf painted with forget-me-nots and decorated with sequins, circa 1920. £20

A large tambour worked German fan with unusual blackwood sticks, circa 1890.£45

Mandarin fan made for the export market with lacquered sticks and original box, circa 1880. £60

An unusually shaped satin leaf fan with finely carved and pierced ivory sticks, circa 1850. £75

Buffalo horn fan from Sumatra with sequinned decoration. £25

Victorian fan with silver painted and pierced wooden sticks and having gauze leaf inset with lace, circa 1880. £40

A French Art Nouveau style fan having painted lily of the valley on gauze and carved and shaped wooden sticks, circa 1900. £45

(Janet Maund)

144

Late Victorian fan with mother-of-pearl sticks and white silk leaf decorated with sequins, circa 1880. £55

An 18th century French bleached horn fan of pierced Gothic style, circa 1790. £30

A large red satin leaf fan painted with gilded birds and having gilded blackwood sticks, circa 1890. £40

A fine quality hand-painted satin leaf fan with pierced and carved ivory sticks, circa 1880. £45

French, shaped fan with green plastic sticks and leaf painted hunting scene, signed, circa 1900. £45

Spanish cockade fan with inlaid support, made for tourists, circa 1910. £10

Early 20th century black silk fan with hand-painted and gilded decoration and mother-of-pearl sticks. £60

Advertising fan with silk leaf and wooden sticks decorated with an Oriental scene, dated 1921. £25

(Janet Maund)

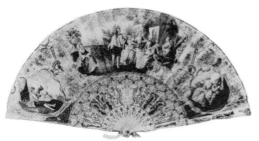

European 18th century folding fan
with pierced and painted ivory
sticks, guard length 11.1/8in.
(Robt. W. Skinner Inc.)   £110

Late 19th century lace fan, fine
needle lace on pierced, gilded pearl
sticks, guard length 10¾in. (Robt.
W. Skinner Inc.)   £327

Framed fan, gouache on paper,
pearl sticks with multicolour
foil floral decoration, France,
circa 1880's, guard length 12¾in.
(Robt. W. Skinner Inc.)   £206

Folding fan, depicting Rebecca at the
well, gouache on vellum, circa 1740,
guard length 11½in. (Robt. W. Skinner Inc.)   £155

19th century Chinese fan with sticks of
stained and pierced ivory decoration.£31

Late 19th century framed fan, Louis
XVI-style, with pearl sticks, guard
length 10½in. (Robt. W. Skinner Inc.)
      £189

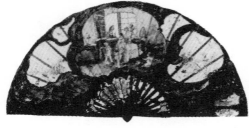

French double-sided fan with tortoiseshell
guardsticks, circa 1880, 7in.   £160

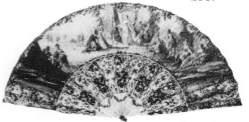

French fan with mother-of-pearl
sticks, circa 1760, 7in.   £400

FINGER PLATES

Of all door fittings, the finger plate offers the greatest scope for decoration and through-out the ages they have reflected fashionable taste and current architectural design.

The early examples were made from solid brass, steel, cut glass or fine quality porcelain and many were very ornate indeed. As a general rule, the earlier, the better the quality. Around the mid 1920's finger plates came into more common use and there are some fine Art Deco designs made from bakelite, tin or perspex.

It is clearly demonstrated, by price alone, that the colourful enamel advertising finger plates are the most popular of all. These were designed to be affixed to the outside door of the dealer's shop and, some are still to be found on older properties, often under many layers of paint.

There was also a version made for use inside the shop and, wherever appropriate, this incor-porated a match striker.

Spratt's Bird Seeds, match striker and plate.   £50

Art Nouveau style pressed brass plate.   £5

Player's Navy Cut, match striker and plate.   £50

Mid 19th cen-tury pressed brass plate.£8

Green's Lawn Mower, 'For British People'.   £45

French ormolu finger plate, circa 1860.£15

Sunlight Soap, 'Less Labour, Greater Comfort'.   £30

Victorian solid brass cupid finger plate. £12

Thomson's Dye Works Perth.   £20

Morris's Blue Book Ciga-rettes, match striker and plate.   £75

(Street Jewellery Society)

FIRE EXTINGUISHERS

Until about 1850, the inhabitants of many rural areas had no alternative but to pay an insurance premium to a private fire service in the sometimes vain hope that the firefighters would arrive at the scene of the fire before the building was burned to the ground.

Most hedged their bets by stocking up with the primitive fire extinguishers available at that time. These early devices were made of glass and of a globular shape. They were coloured blue, green or amber and contained a liquid which was a mixture of various ingredients combined with hydrogen peroxide. Grenades were sold in boxed quantities to be distributed around a premises and hung in specially designed wire baskets. These were the first commercially produced fire extinguishers and they carried the only possible instructions......... 'In case of fire — the grenade should be thrown into the heart of the fire'! Today, these are worth about £30 each.

In time, round and tubular appliances were produced by Harden, Imperial, Star, Swift and Spong; followed by the wall mounted type of device more or less similar to those in use today but showing many variations in case type and contents. The earliest examples of this type were made of brass and some were chrome plated for effect.

Red painted, metal cased fire extinguishers were introduced along with standard fire regulations. Many of the earliest still feature brass fittings and were supplied with wall mountings.

1930's 'Firene' plated brass fire extinguisher.   £15

Minimax fire extinguisher, model no. 4AW, a gas pressure water type with brass fittings.   £6

Minimax blue glass fire extinguisher.£35

Romac brass fire extinguisher complete with wall fitting.   £10

Copper fire extinguisher with a fine oval brass plaque, circa 1930, 29in. high.   £75

Minimax, one gallon glass fire extinguisher refill.   £5

A Harden Star fire grenade in blue glass.   £30

Minimax one gallon type G fire extinguisher with brass fittings.   £8

(Paul G. Sheppard)

FIRE IRONS & FENDERS

An open fire burning brightly in the hearth will tend to monopolise attention in any room and a great deal of expense and attention to detail went into the design and production of the focal point — the fireplace.

Catering for the practicalities of keeping a good fire going without razing the house to the ground led to the production of such necessary tools and accessories as Fire dogs, Fire irons and Fenders. These were produced mainly in materials such as brass, steel, wrought iron, cast iron or copper and fashioned in a variety of designs according to the period and fashion of the day.

A typical set of fire irons may include a shovel, brush, tongs, poker and some sets even incorporate bellows. Long handled irons were produced from the mid 19th century and these were displayed either resting on fire dogs or, where provision was made, in specially designed notches against the fender. The principal function of the fender was to give protection against burning logs and hot coals tumbling from the hearth but the beautiful designs and good quality materials used in their production soon assured that the fender also became an important feature of the room. One of the most impressive examples, introduced to Britain around 1860, is the Club Fender which apart from a practical function offers quite comfortable seating with its broad, upholstered top running the full length of the hearth.

In recent years there has been something of a revival in the popularity of the open fire with resulting demand for all fireplace furnishings and, while the value of examples once on the market is quickly recognised, these are just the type of pieces that get stashed away in the attic when central heating is installed or the old fireplace removed. They are well worth resurrecting.

A heavy set of Victorian brass fire irons, 32in. long. £85

An Edwardian brass companion set, 21in. high. £38

Victorian brass barley twist fire irons, 30in. long. £90

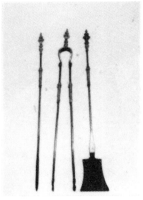

A fine set of Georgian steel fire irons, 32in. long. £145

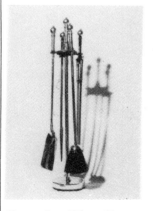

Four-piece Edwardian brass companion set, 30in. high. £85

An early set of steel and brass fire irons, 32in. long, circa 1810. £110

(Shirley A. Butler)

149

An ornate Victorian brass fender, 51in. long, circa 1870. £150

Cast iron fender with ornate brass relief decoration, 44in. long, circa 1895. £85

Victorian brass rail fender, 40in. long, circa 1870. £165

19th century polished steel fender with copper relief, 36in. long. £125

An early 19th century polished steel fender, 46in. long. £140

A Welsh steel fender, 48in. long, circa 1880. £48

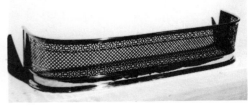

Mid 19th century brass rail fender, 54in. long, circa 1850. £220

A finely pierced early 19th century polished brass fender, circa 1810. £190

(Shirley A. Butler)

A fine quality pierced brass fender, 50in. long, circa 1870.   £200

Georgian serpentine-shape steel fender with cast brass embellishments, 60in. long. £295

Victorian brass bobbin fender, 46in. long.   £185

An early Victorian brass fret fender, 66in. long.   £375

A copper and brass Art Nouveau style fender, 42in. long.   £175

Victorian brass fender with scroll ends, 48in. long.   £140

Brass Art Nouveau style fender, 46in. long.   £125

Deep brass fret fender, 56in. long, circa 1830.   £200

(Shirley A. Butler)

Pierced steel fender, 48in. long, circa 1810.
£185

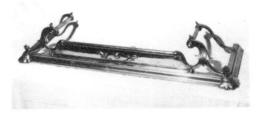

Victorian brass fender, 46in. long, circa 1885.
£145

Cast iron and copper Art Nouveau style fender, 52in. long.
£165

A small Victorian cast iron fender, 24in. long.
£60

A very ornate iron fender, 7ft. long, circa 1890.
£285

An unusual steel half-moon fender with matching irons, circa 1790.
£385

Victorian brass rope twist fender, 56in. long, circa 1850.
£220

Late Victorian cast iron and brass rail fender, 42in. long.
£125

(Shirley A. Butler)

Most of us have, at some time or another, tucked away a few stamps, envelopes or first day covers for no particular reason other than that they seemed attractive at the time. Today, many of these have some monetary value and some rare examples can be worth a lot of money. It is a fact that many valuable first day covers and stamps, including the famous penny blacks, have turned up in the proverbial 'shoebox' stashed away in a corner of the attic.

For the philatelist whose first love is the stamp itself, first day covers have the added attraction of presenting a decorative envelope bearing a special cancellation which, in some cases, comes together with an informative card insert.

With only one or two exceptions, the Post Office issued the first of the 'official' illustrated covers in 1964 to mark a particular issue of stamps commemorating Shakespeare. As far back as 1890 however, they issued a jubilee cover to commemorate fifty years of penny postage, and this is generally accepted as the first illustrated special event cover with related postmarks. These items can be worth up to £25.

Another exception must be the 1840 Mulready 1d. & 2d. envelope which can be worth up to £5,000 — but these are extremely rare.

Various factors effect the pricing of covers. Condition, clarity of cancellation, type of cancellation, errors, additional postage marks, etc.
Since the early 1980's first day covers have become much more commercialised. New covers appear with surprising regularity in commemoration of some quite unexceptional events. It would be fair to say that because these are produced in such large quantities, most are worth no more than a few pounds each.

'British Explorers', P.O. Souvenir Cover, Branch Office postmark. £2

Centenary of postage stamps commemorative cover from Red Cross Exhibition, London, 6th May 1940. £25

'British Textiles', First Day Cover 23 July 1982, 15½p., 19½p., 26p., 29p. £3

First Day of Issue Scottish £1 coin, official Royal Mint issue £1 stamp, Special Cover, handstamp and encapsulated Scottish £1 coin. £5

(Paul G. Sheppard)

FIRST DAY COVERS

'County Cricket', P.O. Commemorative Cover, Branch Office postmark.   £3

Mulready envelope July 23rd 1840, red Maltese Cross cancellation.   £45

'Rhodesia', Inauguration of the Posts and Telecommunications Corporation, 1 July 1970.   £3.25

First Day of Issue, South African stamps 1973, 'Music', Private Cover.   £1.50

Royal Mint Official Issue to commemorate First Day Issue of £1 coin. Cover has £1 stamp, Special Cancellation and real £1 coin in plastic capsule, plus information card inside.   £5

Cover to commemorate 'The Mayflower' 1620-1970, 15 August 1970. Special cancellation and enclosure.   £3

Commemorative postmark on 11½p. stamp on cover, Official Naming of the Tynemouth Lifeboat, 28th June 1980.   75p

'British Trees', the oak P.O. Souvenir Cover, Branch Office postmark.   £1.25

(Paul G. Sheppard)

New Definitive Values for Wales, P.O. First Day Cover 8 Apr 1981, 11½p., 14p., 18p., 22p. stamps.   £2.50

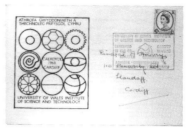

University of Wales Institute of Science & Technology, Commemorative Cover and postmark 4d., definitive stamp 19th April 1968.   £1.75

Isle of Man Souvenir Cover, 'House of Keys Election Act' 5th Jan 1981, 7p. and 1p. stamps.   £2

'British Textiles', P.O. First Day Cover 19½p. stamp only.   £1.25

'Sports', First Day of Issue, First Day Cover 10th October 1980, 12p., 13½p., 15p., 17½p stamps.   £2

1890 post office Jubilee cover (envelope) with set of King Edward VII stamps posted on First Day of Issue January 1st 1902.£500

Parcel Post Centenary Postcard 1883-1983, special cancellation with £1.30 parcel post stamp on postcard.   £3.50

Silver Jubilee Souvenir Presentation Pack of Stamps 8½p., 10p., 11p., 13p.   £2.75

(Paul G. Sheppard)

155

FIRST DAY COVERS

First Day Cover 'British Paintings' 4th July 1973, 3p., 5p., 7½p., 9p. Nice decorative illustrations with enclosure.   £2

Post Office picture card SWPR 17 Royal Mail Delivering in Plymouth Dock. First Day of Issue of 'Cars' stamp 19½p. and postmark 13 Oct 1982.   £1.25

Mulready cover red Maltese Cross, reverse stuck to album page.   £20

Exhibition Souvenir Cover 'Energy Conservation' set of folklore stamps, special exhibition handstamp 25 March 1981.   £2.25

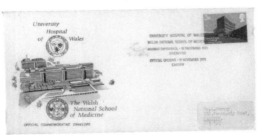

Official Commemorative envelope 'University Hospital of Wales'. Official opening 19 November 1971, 3p. Aberystwyth stamp. Special handstamp.   £2.50

'150th Anniversary of the Birth of Florence Nightingale', 2 x 9d. stamps. 'The Lady with the Lamp'.   £2

Commemorative Cover April 26th 1948, 'Silver Wedding', 4 x 1½d. Swaziland stamps posted 1st Dec. 1948.   £2.50

Rare First Day of Issue Mulready envelope with Maltese Cross postmark and date stamp, 6th May 1840.   £1,000

(Paul G. Sheppard)

FIRST DAY COVERS

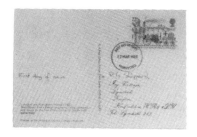

P.H.Q. card No. 42(a) Liverpool and Manchester Railway 12 March 1980.   £1

Post Office Commemorative Cover 'The last day of the British postal services in the Isle of Man 4th July 1973', Douglas postmark, 4 definitive stamps.   £6

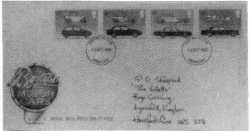

'British Motor Cars', Royal Mail First Day Cover 15½p., 19½p., 26p., 29p. stamps. First Day postmark 13th October 1982, cars Austin, Ford, Jaguar, Rolls Royce.   £3.25

National Trust Series No. 1 'Official Opening of the Old Post Office Tintagel, Cornwall', 9d. philympia stamp, special handstamp, 2 June 1971.   £3.50

'Music — British Conductors', P.O. First Day Cover 10th Sept. 1980, 17½p., 15p., 13½p., & 12p. stamps. Sir John Barbirolli, Sir Malcolm Sargent, Sir Thos. Beecham, Sir Henry Wood.   £1.75

'Cattle' P.O. First Day Cover, single 26p. stamp 'Hereford Bull', special Hereford Commemorative handstamp 6.3.84.   £2

Post Office Official First Day Cover 'Horses' 5 July 1978, 9p., 10½p., 11p., 13p. stamps.   £2.50

'International Year of the Disabled', Special Exhibition Official First Day Cover with Special Exhibition handstamp 14p., 18p., 22p. and 25p. stamps.   £4

(Paul G. Sheppard)

FIRST DAY COVERS

First Day Cover 'Liverpool & Manchester
Railway' , strip of five 12p. stamps, all
different Welsh First Day cancellation 12
March 1980.   £2.50

P.H.Q. card Serial No. PHW7(d) with res-
pective stamp 10p. 'Medieval Warriors',
issued 10th July 1974, posted to S. Africa.
£9

Official First Day Cover 'Information
Technology', 8 Sept. 1982, with explanatory
insert.   £2

'The Royal Wedding', P.O. First Day Cover
to celibrate the marriage of Prince of Wales,
29th July 1981, 14p. & 25p. stamps. £2.25

Trinidad and Tobago envelope cover, 1c.,
2c. stamps, 20th May 1940.   50p

First Day Cover to commemorate 350th
Anniversary, 29th Sept 1982, of Lady
Hawkins School, special handstamp together
with information card.   £3.50

Christmas 1980 single 12p. stamp — Special
Cancellation 'The Regent Street Association
wish you a Very Happy Christmas', 19.11.80.
£1

Christmas cards 1982, P.O. First Day Cover
17th Nov. 1982, 5 stamps 12½p., 15½p.,
19½p., 26p., 29p.   £3.50

(Paul G. Sheppard)

158

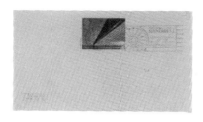

Borough of Sandwell 'Industrial hub of West Midlands' slogan, handstamp.   50p

P.O. First Day Cover £1 book of stamps, the story of Wedgwood, 24th May 1972.   £40

The Announcement of the Betrothal of H.R.H. Prince of Wales to Lady Diana Spencer 24th Feb. 1981, St. Valentine's day stamp special Windsor handstamp.   £5

Spanish Souvenir Commemorative Cover, seven different pictorial Spanish stamps 1978.   £2.25

'British Gardens' First Day Cover 4 stamps 31p., 28p., 20½p., 16p. with Special First Day Cancellation 24th Aug. 1983.   £2.50

'London 1980 International Stamp Exhibition', P.O. First Day Cover miniature sheet 7th May 1980. (P.O. Third miniature sheet).   £1.75

'Hodge Life Assurance' advertising First Day Cover 25 Nov. 1970. Single 5d. stamp, special handstamp cancellation.   £1.25

Lithograph envelope by Valentine of Dublin, pen and ink drawings of 'trick mules' inside, unused.   £18

(Paul G. Sheppard)

FIRST DAY COVERS

Gibraltar Uniform Issue, Official First Day Cover 21.8.74. £2.60

'London Landmarks', P.O. First Day Cover 7th May 1980, 5 stamps 17½p., 15p., 13½p., 12p., 10½p. £2

(788) Mulready envelope to Chipping Norton 1840, red Maltese Cross. £50

Souvenir postcard from San Marino 9.3.1960, nice stamps. £2

'Christmas 1972', P.O. First Day Cover 18th Oct. 1972, 2½p., 3p., 7½p. stamps. £1.50

'Christmas 1981', P.O. First Day Cover 18th Nov. 1981, 5 stamps 25p., 22p., 18p., 14p., 11½p. £3

'Prince of Wales 21st Birthday', P.O. Cover with commemorative stamp and Caernarvon postmark 14th Nov. 1969. £3.50

First Day of Issue of 2½d. 'Silver Wedding' stamp 26th April 1948, plain envelope cover. £2.50

(Paul G. Sheppard)

FISHING REELS

Epitomising the art of angling the fishing reel is without doubt the most sought after and worthy star attraction in the whole field of collecting fishing tackle.

Invariably well engineered and each designed for a specific job they have the added advantage of taking up very little space and can be arranged in a most attractive display.

Other items of collectible tackle and associated ephemera include fly boxes, fly wallets, pen knives, creels, gaffs, nets, stuffed fish, licences and a host of smaller articles.

A Hardy Bros. Ltd. 'Fortuna' alloy sea reel with 'ship's wheel' tension nut and double handle, 7in. diam. (Christie's) $391 £270

A Hardy Bros. Ltd. 'St. George' multiplying alloy fly reel with ebonite handle. (Christie's) $117 £81

A Watson, Inverness, brass reel, with horn handle and smooth brass foot, 3½in. diam. (Christie's) $44 £30

A Hardy Bros. 1896 pattern all brass 'Perfect' reel with ivorine handle, 4¼in. diam. (Christie's) $561 £453

A Malloch's Patent spinning reel with horn handle, 4¼in. diam. (Christie's) $71 £49

A Hardy Bros. Ltd. large alloy sea-fishing reel with 'ship's wheel' tension nut, 9in. diam. (Christie's) $626 £432

A Hardy Bros. Ltd. The 'Perfect' alloy reel with ivorine handle and smooth brass foot, 4in. diam. (Christie's) £119

A Dreadnought Casting Reel Co. Ltd. alloy reel with ivorine handle brass check-nut, 3¼in. diam. (Christie's) £30

A Hardy Bros. Ltd. 'St. George' multiplying alloy reel with ebonite handle and ribbed brass foot. (Christie's) £119

A Hardy Bros. Ltd. The 'Longstone' alloy reel with ebonised wooden handles, 4¼in. diam. (Christie's) £45

A Malloch's Patent bronze reel. (Woolley & Wallis) £65

An A. C. Farlowe & Co. Ltd. brass faced alloy reel with ebonite handle, 4.3/8in. diam. (Christie's) £97

A Hardy Bros. Ltd. The 'Perfect' alloy reel with ebonite handle, 4¼in. diam. (Christie's) £130

A Hardy Bros. Ltd. 'Silex' No. 2 alloy spinning reel with ivorine handles, 4½in. diam. (Christie's) £52

A Hardy Bros. 'Perfect' brass reel with ivorine handle, 4in. diam. (Christie's) £346

A Hardy Bros. Ltd. The 'Perfect' alloy reel with ebonite handle, 3.7/8in. diam. (Christie's) £59

A Hardy Bros. Ltd. The 'Silex' No. 2 alloy sea reel with wooden handles, 7in. diam. (Christie's) £86

A Hardy Bros. Ltd. 'St. George' multiplying alloy fly reel, 3¾in. diam. (Christie's) £367

A Hardy Bros. Ltd. The 'St. George' alloy reel with ivorine handle, 3¾in. diam. (Christie's) £54

An Ocean City 'Automatic Go' (Philadelphia, USA) alloy reel with ivorine handles, 3½in. diam. (Christie's) £13

A brass reel with foliate engraved band to the front plate, horn handle, 4in. diam. (Christie's) £35

A Hardy Bros. 'Perfect' nickel plated brass reel with ivorine handle, 4in. diam. (Christie's) £346

A Hardy Bros. Ltd. 'Perfect' alloy reel with ivorine handle and smooth brass foot, 4¼in. diam. (Christie's) £81

A Hardy Bros. all brass 'Perfect' reel with horn handle, smooth foot and oval logo, 2.3/8in. diam. (Christie's) £346

An Allcock's 'Aerial Popular' reel, solid front rim, adjustable drag and optional check, circa 1935, 3in. diam. (N. J. Marchant Lane)   £20

Brass salmon reel with ivory handle and ventilated drum, by Broddell of Belfast, circa 1900, 4¼in. diam. (N. J. Marchant Lane)   £80

A Hardy Bros. Ltd. 'Sea Silex' alloy reel with smooth brass foot, ebonite handles and ivorine check handle, 7in. diam. (N. J. Marchant Lane)   £200

A Julius Vom Hofe alloy and ebonite sea reel with ebonite handle, 6in. diam., circa 1890. (N. J. Marchant Lane)   £150

A Julius Vom Hofe salmon fly reel, circa 1896, 4½in. diam. (N. J. Marchant Lane)   £130

A 'Featherlight' brass star back reel with perforated plates and foot, horn handle, patent Jan. 14.96, 2.5/8in. diam. (N. J. Marchant Lane)   £5

A large ebonite 'Starback' sea reel by Farlow, with brass star, foot and leather-bound Bickerdyke line guide, circa 1910, 5¾in. diam. (N. J. Marchant Lane)   £60

A Hardy Fortuna 7in. centre-pin sea reel, fitted with dual ebonite handles and brass star drag. (N. J. Marchant Lane)   £150

The 'H.J.S.' multiplying reel, blacked alloy with grooved alloy foot and nickel-plated thumb bar, 2.1/8in. diam. (N. J. Marchant Lane)£220

FISHING TACKLE

This particular collecting 'bug' has bitten both fisherman and collector alike and with over three million anglers in the country one may reasonably predict that it is a growing market. Most of the early tackle available dates from the 19th century and certainly very little was made before 1800.

The most notable makers of fine quality fishing tackle was the firm Hardy Brothers of Alnwick, established in 1872, but other well known makers include Allcocks of Redditch, Farlows of London and Mallochs of Perth all of whom made excellent equipment.

With the exception of lightweight split cane trout rods and other useable items, rods are, in general, not considered to be very much in demand. They tend to deteriorate rapidly and examples in poor condition are of little value. Rods also have the disadvantage of being difficult to display.

A Mallochs Patent japanned tin salmon fly reservoir, book-shape with two leaves, 11¾ x 7½ x 1½in. Inside is a collection of over 250 salmon flies, over half of which are gut-eyed. £200

A 'carry-all' style wicker creel with leather straps, circa 1910. £55

A galvanised live-bait can, with removable perforated interior container, perforated lid and folding handle, circa 1900, 10 x 7in. £15

A superb case of mixed fish caught 1895, pike, perch, roach, rudd, trout and carp, 3ft. x 2ft. £450

(N. J. Marchant Lane)

FISHING TACKLE

A two-section brass and steel telescopic gaff with rosewood handle, 36in. extended, circa 1910.   £40

Extending 'trout gaff' in brass.   £22

A stuffed sea trout, the boldly spotted 20¼in. fish mounted against reeds and grasses in bow-fronted case, 27¼ x 6¼ x 13½in.   £180

Two perch in bowed glazed case caught by H. Lord at Dogdyke, August 1903, 34½in. wide.   £190

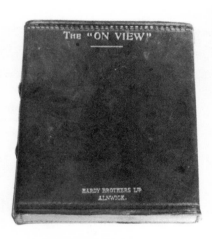

A 19th century mahogany fly box containing approximately 120 gut-eyed salmon flies.   £200

A Hardy Bros. The "On View' Fly Wallet, circa 1930.   £10

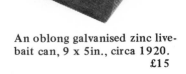

A 19th century fisherman's salmon gaff with turned beechwood handle and brass collar, circa 1870, 17¾in. long. (Christopher Sykes)   £29

Late 18th century salmon fishing spear, 6ft.6in. long.   £45

An oblong galvanised zinc live-bait can, 9 x 5in., circa 1920.   £15

(N. J. Marchant Lane)

FURNITURE FITMENTS

If you are in the least bit interested in furniture fittings, then a very pleasant hour, or two, may be spent browsing through the trade catalogues published during the last century. There you will find illustrations, descriptions and prices for many thousands of fittings including, ornate brass feet, castors, candle sconces for mirrors and pianos, key escutcheons and handles — and more handles.

A quick glance will confirm that, comparitively speaking, good quality fittings were just as expensive then as they are today. Most originate from Birmingham for that was the centre of the trade.

Before the 1770's, fittings were usually made of hollowcast brass but that was all to change with the invention of a machine capable of stamping fittings from a thin sheet brass.

Of all the fittings one is likely to come across, handles are the most common.

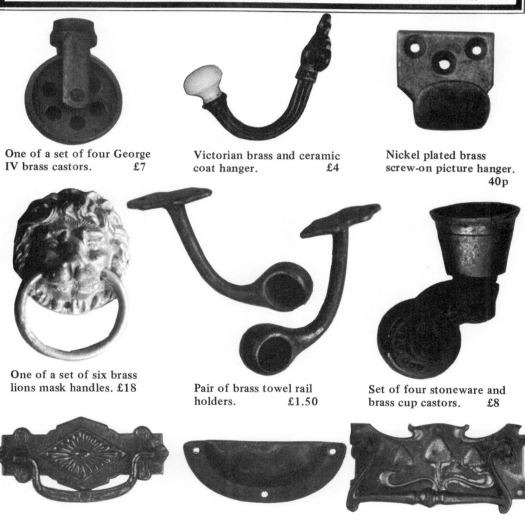

One of a set of four George
IV brass castors.   £7

Victorian brass and ceramic
coat hanger.   £4

Nickel plated brass
screw-on picture hanger.
40p

One of a set of six brass
lions mask handles. £18

Pair of brass towel rail
holders.   £1.50

Set of four stoneware and
brass cup castors.   £8

Set of four Edwardian
brass drawer handles. £5

One of a set of eight
coppered tin drawer pulls.
£3

Set of six Art Nouveau
coppered brass drawer pulls.
£10

(Paul G. Sheppard)

167

FURNITURE FITMENTS

Set of four brass key escutcheons.   £5

One of a set of eight brass key escutcheons.   £3

Set of four brass drop handles.   £4

A Victorian heavy bronze door knocker of Regency design, circa 1850, 5in. diam. (Christopher Sykes)   £40

Victorian brass candle holder.   £10

Victorian brass cabinet door lock.   £4

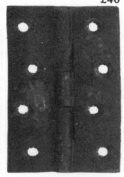

Pair of 3½in. brass door hinges, by S. J. & W. £4

Etas No. 5 brass lavatory lock.   £50

A 17th century William and Mary period brass door lock, keeper key escutcheon and key. (Christopher Sykes)   £245

Sheet brass fleur de lys screw-on picture hanger.   50p

Victorian brass door knob.   £3

Pair of brass curtain rail ends.   £3

(Paul G. Sheppard)

GAMES

The endless quest of mankind, to fill his leisure hours with entertaining pursuits, has left a legacy of games for today's collectors.

Most of the Victorian examples offer a degree of education as well as amusement, and games in their original boxes, complete with gaming pieces, dice and instructions will always make good money.

With the advent of the silicon chip, most of the mechanical machines from the end of the pier arcades have been replaced with more demanding modern delights. This has created a nostalgic fascination for such as the old 'Pussy Shooter' and 'Test your Strength' machines, many of which now sell for hundreds of pounds.

With the pace of life moving ever faster, even some of the 70's pin-ball machines have now become collector's items.

Early 20th century tartan-ware whist marker. £5

Leatherette wallet with integral domino set. £3

Late 19th century parquetry folding cribbage board. £5

'Improved Greek Architecture' wooden puzzle. £25

Victorian box of wooden building bricks, 9in. square. £8

Victorian set of bone dominoes in an oak box. (Christopher Sykes) £48

Victorian wooden building game in a fine pictorial box. £35

(Paul G. Sheppard)

169

A 'Little Wonder' Allwin-type machine, circa 1925, 32½in. high. £132

A 19th century random number selector, signed Jno. Wright Sept. 1897, 10in. wide. £77

Coin operated mechanical sweepstakes game, manufactured by RMC, trademark Rock-Ola, circa 1930?, 12in. high. (Robt. W. Skinner Inc.) £348

Coin operated mechanical football game, manufactured by The Baker Novelty Co., circa 1933, 17½in. high. (Robt. W. Skinner Inc.) £155

Brooklands Totalisator bandit with coin slot, circa 1939, 24in. high. £121

The French Execution Coin-slot Automaton, circa 1935, 84in. high. £495

A 'Stars of the Silver Screen' machine, circa 1935, 27in. high. £352

Rare prohibition gambling machine with metal body, circa 1930, 6in. high. £143

An Aeroplane Allwin-type machine, circa 1940, 33in. high. £99

GLAMOUR POSTCARDS

When compared to the standard of todays equivalent, these glamour postcards represent a return to an earlier age of innocence.

Glamour cards, always a keenly collected subject, were particularly popular with soldiers of the 1st World War who carried the cherished pin-up into the trenches with them.

The French, as always, were much bolder and their more permissive attitude is demonstrated by the disproportionate number of cards of French origin currently available.

It is difficult to imagine that contemporary collections were kept hidden in secret places and, for obvious reasons, a card which has successfully passed through the postal system would be an extremely rare item.

Glamour is still an inexpensive collectible with an appeal which lies mainly in the nostalgia content.

Marilyn Monroe, (printed in Germany).   £7

Birgit Nielsen, 1st Series, 50's 60's, deckle edged, colour.   £2.50

Terry Moore, (printed in Germany).   £3.50

Ziva Rodan, 1st Series, (printed in Germany).   £2.50

Brigitte Bardot, 1st Series, 50's, 60's, colour.   £3

Jayne Mansfield, Melissa Klasik Kards, (printed in Italy).   £1.50

(Paul G. Sheppard)

171

R. L. & K. Series, photographic study with flowers.
£1

Art Deco Glamour by Marte Graf, 'Falto' Series, 'The Difficult Ball'. £7

Corona Publishing Co., Blackpool, (printed in Italy), British Beauty. £1

French 'Bathing' Glamour, hand-tinted photo type.
£1.50

P.C. Paris Series No. 1519, lingerie study. £3.50

ARS Series 'Bonne Fete', vivid colours, hand-tinted with applied dots, 1930.
£4

French hand-tinted photo type 'beauty' card with cat interest. £1.50

Art Deco Glamour by Marte Graf, 'Falto' Series, 'The Monkey and the Hoop'. £7

Salon de Paris No. 98, S.P.A. Series 'Voluptuous', by I. Seeberger.
£6

(Paul G. Sheppard)

GLAMOUR POSTCARDS

Blenet 1926 French photo type, hand-tinted, vivid colour.   £3.50

Art Deco Glamour by Marte Graf, 'Falto' Series, 'Getting It Through The Gate'.   £7

P.C. Paris Series No. 2320, French beauty, 'Purple-tone' photographic.£1.50

Carte Postale French hand-tinted Glamour study photographic.   £2

Paris Series post-card No. 1445, silk stockings and frilly knickerbockers, partially dressed study.   £3

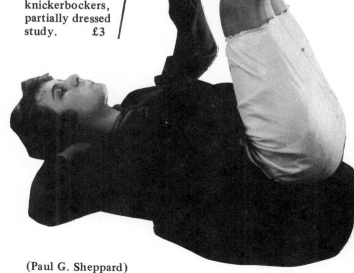

P.C. Paris Series No. 1831, a temptatious study in silk.   £4

(Paul G. Sheppard)

173

GLAMOUR POSTCARDS

Salon de Paris No. 63,
'After the Tub', by D.
Enjolras.   £7

Rotary Photo Co. London,
British Beauty.   £1

French VAW Series No.
8004, Erotic Study with
model cat.   £3.50

Miss Vernon.

Marilyn Monroe (Camden
Graphics repro.)   40p

G.P. Paris No. 139, Nude
Study with lace.   £5

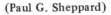

Salon de Paris, study by
Pereira da Silva, titled
'Salome'.   £5

(Paul G. Sheppard)

C.A. Paris No. 101, Nude
study poised on chair.
                £5

GLAMOUR POSTCARDS

Glamour/Fantasy, Girl in Bubble, NPG Series. £9

'In the Serene Evening' by J. Georges Bertrand, Paris Salon de 1914, Art Glamour. £4

Rotary photo No. A598-6, British Beauty Series, Miss Drina Verchesi. £2

C.A. Paris No. 127 Nude study sitting with roses. £4.50

Jayne Mansfield 1st Series 50's, 60's, colour. £3.50

M.K.B. Germany 'Triumphant Love' by G. Rienacker. £2

B.G. Paris No. 191 Nude Study with mirror, dressing-room scene. £5

Art Deco Glamour by Marte Graf, 'Falto' Series, 'Ice-skating'. £7

(Paul G. Sheppard)

Fantasy/Glamour 'Light-prayer', photographic, German. £4.50

GLAMOUR POSTCARDS

VAW Series France, Reclining Study with Buddha (real photograph).   £3.50

Rotary photo, Miss Constance Worth, British Beauty, photographic.   £1

WKP Series tinted phototype Glamour/ Fantasy card.   £3

A.R. & C. Co. Germany, Glamour with Equestrian Mythological subjects.   £2

Salon de Paris No. 137, 'The Spring' by C. A. Lenoir.   £2

Photographic study of reclining nude, circa 1916.   £5

Salon de Paris No. 103, 'Careless' by G. Seignac.   £6

Woodbury Series No. 244 'A Summer Night' by Albert Moore (Walker Art Gallery), sepia collotype.   £1

(Paul G. Sheppard)

GOLFING

Almost everything to do with the sport of golf is enthusiastically collected; from bags, which made their first appearance around the 1880's, to trophies and other commemorative pieces. Even the most ordinary artefacts, when related by design to golf (like a hatpin in the form of a club), will fetch a much higher price than could otherwise be expected.

The earliest golf balls were made of leather and filled with a concoction of boiled feathers. They were then hammered to a round shape and painted white. In time, these were followed by the 'gutta-percha' balls which were of smooth appearance and patented by a Dr. Paterson of St. Andrews. The balls came into common usage by 1850 and were superseded by the mass produced moulded 'hammered' ball used today.

During the late 19th century various other designs were patented and these are now considered to be very collectible.

A Feather golf ball, no name. (Christie's)
£626

A brass Gutta golf ball mould for the Trophy golf ball, bramble pattern No. 11917, by J. White & Co., Edinburgh. (Christie's)
£324

A Gourlay feather ball, size 25, mint condition. (Christie's)
£1,350

A collection showing the development of the Silver King ball comprising: a smooth gutta ball; five machine made Silver Town gutty balls and four Silver King rubber core, all mounted in an ebonised case, 12 x 6in. (Christie's)
£486

A scared head long-nosed spoon by McEwan, the head so stamped, circa 1875. (Christie's)
£886

Hickory shafted mid iron by Stanhope. £8

A scared head long-nosed grassed driver by Wm. Park, Snr., circa 1870. (Christie's) £626

One right-handed cleek by Nicholson of Pittenweem, circa 1890. (Christie's) £140

A mallet headed 'cross-head' club, owned by Sir G. Alexander, circa 1900. (Christie's) £302

Hand forged mashie by J. Coleman, Surbiton. £10

Hickory shafted mashie niblick by J. Bremner, Scotland. £12

A scared head long-nosed short spoon by Tom Morris, circa 1875. (Christie's) £702

A scared head wooden putter by Tom Morris, regripped. (Christie's) £486

A scared head putter by
Jackson of Perth, circa
1870. (Christie's)
£886

Hickory shafted club by
Lillywhite, London.   £8

A scared head long-nosed
spoon by W. D. Day.
(Christie's)   £248

A special niblick by T.
Stewart, St. Andrews. £15

A scared head long-nosed
driver by Jack Morris, with
greenheart shaft. (Christie's)
£540

One left-handed cleek by
John Gray, circa 1875.
(Christie's)   £140

A Carrick rut iron, the
shaft stamped John Wisden,
London, circa 1870.
(Christie's)   £648

Hickory shafted wood by
A. R. Jeffery.   £6

A Hickory shafted roller
headed club, the nose stamped patented July 1907.
(Christie's)   £259

A French pottery Art Deco style jardiniere by Jerome Massier, circa 1920, 7in. diam. (Christie's)

£183

Bobby Jones double sided 'Flicker Book', published by A. G. Spalding & Bros., 2½in. high.   £6

A Royal Doulton bowl printed and coloured, the interior with a golfer about to putt, 8¼in. high. (Christie's)

£270

A bronze figure of Harry Vardon by H. S. Ludlow, cast by Elkington & Co., circa 1900, on oak base, 5in. high, 7½in. overall. (Christie's)   £864

A Royal Doulton two-handled vase printed and coloured with two golfers and a caddie below a landscape of a golf course, 8in. high. (Christie's)

£226

A composition painted caricature figure carrying a golf bag of clubs advertising the 'Dunlop' golf balls, 17in. high. (Christie's)

£226

A Royal Doulton Kingsware mug, the raised decoration of a golfer and his caddie, circa 1910, 5¾in. high. (Christie's)   £216

A composition painted caricature figure of an early golfer advertising the Penfold golf ball, 21½in. high. (Christie's)   £324

A Royal Doulton oviform jug decorated in the style of Chas. Crombie, circa 1910, 9¼in. high. (Christie's)   £226

GREETINGS CARDS

Examples of some of the finest printing skills are to be found in this category.

Many of the most highly acclaimed artists and illustrators designed greetings cards and had their designs overprinted with seasonal messages. All artist drawn cards are worth more if the work can be identified.

The more unusual the subject the better and cards designed to celebrate Halloween, Krampus (counterpart of Santa Claus — Father Christmas traditionally rewarding good children; Krampus punishing naughty ones) and the Jewish New Year are highly prized are often quite rare and valuable.

The embossed deckle edged greetings cards produced from 1918 until 1945 presents an interesting variety for collectors and most of the photographically reproduced, sometimes hand tinted specimens can still be bought for between 10p. and 50p. Many popular examples were produced in the Beagle and Rotary series.

'Loving Birthday Wishes', real photo of a girl and dolls/toys in a wheelbarrow. 50p

'New Year Greetings' 1915, Whitney Series (U.S.A.) chromo litho with gold applique showing the sands of time running out and in, embossed.   £2.50

Eight-sided Christmas and New Year chromo litho card edged with satin. £5

Envelope type Christmas card chromo embossed applied glitter 'acorns'.   £4

11th Birthday card, hand-tinted real photo with large numbers for age and verse 'May Your 11th Birthday Be A Very Happy One'.
£1.50

Better than average example of deckle edge greeting card by Beagles, real photo with rural interest, posted in 1912.   50p

(Paul G. Sheppard)

GREETINGS CARDS

Padded envelope 'blessing card' applied scraps with printed silk verse.
£5

A Christmas Greeting card, chromo embossed with nice Greenaway style artwork.   £3.50

Christmas card by Pollards Ltd., Exeter, verse printed on reverse, hand-tinted Father Christmas in green robes.   £3.75

Woven silk birthday card opening out to reveal verses in centre ovals surrounded by chromo litho floral artwork.   £18

New Year Greeting chromo litho card by Raphael Tuck, Serial No. 1234, 125 x 55mm.   £1.50

'Wishing You Many Happy Returns of the Day', real fur, velvet and silk.   £10

Embossed deckle edged card with applied scraps and verse 'Love's Offering'.   £1.60

Gilt edged stiff chromo litho card 'God Bless You with a happy New Year', by J. F. Schipper & Co., London.   £1.50

Chromo litho embossed 'A Happy Christmas', flowers and cross. £1.25

(Paul G. Sheppard)

GREETINGS CARDS

A Christmas card by Rotary with real photo of Mabel Love 'The Best of Xmas Wishes'. 50p

'Battle Bravely' by Charlotte Murray, chromo embossed Christmas book card, three pages of verse, bound with pink ribbon. £6

'A Sincere Wish', Christmas greeting card with verse, Carlton Series No. 3459/4. Postally used in 1912. £1.50

'Many Happy Returns of the Day', chromo card, verse and design on reverse. £1.50

'With kindest wishes for the the New Year', chromo litho card by Castell Bros., printed in Bavaria. £1.50

'A Happy Birthday Be Thine', 'Court' chromo litho greeting card by royal letters patent, size 130 x 150mm., lace cut-out edge. £4

'Many Merry Greetings', New Year, embossed chromo litho card by Raphael Tuck. £3

'Greeting' chromo embossed 3-fold Xmas & New Year card with verse inside. £1.75

Embossed opening card 'Remember Me', with applied chromo scraps. £2.50

(Paul G. Sheppard)

'Glad Days Be Yours , Xmas 1902 to wish you for Auld Lang Syne A Happy Xmas and a Glad New Year', Caldmore Conservative Club, Walsall. £2

'A Casket of Good Wishes', 150 x 100mm., embossed, opens up to reveal verse. £6.50

Lace cut-out type romantic card 'Accept my heart its truthful love from thee' . £1.75

'The Latest News', 'To Wish You A Happy Xmas', real photo by Davidson 1908.50p

'Happy Birthday Wishes', Valentines Series, illustration and verse inside. 75p

'Best Wishes for Xmas' by Rotary, real photo of child with dolls. 50p

'To Greet You and Wish You a Happy Christmas', photo bromide series, real photo. 75p

Embossed chromo litho and glitter Christmas card which opens to reveal verse. £2

'Best Luck for Christmas' 1907, red robed Father Xmas and children, chromo litho. £4

(Paul G. Sheppard)

Lace type cut-out with pop-up scrap to reveal verse 'Firm and faithful fond and true such my love I'll be to you'. £4.50

'God Bless Your Christmas', embossed chromo litho card with nice design and cut-out edge. £2.50

Embossed parchment paper Christmas greetings card, verse inside remembrance, coloured flags, cotton binding, 1914-18. £1.50

'God Save The Queen', Diamond Jubilee 1897, chromo litho card by Raphael Tuck. £40

Embossed birthday card 1925 'Good Luck be with you', fairy interest, 110 x 160mm. £1.50

Chromo litho embossed Kate Greenaway style 'letter type' greeting card with verse inside. £2.50

'Christmas Greetings and all Good Wishes', chromo embossed blue robed Father Christmas with gilt decoration. £10

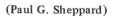

Chromo litho embossed 'Sweet Joys be thine this Christmas' with birds and flowers. £2

'To Greet You At Christmas', chromo embossed red robed Father Xmas, B.B. Serial No. X250. £5

(Paul G. Sheppard)

HANDKERCHIEFS

The use of handkerchiefs originated in Italy then, gradually, the custom spread throughout Europe.

At first, any old shape was considered suitable and it was only later that the traditional square shape was adopted. It was, actually, more by proclamation than adoption, for it was Marie Antionette, Queen of France, who first suggested the traditional shape and on 2nd January, 1785, a royal decree was announced to the effect that 'Henceforth, all handkerchiefs will be square in shape'.

A collection may follow one of a dozen or more themes such as heraldic, comic, silk, lace, initialled etc., and the price range is wide enough to cater for everyone.

An Edwardian box trimmed handkerchief with original trade sticker.   £3

A printed George Washington handkerchief, probably England, circa 1800, 12½ x 11½in. (Robt. W. Skinner Inc.)   £326

A handmade Bedfordshire bobbin lace handkerchief, large. (Iris Martin)   £6

Souvenir of Ypres embroidered handkerchief.   £5

Early 19th century printed handkerchief apotheosis of George Washington, England, 26 x 19½in. (Robt. W. Skinner Inc.)   £634

An Edwardian embroidered cotton handkerchief.   £3

Late Victorian embroidered handkerchief with floral designs. (Paul G. Sheppard) £5

20th century cotton handkerchief with finely embroidered floral spray. (Paul G. Sheppard) £3

Early 20th century linen handkerchief with lace border. (Paul G. Sheppard) £2

'Greetings from France' embroidered handkerchief, 1914-18. £6

Copper plate printed handkerchief, England, circa 1800, 18½ x 21in. (Robt. W. Skinner Inc.) £451

Early 19th century printed handkerchief, printed in red on linen, 32 x 25½in. (Robt. W. Skinner Inc.) £555

Late 19th century cotton handkerchief with embroidered initial and floral sprays. (Paul G. Sheppard) £3

Late 19th century handkerchief with central medallion and all-over floral pattern. (Paul G. Sheppard) £4

Nylon trimmed handkerchief with original trade label. (Paul G. Sheppard) £1

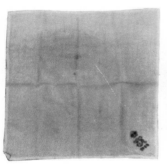

Cotton handkerchief embroidered 'E.R. 1953'. £2

Royal Corps. of Signals silk and satin handkerchief. £8

1930's lace handkerchief in cotton. £3.50

HATS

Most people have accumulated what amounts to a collection of hats, before they realise they are doing it. Having bought a few cloche hats because you approve of their snug fitting elegance and, of course, as pure contrast, that dusty hat from the music hall days, still with a faded scent lingering to the ostrich feathers and disintegrating array of fruit and flowers clinging gamely to the brim, how then, can you resist the collapsable opera hat, in nearly perfect condition? — You can't.

If you are brave enough, you might wear them out of doors. If not, they look spectacular displayed on a bentwood hatstand or on a wig stand.

If you have just come across a boxful of hats in the attic and you wish to sell them, then you have marketable goods. Nowadays, it is not only collectors who are looking for different models; it is the fashionable trend for wearing hats of all shapes and sizes, the more unusual the better, that is creating the current demand.

An officer's peaked cap of The Royal Scots, diced headband, patent leather peak with gilt, silvered and enamel badge. (Wallis & Wallis) £45

Black velvet covered riding hat by Moss Bros. of Covent Garden.　　　　£6

1930's lady's felt hat with satin band.　　　　£3

A lady's flat wide-brimmed hat of black figured silk laid over plaited straw, circa 1770, 15¼in. diam. (Christie's S. Kensington)　　　£600

19th century Welsh 'Cardigan' hat with lace trimming.　£60

An Italian cocked hat of The Carabiniers with white metal grenade badge. (Wallis & Wallis)　　£110

Top hat by O. Parsley of Bristol.　　　　£6

A Nazi Panzer NCO's peaked service cap with dark green band. (Wallis & Wallis) £110

A 1920's rubber bathing cap.　(Phillips) £15

(Paul G. Sheppard)

HEARING AIDS

A good representative collection of hearing aids would span a century or more, and demonstrate a succession of devices from a simple ear trumpet to the highly sophisticated microchip technology of today.

The first electric hearing aid was the Acousticon patented in November 1901 and developed by the man who invented the Klaxon horn. These early examples worked on the principal of a 'telephone-type' receiver powered by a very large battery.

The important patronage of Queen Alexandra, who asked for a hearing aid to be made available to her during the Coronation of 1902, gave support and encouragement to other would-be users. Victor Ketjet, the inventor of the particular device used by the Queen, was awarded a medal denoting his achievements.

The next major development came in 1935 with the Amplivox and a battery unit small enough to be clipped to a pocket.

Early 18th century ear trumpet, maker's mark E.M., circa 1740.   £550

Silver ear trumpet by Rawlings & Sumner, 1833.   £750

Medresco Hearing Aid, battery type, with case and leads.   £3

A leatherette covered box containing a battery operated deaf aid, by R. H. Dent, London, circa 1930, box 8 x 2¾ x 3½in. (Christopher Sykes) £35

Victorian ear trumpet with ivory earpiece, by Hawksworth Eyre & Co., Sheffield, 1845.   £700

A Victorian telescopic hearing aid made of simulated tortoiseshell, diam. of trumpet end 3½in. x overall length 12¾in. (Christopher Sykes)   £185

HORSE TACK

There is a long held tradition for collecting horse tack, not least for its ornamental value. Tack is, invariably, very well made from good strong materials and very little of it was ever thrown away unless it was damaged beyond repair. The chief sport is in identifying and dating pieces.

Bronze was often used in the fittings and ornamentation of the very early days and these items can still be found. Stirrups can be dated by identifying the style of footwear they were designed to accommodate. Collars and hames vary in age and size from the draught horses of the middle ages to the pit ponies of the last century. Early horse trappings are very attractive but not as easy to find as the ubiquitous horse brasses produced in masses after 1850 and reproduced in equally large quantities. Horse shoes date back to Roman times and may provide an interesting area for study.

A pair of English latten spurs, circa 1570, each with shaped 5 spike rowels supported by bridles. (Wallis & Wallis) £90

Early 20th century canvas feeding bag. £5

Early 20th century hand-operated horsehair clippers. £5

One of two straps, each hung with a relief stamped scallop shell, together with two other brasses. (Lawrence Fine Art) £88

A silver horse bell, the bulbous body applied with silvered copper strapwork, 2¾in. high. £990

First World War canvas nosebag with U.S. insignia. £5

A silver George III driving plate by W. Pitts and J. Preedy, 1792 and 1793, 12in. long, gross 53oz. (Christie's) £2,808

(Paul G. Sheppard)

HOT WATER BOTTLES

Before the introduction of the rubber hot water bottle — and long before the electric blanket, 'hotties' were made of a very heavy stoneware material.

The bottle is flat based with an arched top and is sealed by means of a stoneware threaded screw stopper, secured by a rubber washer. Children commonly referred to bottles as 'piggy' bottles because of the squat, flattened nose shape of the handle. Some carry printed trademarks or early advertising slogans.

There are miniature versions designed to be carried within a muff and used as a hand-warmer and a special version designed to be used as a footwarmer for the comfort of coach and carriage travellers.

A decorative Victorian stoneware hot water bottle. £5

Late 19th century copper hot water bottle with screw plug, 7½in. diam. £12

Decorative stoneware hot water bottle, 9in. long. £3.50

Late Victorian plain stoneware hot water bottle. £3

Late Victorian footwarmer with carpet top and concealed metal water container, 10in. square. £15

Stoneware 'Sunrays' footwarmer, 8in. wide. £7

(Paul G. Sheppard)

HOT WATER BOTTLES

A decorative two-tone brown stoneware hot water bottle. £5

Stoneware hot water bottle in the form of a Gladstone bag. £20

Victorian stoneware hot water bottle stamped 'Footwarmer'. £4

'Handy' stoneware hot water bottle. £8

'The Adaptable Hot Water Bottle & Bed Warmer'. £15

Stoneware hot water bottle, late 19th century. £3

An early example of an English made Beta hot water bottle. 50p

'The Bungalow Footwarmer' by Denby Stoneware. £20

An early example of a Russian made rubber hot water bottle. 50p

(Paul G. Sheppard)

INDIAN BRASS

Much of the chased and embossed brassware, loosely referred to as Benares ware, was brought to this country by Anglo-Indians or intrepid travellers in the days of the Grand Tour.

Early pieces were of excellent quality metal, burnished and decorated with intricate patterns and fashioned in the most pleasing shapes.

It was popular with tourists then, as now, and by rights, we should be knee-deep in the stuff. The best work was produced before the tourist trade was catered for in a commercial way, which resulted in a marked decline in the quality of materials, decoration and finishing.

Now that the solid brass artefacts originating in Britain have become pricey, a new interest and appreciation is developing in Benares ware, once considered only a poor substitute for the real thing.

A South Indian figure of Parvat, 30cm. high. (Lawrence Fine Art) £77

An Eastern brass bowl with serpent handles.   £14

An Eastern brass bell complete with wall bracket.
£20

A pair of Indian brass circlets.   £22

Large Benares ware brass vase with incised decoration, 12in. high.   £15

A figure of a Boddhisattva seated crosslegged, 35cm. high. (Lawrence Fine Art) £132

Indian brass circular jardiniere with ring handles. £40

Eastern brass jug and cover with hinged lid.   £24

A Bidri ware brass jug with ornate handle.   £20

(Paul G. Sheppard)

Late 19th century Indian brass travelling altar, 22in. high. £85

Kurdistani brass dragon horn. £50

Eastern brass pot with embossed decoration, 8in. tall. £15

Late 19th century brass incense burner. £20

An Indian brass rabbit with chased and inlaid decoration, 5in. tall. £12

Indian, solid brass opium spoon, 6in. long. £9

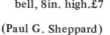

19th century Eastern brass bowl and cover on paw feet and with bird finial, 7in. tall. £22

Indian brass table bell, 8in. high. £7

An Indian inlaid 'Peacock' brass wall plaque. £10

(Paul G. Sheppard)

INHALERS

Collectors of medical antiques and memorabilia will be aware of the compulsive interest in health held by the more affluent of our forefathers. This led to an expansive and profitable market for the manufacturers of medications and medical equipment.

Although relief from coughs and bronchial troubles could probably be obtained effectively by simply inhaling some of the vapour straight from a bowl of boiling water containing some of the prescribed preparation, manufacturers produced a variety of inhalers, some boasting various claims and others bearing attractive motifs.

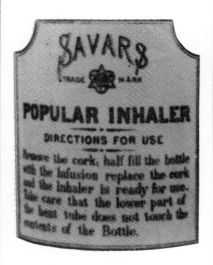

Small portable inhalers were designed specifically for use when travelling and for convenience, the medication could be introduced beforehand and hot water added when required.

Today, although some searching must be done for the more desirable examples, inhalers can provide a varied and unusual theme for the collector, offering a range from the bizarre to quite beautiful.

A small portable inhaler with sepia and blue design.   £10

Savars 'Popular Inhaler' attractively mottled in pink.   £50

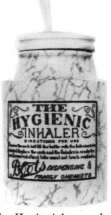

'The Hygienic' an early inhaler produced for sale by Boots Dispensing & Family Chemists.   £30

The Westminster Inhaler, sepia printed with floral decoration.   £60

The Oxford Inhaler, sepia printed with birds and floral decoration.   £60

The Bournemouth Inhaler, sepia printed with floral decoration.   £60

(R. J. Lucibell)

Saunders 'Family Inhaler', an early blue mottled bulbous-shaped inhaler without the built-in air vent by Ayrton & Saunders.   £40

Hockin's Acme Inhaler with white body and shoulder design of grey leaves with orange-brown flowers. £50

The Simplex Inhaler with white body overprinted with directions in black.   £40

Improved Earthenware Inhaler by S. Maw Son & Thompson with attractive marbled effect.   £25

Dr. Nelson's Improved Inhaler of bulbous-shape with built-in vent to replace air taken through the mouth-piece, circa 1880.   £10

S. Maw Son & Thompson earthenware inhaler the 'Double Valve' complete with top.   £50

The Universal Inhaler produced by Bourne, Johnson & Latimer of London, in white with lavender mottling, white with pink mottling and a blue background with black mottling.   £40

Maw's Vel-Fin Hygienic Inhaler of jug form complete with top.   £30

Hockin's Acme Inhaler with all-over floral design in sepia and blue colouring. £50

(R. J. Lucibell)

INSTRUMENTS

If ever there was an age of discovery, it must have been the second half of the 19th century when new theories and inventions were being created daily. It would appear that the whole populus was fascinated by science, with hardly a magazine or newspaper not devoting acres of column inches to the likes of Darwin, Eddison and Bell. This has left a legacy of finely made instruments with many, such as the microscopes and telescopes, adequately fulfilling today, the function for which they were designed.

It is not only the scientific instruments such as circumferentors, theodolites, equitorial dials and graphometers which are sought after but domestic instruments as well, such as telephones, typewriters and telegraphs.

All, when cleaned and polished, make an interesting display, a tribute to fine Victorian craftsmanship and inventiveness.

A 19th century wooden pillar dial, signed W. Burucker, 145mm. high. (Christie's) £550

A Victorian brass binocular microscope by Smith & Beck, London. (Reeds Rains) £420

Late 18th century iron way-wiser. £40

Late 19th century Negretti & Zambra walnut table stereoscope, 17in. high. £209

Mid 19th century brass kaleidoscope with 4in. diam. tube, 11in. long, in wooden carrying case. £3,300

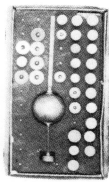

An early hydrometer with float and thirty brass weights, English, 1750-80, 7½in. long. £165

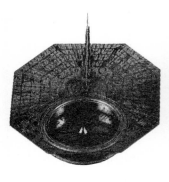

A brass Butterfield dial, signed Butterfield a Paris, 'Premier Cadran', 65mm. long. (Christie's) £550

A French brass circumferentor, signed Charot a Paris, circa 1775, 23cm. diam. (Christie's) £733

Gregory's System of Weight Measure in a mahogany case. £40

Early 20th century tachometer by Smiths. £30

Mid 19th century Savigny & Co. cupping and bleeding set, 6¼ x 6¼ x 4in., English. £660

A brass theodolite by Stanley, London, on three adjustable feet, 12in. high. (Neales) £240

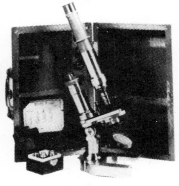

A mid 19th century brass and mahogany travelling scale set, 9½in. wide. £60

An English brass universal equatorial dial, signed Dollond, London, circa 1800, 110mm. diam. (Christie's) £1,173

A German brass monocular microscope, signed E. Leitz, Wetslar, dated 1879, 250mm. high. (Christie's) £256

IRONS

Victorian flat irons came in an immense variety of designs and styles — some of the later versions with built in heating units powered by coke, gas or even petrol.

No Victorian housekeeper worth her salt, would have had anything less than a battery of irons designed to cope with the challenge of laundering fabrics which required pleating, crimping, goffering and finishing.

Because the early flat iron had to be heated directly at a fire or on a laundry stove they were often sold in pairs or sets, so that there was always a hot iron ready for use. These irons were pretty heavy and, since the handles also got hot, they were difficult to manage. (A set of irons with interchangeable handles was produced in America in 1871.)

There are many hundreds to choose from and a good collection might include some of the ornately cast iron stands, many bearing the maker's trademark, or even a laundry stove. Some stoves had the capacity to heat up to forty or fifty irons all at the same time.

An Italian iron by Archibald Kenrick & Sons, circa 1870. £25

An unusually small late 19th century iron complete with stand. £12

A small Kenrick box iron complete with stand, 5in. long. £20

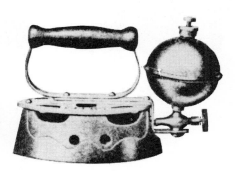

An Archibald Kenrick petrol iron, circa 1926. £25

Late 19th century crimping iron. £35

A cast snooker table iron by J. O'Brien, Manchester. £10

(Paul G. Sheppard)

Premier 850 electric iron with wooden handle. £3

An early electric iron complete with stand. £10

19th century box iron complete with iron stone. £25

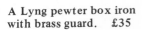

A Lyng pewter box iron with brass guard. £35

An unusual charcoal heated iron by William Cross. £35

Early 19th century slug-type iron with brass fittings. £15

Beatrice gas iron of dull nickel with polished face. £20

Patented No. 8 iron. £3

(Paul G. Sheppard)

Beatrice 'O.K.' gas iron with wooden handle. £20

JIGSAW PUZZLES

The forerunner to the modern jigsaw puzzle was invented by a map maker in London during the 1760's and designed to facilitate the teaching of geography.

The puzzle was referred to as a 'dissecting map' and was hand made by mounting a map on a sheet of mahogany which was then cut by a fine marquetry saw. Lines were cut to define areas and the pieces fitted together to form a fairly accurate map. The puzzles were presented in a wooden box with a sliding lid bearing an engraved label.

Early puzzles were hand made and therefore expensive to produce, but their popularity with both adults and children soon led other manufacturers to appreciate their market potential as a learning aid and the range of subjects widened to encompass history, the three R's, religion, mythology and so on. Manufacturers best known during this period were J. Wallis, W. Darton, J.W. Barfoot, W. Peacock, Dean & Son and J. Betts and puzzles by these names are eagerly sought after.

Towards the end of the nineteenth century, boxes began to bear hand-coloured pictorial labels and these have now become collectible in their own right.

The 20th century saw the introduction of mass production techniques and the use of plywood and motorised fretsaws with hundreds of manufacturers responding to the jigsaw 'craze' of the 1920's and 30's. Notable British firms producing during this period are Raphael Tuck (Zag Zaw), Chad Valley (GWR, Cunard/White Star Line), Fredrick Warne (Chandos, Bedford), Victory (Supercut, Artistic), Holtzapffel (Figure-it-out), Salman (Academy), Delta fine cut, Zig Zag, Huvanco and A.V.N. Jones.

'Morning Catch', a typical postcard-sized puzzle of the 1920/30's, 4 x 6in.   £3

'Coronation 1953', a characteristic commemorative puzzle of the 1950's by Victory, the box is large enough to take the fully assembled puzzle, 8 x 10in.   £18

'Sporting Days', a 1920's Raphael Tuck 'Oilette' picture puzzle by H. Drummond, 6 x 9in.   £17

(Kevin Holmes)

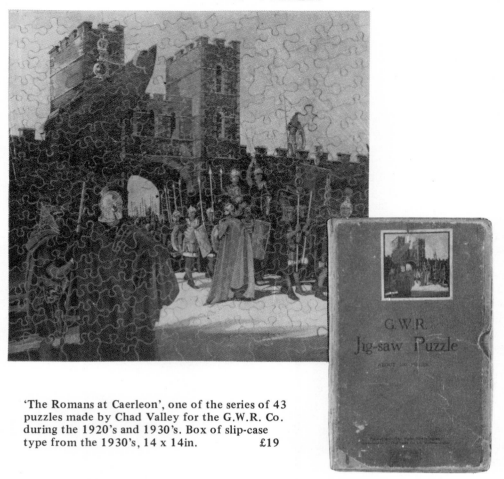

'The Romans at Caerleon', one of the series of 43 puzzles made by Chad Valley for the G.W.R. Co. during the 1920's and 1930's. Box of slip-case type from the 1930's, 14 x 14in.   £19

'The Eton Coach', popular or fashionable artists' works were often the subjects of jigsaw puzzles between the wars. This one, of a Cecil Aldin painting, has been cut in the style of the Huvanco firm, 6 x 19in. £14

(Kevin Holmes)

JIGSAW PUZZLES

'The Horse', one of a series of 'Graphic illustrations of animals showing their utility to man', by Roake & Varty, circa 1840, 12 x 15in.   £70

'Primrose and Violet', with traditional shapes, an early Victory (Hayter & Co.), with interesting box design showing common pictorial theme of the period, 1920's, 11 x 13in.   £17

(Kevin Holmes)

'The Victory', one of The Delta Fine Cut
'National' Series of puzzles from the 1930's.
The box lid bears a traditional design that
has a family resemblance to the Victory box,
13 x 18in.   £19

'The Milkmaid', 1930's 'Chandos' puzzle by Frederick Warne, it has a
distinctive and easily-recognisable style of cut which can make it
awkward to assemble, 7 x 9in.   £10

(Kevin Holmes)

'First Whiff', a Lawson Wood cartoon made into a puzzle, probably by an amateur, 1930's. Humour was always a popular subject for amateurs (who often cut to professional standards, and usually with an interpretive flair) and Lawson Wood has become highly collectible now, 10 x 8in. £14

Double sided puzzles became very popular during the inter-war jigsaw 'craze' years; they were mass produced on a large scale, since they offered 'two for the price of one'. This one has typically sentimental subject for each side, 7 x 10in. £7

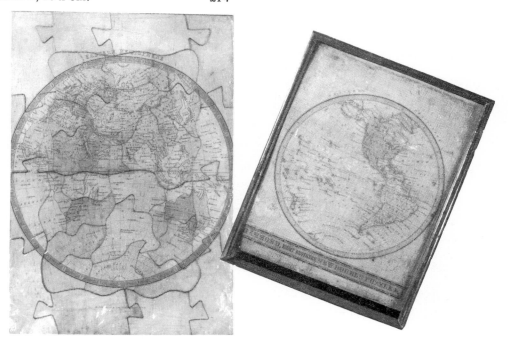

A rare Barfoot puzzle, a double sided map dissection, showing the Eastern and Western hemispheres (normally Barfoot had a non-map picture — eg historical or mathematical tables — on the reverse side of a map), 12 x 8in., circa 1855. £220

(Kevin Holmes)

'Journey into Egypt', probably amateur cut, all pushfit pieces, typical of its type and style for the period, 1920's, 9 x 7in.   £9

'A Labour of Love', 'Society Dissected Picture Puzzle — The Latest Craze' made for Hamley Bros. to sell in their store in London during the 1920's. The box label is typical of those made also for other stores, who had their names printed in the space provided, 8 x 6in.
£8

'Captain Cuttle', one of a series of twelve Dickens characters made into puzzles and issued by A. V. N. Jones in the 1930's, 10 x 8in.   £19

(Kevin Holmes)

'Good Companions', 1930's example of a Douglas Jigsaw Library Puzzle, with its unusual and unrepetitive shapes that make it more challenging to assemble, 14 x 18in.   £15

'A Welcome Intrusion', a 1930's Chad Valley puzzle with its characteristic patented— 'book-box' design of container with guide picture, 10 x 14in.   £12

(Kevin Holmes)

KEYS

Key collecting is a complex subject and an extremely specialised field.

Old lock and key sets rarely appear on the market still united for the obvious reason that while it may ruin a piece furniture to remove an ornate lock, keys, as we all know, tend to change hands or, when not in use, become misplaced or lost — only to turn up centuries later at a high price!

Keys are usually made of steel, iron or brass though rare examples are found in gilded wrought iron or pinchbeck. Some are very ornate indeed, with bow patterns featuring elaborate birds and flowers.

Sturdy Victorian keys are collectible and all the more so when a little is known of the history or original source but the modern mass produced keys generate very little interest usually selling for pence rather than pounds.

Yale A.A. type key.   25p

Early 17th century Italian steel key, the bow pierced and cut with scrolling foliage, 3¾in.
£198

A set of Georgian cabinet keys with original label.   £2

Early 18th century French iron masterpiece lantern key, 5¾in. long.   £2,640

17th century French Renaissance key, the bow cut with adorned griffins, 5½in. long.
£385

A 15th/16th century Venetian key, 6in. long.   £100

Pair of Georgian cabinet keys.   £3

A large iron key converted into a corkscrew.
£20

An 18th century French casket key, the gilt bow cast and chased in the form of entwined dolphins.   £85

Victorian security lock key in brass. £2.50

(Paul G. Sheppard)

KEYS

An 18th century Netherlandish key, with circular bow, 4¼in. £165

Shaped Yale key. 30p

An all steel patent safe key, 3in. long, 'Climax Detector Birmingham'. (Christopher Sykes) £35

19th century iron key, 4in. long. £5

Set of Yale lock keys. £1.50

H. & T. Vaun key. 40p

A North Italian key, the bow cast and chiselled with scrolls, circa 1600, 8¼in. long. £308

Late 18th century iron door key, 5in. long. £7

Late 17th century French Renaissance key, the bow cut as two stylised dolphins, 6in. long. £220

Italian 18th century iron casket key, 4¼in. long. £3.300

Numerous 1960's car keys. £2

'His Master's Voice' cabinet key. £1.50

(Paul G. Sheppard)

KEY RINGS

'Don't chuck the baby out with the bathwater!'
While a single keyring may be considered an insignificant little object, and many are just that, some can be worth money. Nobody in their right mind, would overlook a hallmarked gold Rolls Royce keyring and its potential value but, many early 'seaside viewers' and the like, look pretty ordinary until their mechanism is discovered.

Production has been prolific and designs cover every subject imaginable. There is a super-abundance of advertising merchandise and while interest would certainly be shown in the first edition of the Michelin Tyre Man, made of rubber, collectors can afford to be choosy.

Keen collectors display their carefully selected and colourful treasures in a variety of ways. The most popular method is to arrange the collection on a display board fitted with hooks, which can then be glazed and framed.

'Bomb Dropper' key ring.   £2

'He who holds the key can open my heart'.   £2

'Audi' key ring.   50p

I can do a ton. £1

Skeleton hand key ring.   75p

Double hamburger.   £1.50

Aubrey Beardsley painting.   £1

Plastic E.T. key ring.   £1

'Clown' watch face.   £1.50

Donald Duck key ring.   £2

(Hilda White)

210

KEY RINGS

World's Greatest Bingo Player. £1

Super Multigrade, Unipart. £1

'Shandy Bass' when you want a real shandy. 50p

John Player Special 50p

Whitbread Tankard. 50p

'Mini' key ring. 75p

Male Chauvinist. 50p

'Good Morning' emergency pack. £1.50

Associated Tyre Specialists. 50p

Carlsberg Beer 'The Glorious Beer of Copenhagen'. 25p

'Nude' key ring. 50p

'Join the Boy's Brigade', the key to success. 50p

Electronic Poultry Aids Ltd. 75p

Team Gulf key ring. £1

Borth with Welsh dragon. 50p

(Hilda White)

KEY RINGS

Ritz key ring. £1

'Clunk Click every trip'. £1

Six shooter key ring. £2.50

Unipart key ring. 50p

'Cornwall' with coat-of-arms. 50p

  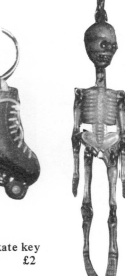  

Kermit the frog. 75p

Roller skate key ring. £2

Enjicolor F11 film can. £1

Heineken lager beer. 50p

Plastic skeleton key ring, 2½in. long. £3

'10 Downing Street', London. £1

Football. 50p

'B.M.W.' key ring. £1

'My little book'. 75p

Lloyds Bank key ring. 50p

(Hilda White)

KITCHEN EQUIPMENT

Times change, and fashions with them, but one branch of the antiques business which goes on forever is that dealing in kitchenware — particularly from the Victorian period.

It all began as a reaction against the vogue, some years back, for plastic laminated antisepsis in the kitchen. Doubtless influenced to some extent by the country-kitchen, full-colour photographs on the cookery pages, people began to react quite strongly against the characterless rooms in which they were expected to create culinary marvels. Storage jars, pestles and mortars, the odd copper saucepan or two, gradually the demand grew from a trickle to a steady stream.

For centuries, the kitchen in upper and middle class houses was a purely functional room used only by servants for the preparation of their masters' meals. No attention was paid to comfort, decor or labour saving.

As the years passed meals were no longer prepared by servants but by the mistress of the household who became not only the cook, but nanny and bottle washer into the bargain. And now the wheel has turned still further; the kitchen has become a fashionable room. Food is not only cooked here, but often eaten too, and the kitchen is becoming one of the main living rooms of the house — often being recreated as a place in which to relax and sometimes even entertain.

For this reason alone, the utensils of the great kitchens of the past are much sought after for their decorative qualities. The Victorian kitchens with their copper and brass, their intricately carved wooden implements and their stone and steelware have a lot to offer, particularly since all these things were made in the days when mass production was in its infancy and individual artisan skills were given full rein.

Lister ball bearing cream separator. £15

Late Victorian wooden handled chopper, 15in. long. £8

An unusual home canning machine complete with instruction book. £10

Pair of 19th century steel sugar cutters. £16

Late Victorian chopper with turned wood handle. £7

(Paul G. Sheppard)

213

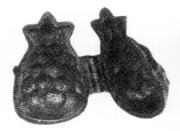

19th century pewter pineapple butter mould, 3¾in. long. (Christie's)   £60

An English pewter two-handled colander, touch mark in the centre, circa 1780, 10¾in. diam. (Christopher Sykes)£245

A small French electroplated travelling burner.   £6

Victorian cased set of icing bag barrels.   £18

Enamelled tin breadbin marked bread.   £5

Late 19th century cast iron mincer 'Rollman Food Cropper', No. 15.   £3

Plated tin tongue press, circa 1900.   £15

Late 19th century plated tin milk can, ½ gallon. £8

Kitchen grater of tin with three variations, circa 1900.   £4

(Islwyn Watkins)

KITCHEN EQUIPMENT

Set of four 19th century troy brass weights 2oz., 1oz., ½oz. and ¼oz. £10

Twin handled steel chopper.
£9

The Seamless Stove, a small travelling burner in brass.
£6

Farmhouse individual butter churn, late 19th century.
£12

A small late 19th century wooden handled scoop. £3

Beatrice cast iron combined heater and cooker.
£7

An early bentwood quart measure.   £18

Late Victorian wooden masher.   £5

(Paul G. Sheppard)

Victorian turned wood crumpet pricker with steel spikes.
£7

Set of eight tear-shaped pastry cutters, circa 1890. £12

Late Victorian boxed set of 12 tin petit four cutters. £14

Boxed set of wavy pie top cutters. £12

Set of six late 19th century shaped pastry cutters. £18

Late 19th century boxed set of petit four cutters. £12

A Victorian boxed set of nine tear-shaped pastry cutters. £18

(George Court)

Pineapple-shaped cream cake moulds. £6

Set of six late 19th century tin moulds. £6

Set of four Victorian shell-shaped tin moulds.
£5

A set of six Victorian moulds in the form of walnuts and strawberries.   £4

Set of five boat-shaped tin eclair moulds. £6

Set of nine small late 19th century shaped moulds.   £8

(George Court)

Victorian brass egg cup. £5

19th century stoneware filter by Gorton of Manchester. £35

British made alloy juice extractor 'Instant No. 1'. £5

Early 19th century japanned tin plate warmer with cast metal carrying grips, 27in. high. (Lawrence Fine Art) £1,430

Sheet tin bread board and rolling pin, 11 x 18½in. (Robt. W. Skinner Inc.) £225

A large Reliance mincer made in Sweden. £4

Victorian earthenware pie centre. £1

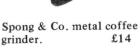

Spong & Co. metal coffee grinder. £14

A large stoneware wine jar by Savage & Son, Wolverhampton. £10

(Paul G. Sheppard)

KITCHEN EQUIPMENT

Early 19th century American wire potato boiler, body diam. 11in. (Robt. W. Skinner Inc.)
£208

Pair of cast iron scales by Smith & Sons, Lancaster.
£20

Edwardian EPNS herbal tea dipper.　£2

Late 19th century brass kettle with bone handle.
£18

A set of six Hovis baking tins.
£18

One of two 19th century copper jelly moulds of castellated form, 4in.
£121

A Beatrice 324159 mincer.
£7

Late 19th century tin scoop.
£7

Toleware spice box complete with contents and central nutmeg grater, circa 1835.　£28

(George Court)

KITCHEN EQUIPMENT

White glass rolling pin painted with sailing ships. £20

A 19th century steel and beechwood meat cleaver, stamped W. & O. Wynn, 11in. long. £49

Victorian pitch pine rolling pin. £3

A large wooden fork, 11in. long. £3

Small late 19th century wooden handled butcher's chopper. £7

A set of four late 19th century copper plated tin moulds. £15

A 19th century brass and ebony pastry wheel, 8½in. long. £100

18th century iron cleaver, 2ft. long. £40

Wooden rolling pin, circa 1880. £3

Steel sharpener with plated handle. £2

Victorian wooden handled tin scoop. £3

19th century wooden malt shovel used in brewery. £20

Set of scale weights, 8oz. to 4lb. £8

20th century mechanical plated sugar cube tongs. £3

(George Court)

LACE

There is very little evidence of lace of any kind before the 16th century and the earliest examples we have are not much more than embroidery.

Handmade bobbin lace was much favoured by the Stuart Kings of the early 17th century and continued in popularity until the introduction of much simpler fashions at the time of the French Revolution. There was a revival of interest in England between 1840 and 1890 but very little was produced on a commercial scale.

In the 19th century, the introduction of machines capable of producing a much cheaper lace, left the makers of bobbin lace with an uneconomically viable product and the custom of only those wealthy enough to be able to afford the real thing.

Although there was a near fatal decline in the popularity of lace in the 1920's, we are today, witnessing a very healthy revival in all lacemaking equipment and in lace garments, trimmings and furnishings.

A handmade bobbin lace tablecloth with torchon border, 40in. square. (Iris Martin) £25

A handmade Honiton bobbin lace collar. (Iris Martin) £12

A handmade Buckinghamshire bobbin lace neckerchief. (Iris Martin) £5

A machine made lace and embroidery bodice. (Iris Martin) £15

A length of pointe de gaze lace, late 19th century, approx. 16ft. long, 10in. wide. (Robt. W. Skinner Inc.) £325

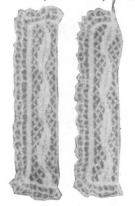

A pair of machine made Bedfordshire lace cuffs. (Iris Martin) £3

A handmade Bedfordshire bobbin lace collar. (Iris Martin) £10

A handmade Bedfordshire bobbin lace collar. (Iris Martin) £10

A machine made lace silk shawl of good quality. (Iris Martin) £16

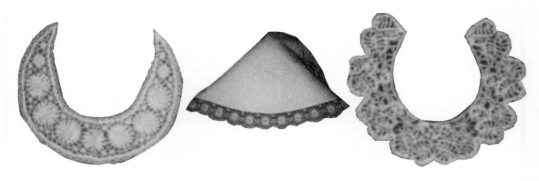

A handmade Bedfordshire bobbin lace collar. (Iris Martin) £10

A handmade Bedfordshire bobbin lace piece, 60in. diam. (Iris Martin) £25

A machine made Bedfordshire lace collar. (Iris Martin) £10

Late 19th century pointe de gaze lace shawl, approx. 8ft. long, 21in. wide. (Robt. W. Skinner Inc.) £243

A machine made lace black scarf of high quality. (Iris Martin) £20

Early 20th century hand-worked bedcover with crocheted and lacework borders, approx. 7ft.2in. x 7ft. 8in. (Robt. W. Skinner Inc.) £528

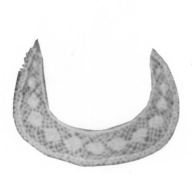

A handmade Bedfordshire bobbin lace collar. (Iris Martin) £10

A machine made lace border on parasol (slightly imperfect). (Iris Martin) £30

A machine made tape lace collar. (Iris Martin) £8

LACEMAKING BOBBINS

A reflection of the recently renewed interest in lacemaking can be seen in the growing number of enthusiasts who scour all of the likely, and some of the most unlikely, sources in a quest for the lovely old traditional lacemaking bobbins.

In the past, it was probably true to say that 'Where there were lacemakers — there were full-time professional bobbin makers' but, it is unlikely that many of the traditional bobbins were made after about 1890.

Bobbins were usually made from inexpensive and readily available materials such as wood or bone which was then turned on a small lathe. Some were plain, some inscribed; some were dyed or decorated with pewter and wire, some with coloured dots and slashes.

Bobbin makers today, often copy the old styles then add their own individual decoration to suit.

A wooden bobbin with pewter decoration. (Iris Martin)   £7

A wooden bobbin with brass wire decoration. (Iris Martin)   £5

A bone bobbin, waisted, with pewter butterfly. (Iris Martin)   £12

A wooden bobbin with brass wire and coloured stripes. (Iris Martin)   £2

A bone bobbin inscribed 'Dear Charlot'. (Iris Martin)   £20

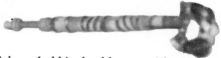

A bone bobbin dyed brown with pewter design. (Iris Martin)   £10

A bone bobbin with coloured dots and stripes. (Iris Martin)   £8

A bone bobbin with brass wire decoration. (Iris Martin)   £9

A bone bobbin with pewter butterfly. (Iris Martin)   £12

A mother and baby bone bobbin. (Iris Martin)   £50

A bone bobbin inscribed 'Jane'. (Iris Martin)   £16

A bone bobbin inscribed 'Joseph Castle hund 1850'. (Iris Martin)   £150

LAMPS

Although early lamps were operated on little more than an oil supplied candle, by about 1860, the wick and paraffin burning table lamp had been perfected and was in common use. Another popular type was the acetylene lamp, which has a small reservoir of water placed above a container at the base, filled with calcium carbide. Drops of water released onto the carbide would produce acetylene gas which, in turn, produced a brilliant white flame. While most people have some idea of the value of a Victorian brass oil lamp there is a possibility that some of the old brass carbide lamps and tilley lamps may be overlooked. These are collected today and have some monetary value.

A long way away from the basic function of providing a source of light, are the shimmering Art lamps of the late 19th and early 20th century. Lamps are often signed and the names to look for are Daum, Emile Galle, Gustav Gurschner, Handel, Lalique, Loetz and many more. These lamps are traditionally made with a cast bronze stem, sometimes in the shape of a plant, and the shade is constructed of multi-coloured glass pieces set in bronze mountings. If you should be lucky enough to find one of these, you could be looking at a few thousand pounds. If however, you hit the jackpot and come up with a lamp by Tiffany, styled as a spider's web, then we are talking about well over £100,000.

Tilley lamp complete with reflector and instructions. £5

A small cast metal hanging oil lamp. £24

Lucas nickel plated brass carbide bicycle lamp. £16

Small oil lamp with screw top base. £2

An Art Deco bronze patinated metal and glass table lamp, signed Vincent 1923, 21in. high. (Andrew Grant) £240

Lucas King of the Road oil bicycle lamp. £14

(Paul G. Sheppard)

A large metal carbide lamp, complete with glass and hood. £20

Table lamp fitted with a Pittsburgh art glass shade, 18in. diam., signed Handel. (Stalker & Boos) £483

An early plated brass carbide lamp. £32

A WMF Ikora Art Deco glass and chrome table lamp, 18in. high, with the original seaweed decorated plastic shade. (Capes, Dunn & Co.) £65

A Miller plated metal dynamo and battery bicycle lamp. £4

A large Tilley lamp, 'Floodlight Projector', Made in Henden. £36

A Chinese made painted tin lamp. £3

A medical vaporizing lamp to destroy germs, together with instructions 'printed in U.S.A.'. (Christopher Sykes) £87

A large Cloham & Son metal cased lamp. £5

(Paul G. Sheppard)

LAVATORIES

The water closet was invented in 1805 by Joseph Bramah but it was some years before the idea really caught on.

The system operated through a leadlined wooden cased cistern which was, in time, replaced by an ornate cast iron version and eventually by a ceramic one.

The lavatory bowls were ceramic and some of the better ones were decorated. The Victorians really took to this transfer-printed ware during the last quarter of the 19th century. As a rule, this decoration is based on a floral pattern, usually in blue and white, though multi-coloured specimens do appear on the market from time to time. The toilet bowl was usually bought en suite with a washbasin and sometimes with a bath.

The best known manufacturers were Doulton, Shanks and Pauls.

1940's Elsan model 44 bake-lite lavatory seat. £9

A 17th century leather close stool, 18½in. wide. (Christie's) £270

Blue and white lavatory pan, 'Niagara'. £150

Victorian pine lavatory seat with brass hinges. £8

English saltglazed stoneware water closet. (Bonham's) £130

An 18th century Austrian walnut bedside commode of tapering form, 84cm. high. £450

(Paul G. Sheppard)

LAWNMOWERS

Edwin Beard Budding of Stroud, Gloucestershire, invented the mowing machine in 1830 and James Ferrabee produced the first example with a cutting width of 19ins., in the same year. By 1833 lawn mowers were produced under Ransomes name and a typical example is the Budding's Patent No. 3157 — now a very rare machine indeed. The Shanks machine, patented in 1842 had a cutting width of 42ins.

To meet the demand, many lesser known makers such as Barnard, Fellows & Bates, Picksley Simms etc., came into production but, for over 100 years, the market was dominated by the 'big three' names — Ransomes, Shanks & Green.

In the 1890's the Leyland Motor Co. produced a steam powered machine with various weights and cutting widths. In 1919, Charles H. Pugh of Birmingham introduced the Atco and in the same year The Derwent Co., of Derby, introduced a side wheel machine named the Qualcast. The first electric mower appeared in 1926.

Qualcast model 61 lawnmower with blade guard.   £7

A large Heaton lawnmower with a 3h.p. Villiers engine.   £65

Qualcast Panther mechanical lawnmower.   £8

Folbate lawnmower model F2, made in Manchester.   £10

H. C. Webb electric lawnmower, made in Birmingham.   £18

Atco four-stroke petrol driven lawnmower. £10

(Paul G. Sheppard)

227

LUGGAGE

Travelling 'light' is a modern concept and one which no self respecting traveller of yester-year would have contemplated. They took their creature comforts with them on long journeys, transported in an astonishing variety of trunks, cases, strongboxes, chests, travelling boxes, carpet bags, hatboxes, picnic boxes and even specially fitted drinks boxes. Because luggage was built to last, we have a legacy of robust and attractive pieces on the market today. A cautionary note to those intending to travel by air — forget about the fabulous old leather suitcases for, even whilst empty, they come very close to the weight allowance permitted for baggage.

Most people nowadays, use the heavier pieces as furnishing features, particularly the old chests. Some were covered in materials such as fine leather or pony skin and decorated with metal studs. Look out for any piece covered in a green, rough textured leathery looking material for this might just be shagreen, a shark skin considered to be very desirable.

Victorian metal uniform case with simulation crocodile skin design. £12

Leather Gladstone bag marked 'Post Office'. £15

A small 1930's leather hand luggage case, 13in. wide. £12

Late 19th century travelling chest. £20

Early 20th century leather suitcase with brass fittings and lever locks. £8

A painted pine blanket chest, possibly American, 1849, with hinged domed top, 55in. wide. (Christie's) £366

(Paul G. Sheppard)

1930's leather suitcase with brass locks and fitted interior. £15

An 18th century French kingwood coffret forte, 12¼in. (Lawrence Fine Art) £506

B. B. H. & Co. metal bound wooden trunk with side handles and double lock. £20

Late 19th century hessian covered wooden case with brass fittings by Lucas Collins, London, 21in. wide. £15

Wooden framed travelling vanity case with metal fittings. £5

A late 17th century French brass bound oyster walnut veneered travelling strongbox, 1ft.10½in. wide. (Anderson & Garland) £2,300

1930's leatherette covered wooden suitcase with leather carrying handle. £10

1930's real leather holdall. £15

(Paul G. Sheppard)

MACHINERY

It is hard to imagine any of our modern machines such as knitting machines, sewing machines, washing machines or typewriters being given pride of place in homes a century hence, but many of the old machines designed for domestic and commercial use are definitely worth a second glance.

Often, a lovely old piece, with its steel fittings polished, its woodwork sanded smooth and clean is transformed into an object d'art, a piece of functional sculpture, worthy of a far better place than the wash house or workshop for which it was made.

These pieces of machinery can be found all over the place, usually in neglected condition. After a quick going over, even the most derelict example will twinkle with gratitude.

Much of the cast iron work is very ornate and prone to damage. If any of the decorative features are missing, an iron filling can be bought for use with fibre glass resin and this, cast in a simple plasticene mould will be almost indetectable.

A wallet pocket adding machine.   £2

Late 19th century cast iron hand knitting machine for small work.   £30

Counselor weighing scales, circa 1937.   £22

Lee Howl & Co. of Tipton bench drill.   £65

Imperial sock knitting machine with bench clamp and all accessories.   £85

A Hopkins-Improved Albion press, by J. & J. Barrett, English, dated 1836, with 21 x 30½in. platen.   £880

(Paul G. Sheppard)

Singer shoemaker's sewing machine. £40

Corona typewriter complete with case. £16

1950's Acme table top mangle with adjustable rollers. £2

A Columbian press, No. 1046, by Clymer & Dixon, dated 1843, the platen 20½ x 26in. £1,320

Vono No. 2 patent knife cleaner. £14

A cast-iron and brass door restrainer made in Boston, U.S.A., patented 1882. £10

Entwistle & Kenyans patent safety mangle. £30

A small German made sewing machine and case. £17

A European sewing machine by The Coventry Machinists Co. Ltd., with hand wheel for bobbin winding. (Christie's S. Kensington) £950

(Paul G. Sheppard)

Late 19th century cast-iron hand-operated
rasping machine.   £10

19th century shotgun cartridge filler. £30

Bacon slicer by Berkel & Parnall, Enfield.
                              £140

A large 19th century cast-iron winch with
wooden rollers.   £30

War Department field telephone in metal
container.   £10

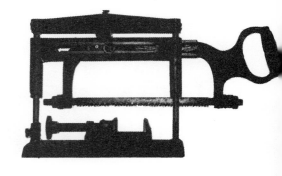

Late Victorian cast-iron hacksaw machine
complete with mitre block and stand.£14

(Paul G. Sheppard)

MAGNIFYING GLASSES

In many professions, a magnifying glass is an indispensable aid, a tool of the trade, and as such they will find a place in specialised collections.

They are sometimes found in cased sets of fine instruments, and may often be found housed in one of the many purpose built compartments of the old wooden travelling boxes which have interiors fitted and equipped for all occupations, from surgeons to butterfly collectors. These glasses, being part of a set, should never be removed and sold separately. Individual magnifying glasses are both useful and attractive with their handles made of gold, silver, pinchbeck, tortoiseshell and turned wood. Many glasses come complete with a shaped case and this will add to the value, particularly if it has some attractive feature. When the lorgnette, quizzing glass and magnifying glass came into fashionable use, each, in turn, was given something of the importance of a piece of jewellery in styling and materials. The modern equivalents seem plain by comparison but still worthy of attention.

Late 18th century scioptic ball, probably English, 5¾in. £2,860

Small tortoiseshell magnifying glass in leather case. £3

A small brass framed magnifying glass, 2in. long. £2

Magnifying glass by Ross, London, No. 164726. £2.50

An early 19th century magnifying glass with turned mahogany handle, 8in. long. £319

14ct. antique yellow gold lorgnette with small octagonal glasses. (Robt. W. Skinner Inc.) £102

1960's Japanese magnifying glass with original box. £3

A 19th century silver plated magnifying glass, 4cm. diam. £10

Gowlands watch maker's glass. £2.50

(Paul G. Sheppard)

233

MATCHBOX HOLDERS

Within a few years of the safety match being invented in Sweden they were brought into use in Britain. By 1900 many people found it a great convenience to carry a box of matches on their person and, since the boxes were produced with little regard for appearance, a decorative holder was devised.

The pocket matchbox holder is a three-sided affair — constructed to leave the end free for the removal of matches and the side open to expose the striker. There are many purely decorative designs and some bearing military insignia or heraldic devices. Official holders were issued to the A.R.P. and C.D. as part of the kit.

The household variety, designed to be placed on a mantleshelf or other convenient spot, was often the work of some of the better known porcelain factories of the day. Conta & Boehme, Doulton and Wedgwood all supplied this trade. The most common examples are the modest earthenware pieces made specifically for the souvenir trade.

1930's enamel matchbox holder. £4

Novelty vesta case in the form of a clenched fist. (Phillips) £160

Silver vesta case inscribed Bryant & May's Wax Vestas. (Phillips) £55

Brass matchbox holder with embossed galleon. £2

A gold match safe, 19th century, with floral and scroll motifs and a gem set clover in central cartouche. (Robt. W. Skinner Inc.) £255

Enamelled metal matchbox holder 'The Wiltshire Regiment'. £4

A Victorian brass matchbox holder in the form of a book. £10

Goss match box holder bearing a coat-of-arms. £30

Second World War metal matchbox holder decorated with 'peace' symbols. £7

(Paul G. Sheppard)

234

MEDALLIONS

Although medallions have been made by hand hammering since the 16th century to commemorate important events, it wasn't until the advent of the mechanical screw press in 1662 that they became symmetrical and uniform in production.

They continued being made on a limited scale until the Great Exhibition of 1851 when they were manufactured in vast quantities to commemorate the event.

This triggered production of medallions to celebrate anything from the opening of a park to the launching of a great ship. As such, there is a wealth of subjects to specialise in be they sporting, transport or religious. Particularly sought after are medallions connected with railways or ships. They should be treated as coins when cleaning.

150th Anniversary medallion for Robert Rakes Sunday School.   £1

'General Nursing Council' silver medallion.   £8

Montgomeryshire Education Authority perfect attendance medallion, silver 1889.   £5

A silver watch fob medallion for 'Rifle Shooting'.   £6

Jason 1930 Aeroplane token.   £3

Silver watch fob medallion for 'Darts Competition' 1946.   £5

Royal Horticultural Society medallion for best kept allotment, 1945.   £1

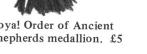

Loya! Order of Ancient Shepherds medallion. £5

Mason Science College medallion to commemorate the opening, dated 1880. £5

(Paul G. Sheppard)

MEDICAL ITEMS

When one surveys the array of medical instruments the Victorians had to endure, it seems a miracle that so many survived at all. And this is the fascination which has given all redundant medical items a ready and eager market.

Cased sets of surgical instruments are particularly sought after by makers such as Hutchinson, A. & S. Maw, J. Milliken and William Pepys. As a rule, wooden, ivory and bone handled instruments are made prior to 1870 and are much more desirable than the later chromium plated examples.

Amputation sets, leech jars, medicine chests and microscopes are all very collectible and can obtain astronomical money for early examples.

Beware, however, of some of the Victorian electrical appliances offered as 'cure alls', for which they had a fascination — try them at your peril.

An all brass medical ear syringe with a three-finger pull one end and the hollow tube the other, 9½in. closed, circa 1870. (Christopher Sykes) £48

Dr. Macaura' 'Blood Circulator' complete with attachments and original box. £12

A surgeon's instrument by 'Weiss London', 7½in. long. (Christopher Sykes) £48

French mid 19th century Charriere amputation set, in fitted walnut case, 16 x 9½in. £605

Vetinary medicine feeder pipe of pewter. £25

A 19th century Magneto Electric Machine for nerves and other diseases, in wooden box with instructions. £12

A Keratometer, an instrument for measuring the curvature of the cornea of the eye, made of brass on a cast-iron stand, circa 1910, 24in. long. (Christopher Sykes) £385

Tube of Tannafax 'For Burns and Scalds', with original box priced 2/6d. £1.50

(Paul G. Sheppard)

236

MILK BOTTLES

About ten years ago, when there were many hundreds of small independent dairies still in operation, it would have been difficult to find anyone who took collecting milk bottles seriously. Nowadays, it is a very different story. Collectors scour their favourite dumping grounds of the countryside and no longer run the risk of derisive remarks when looking for stock in their local antique shops.

Although milk has been sold in glass bottles since the latter part of the 19th century, they did not come into common use until after the Frist World War. They have been produced in many shapes and sizes and most bear the embossed name and location of their origin. Most were made of clear glass but both amber and green were used to a much lesser degree.

The earliest known example, The Thatcher Milk Protector, was devised by an American, Dr. Harvey D. Thatcher in 1884.

Northern Dairies sterilized milk bottle, 1970's. 2p

A vase-shaped bottle by J. W. MacDougall, Clovenfords, 1930's. £5

Matthews Dairy ½ pint, 1970's. 50p

Late 19th century swing stopper. £3

Early 20th century 1 pint 'Special Milk'. £2

1980's milk bottle from Bartonsham Farm. 3p

A late 19th century Thatcher Milk Protector. £150

Late 19th century sterilized milk bottle. £3

(Paul G. Sheppard)

237

MINIATURES

Just about every imaginable artefact has been reproduced in miniature at some time or another.

Some miniatures were made solely as a novelty product, others as commemorative replicas; many are working scale models and others were produced simply for the pleasure they give as ornaments.

Early 'baby houses' were designed to be a plaything for adults. They were fully furnished with precious miniature pieces of the finest quality, some made of silver and other fine materials. Even the kitchens were designed to a working plan and stocked with complete sets of tiny utensils.

The magnificent Queen's Dolls' House gave rise to a prolification of miniature reproductions. Indeed, this work was important enought to warrant a special issue of postcards (40 cards in an album), illustrating in detail the remarkable craftsmanship involved in its construction.

Miniature Hong Kong made hairdressing figure, 3in. high.   50p

A cast metal doll's tea service.   £4

Miniature cast metal vacuum cleaner 'Hoover Model 262'.   £3

Miniature grain-painted chest, simulated bird's eye maple, circa 1840, 10½in. high. (Robt. W. Skinner Inc.)   £337

A mid 19th century mahogany miniature tripod table, circa 1840, 9½in. diam.   £209

A miniature tin dresser, 3½in. wide.   £3

A miniature Federal secretary, America, circa 1830, 13½in. wide. (Robt. W. Skinner Inc.)
£1,832

Pearson's miniature dictionary including magnifying glass, 1¼ x ¾in. £4

An Anglo-Indian miniature ivory bureau cabinet. (Bearnes) £7,200

A miniature apprentice made marquetry top table. £150

A miniature set of die cast 'pots and pans' by Crescent. £5

Novelty miniature pack of Player's 'Bachelor' tipped cigarettes, 1in. square. £3

An American late Federal mahogany miniature chest of drawers, 10in. wide. (Christie's) £733

A miniature cast metal mangle, 5in. high. £7

A George III miniature mahogany chest of drawers, 14¾in. wide. (Barber's Fine Art) £90

Miniature Biedermeier night-stand with marble top and tiny oval mirror, 1in. scale. (Theriault's) £77

Group of 19th century miniature furniture of a cupboard and three chairs, cupboard 7½in. high. (Christie's) £65

Set of tableware in wooden case with red suede lined interior, 1 x 2in. (Theriault's) £65

Miniature raised panelled settle by David S. White. (Theriault's) £27

Miniature Napoleonic-style bed and chairs, 4½ x 4in. (Theriault's) £160

A Federal mahogany miniature chest of drawers, 1790-1810, 14½in. wide. (Christie's) £623

19th century tin piano, 3½ x 4in., in excellent condition. (Theriault's) £60

Part of a set of 19th century miniature maple wood furniture of a Gothic style settee and a set of shelves.(Theriault's) £70

Miniature contemporary canopy bed in walnut with quilted cover, 7½in. high. (Theriault's) £105

MINIATURE BOTTLES

Over the period of the last five years a new collecting field has started to gain in popularity and that is in the acquisition of miniature bottles. A Collectors Club has been established providing the devotee with the opportunity to trade and exchange ideas and information. These little bottles, manufactured in every conceivable shape and size, are produced on a vast scale in most countries of the world and are still relatively cheap and easy to come by. Present day collections are founded on interest rather than on investment potential but enthusiasm is high and, in time, who knows to what lengths the dedicated collector may go to acquire a coveted 'speciality' example.

Incidentally, if you should come across an abandoned collection gathering dust in the corner of the attic you must, at all costs, resist the temptation to sample the contents. Collectors stick, most strictly, to the rule that all miniature bottles must be full!

Taplows 'Plimsoll Line' Rum, cork top.   £10

Bombay Dry Gin.
                £2

Cognac, twisted neck.   £2.50

Gordon's Dry Martini Cocktail, clip top.   £8

Remy Martin Cognac.   £1.50

Royal Wedding Commemorative miniature, watch shape.
                £3

SWN-Y-MOR Welsh Whisky.   £1.50

Dutch 'Advocaat'.
                £1

(Ivy Grant)

241

MINIATURE BOTTLES

'Marille' German
Liqueur.   60p

Black Swan Scotch
Whisky.   £8

Coca-Cola.   £2

'Shipmate' Golden
Jamaica Rum. £2

'Red Hackle' Whisky,
wired bottle.   £10

Taplows 'Crown Vat'
Scotch Whisky, cork
top.   £10

Armagnac, hand-
written label. £10

Canada Dry Orange.
            £2

Gordon's Orange
Gin, clip top. £8

Scotch Whisky jug.
       £3.50

Bols 'Cherry Brandy'.
                £1

Gordon's 'Special
Dry London Gin',
clip top.   £5

(Ivy Grant)

242

MINIATURE BOTTLES

Bell's Old Scotch Whisky. £5

Chequers Whisky Jug. £3.50

QE2 Commemorative Scotch Whisky. £5

The Hunting Squire Scotch Whisky. £8

London Square Gin. £2

Paul Masson 'Rare Cream' Sherry. £5

Bols 'Bananes' Liqueur. £1

Harveys 'Bristol Cream' Sherry. £1

Swnydon, Welsh Whisky. £5

Gordon's Lemon Gin, clip top. £8

Stone's 'Elderberry' Wine'. £2

'Gold Ling' Scotch Whisky. £8

(Ivy Grant)

243

Stone's 'Apricot
Wine'.   £2

Harp Lager. £2

Bols Liqueur 'Move
West', shaped bottle.
£2

'Famous Liqueurs'
Dutch bottle.   £5

Vieille Cure, new
bottle.   £1

Grants Hunting
Sherry.   £2

Booth's Finest 'Dry
Gin', six-sided bot-
tle.   £5

Taplows 'Mountain
Music' Whisky, cork
top.   £10

Canada Dry Lemo-
nade.   £2

Gordon's 'Bronx
Cocktail', clip top.
£8

Gaymers Cider,
screw top.   £3

Martell 'Cognac'.
£1.50

(Ivy Grant)

MODELS

The thing which sets models apart from other 'toys' is that most are hand crafted by skilled individuals and in some cases, as with scale model traction engines, this can mean thousands of hours of work involved. As such, it is not unreasonable when some of these intricate models sell for thousands of pounds at auction. The same applies for model steam trains by Bing, Carette and Marklin and some of the magnificent sailor made shipping dioramas from the 19th century.

Of particular interest are the model ships made by prisoners of the Napoleonic Wars, from the bones left over from their meals; embellished with ivory bought with the proceeds from their skilled carving. Again, these can sell for thousands of pounds.

The Victorian model butchers' shops are sought after as are the Noah's Arks, complete with animals, which were the only toys many Victorian children were permitted to play with on a Sunday.

A 19th century wooden and papier-mache butcher's shop, several pieces marked Germany, 12 x 6in. (Theriault's)   £233

An horizontal cylinder stationary steam engine, built by Negelin & Hubner, 28 x 64in. (Christie's S. Kensington) £500

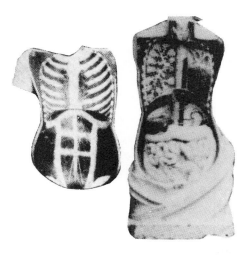

A 19th century four-part model of an anatomical torso. (Phillips)   £940

A large 20th century model bird house. £25

Late 19th century model of a 'Brick Making Machine', 7in. wide, circa 1880. £30

A mid 19th century sailor-made model of the coaster 'Susan Vittery', English, 29½in. long. £500

A Tipp R101 tinplate Zeppelin, German, circa 1930, 25½in. long. £825

A large scale model of the British airship R100-G-FAAV, 10ft. long, with tower, 4ft. (Christie's) £1,070

A 3in. scale live steam coal-fired Burrell single-cylinder agricultural traction engine 'Myrtle', by Dennis Hurn, 45in. long overall. £2,200

An English mid 19th century sailor-made shipping diorama, 30½in. wide. £300

An exceptionally large model Butcher's Shop, 34¼ x 39½in. £660

A 7mm. finescale two-rail electric model of the London and North Eastern Railway 'Coffee Pot' 0-4-0 saddle tank locomotive No. 7230. (Christie's S. Kensington) £220

Die cast model toy aeroplanes have been made in numerous countries and have proved to be very popular and highly collectible. Examples made by companies such as Dinky, Corgi, Lone Star (U.K.), Tootsie Toys (U.S.A.), Tekno (Denmark), Schuco (Germany), Solido and Dinky (France), Mercury (Italy), C.I.J. (France), Aeromini and Tomica (Japan) are particularly popular.

Dinky toys were produced by the Meccano Company, founded by Frank Hornby in Liverpool, 1901. Hornby trains were announced in 1920 and immediatley gained popularity. In 1931 a set of trackside staff was introduced as modelled miniatures for use with Hornby trains and this was the start of Dinky Toys. In 1932 the first vehicles in the model miniature range appeared under the trade name Meccano Miniatures which was very soon changed to the now famous name Dinky Toys.

The first aeroplanes were released as a box of six in June 1934 and given the identification number 60. (The scale used was roughly 1/200 so they were not really suitable for use with Hornby Railway models. The scale of Dinky aeroplane models has varied over the years from 1/150 to 1/200.)

Shortly after the release of the 60 series set, models were released as individual items and sold in boxes of six to the retailer who could then sell them singly. Dinky aeroplanes were issued at regular intervals until the beginning of the war in 1939. Production of the whole range came to a standstill in 1940 but a limited selection from existing stock was still available until well into 1941. This pre-war period was a great era in the history of aviation and the success of Dinky was assured as Meccano produced and updated the range to reflect these important new developments.

The original models were made of lead alloy but at some stage before the war this was substituted by a substance called Mazak which is an alloy containing aluminium, copper, zinc and a small amount of magnesium. Trace elements were also present which in some cases reacted with other metals to cause a condition known as fatigue. This may cause the model to become very brittle, cracks may appear and eventually the model is destroyed. If you should consider buying a pre-war item, which is likely to be highly priced, then you must be absolutely happy about its condition. If it is showing signs of fatigue then it will only get worse. It is advisable to keep a collection of Dinky toys, of all types, in a cool, dry place and out of direct sunlight.

During this pre-war period models were produced in many colours. Probably the most prolific model was the Percival Gull produced from 1934 to 1941 using two basic castings and up to eight or more colour and registration variations.

1940: Before the war and the arrival of the phoney war, the standard finish on the R.A.F.'s day squadrons was aluminium. This was hastily changed to a variety of camouflage schemes on all aircraft and, to follow suit, in 1940, Dinky put some of its aircraft into service camouflage. In this range was the Spitfire, Hurricane, Blenheim, Percival Gull, Fairey Battle, Armstrong Whitworth Whitley, Ensign Airliner, Leopard Moth, Vickers Jocky, Frobisher Airliner and Monospar. Because this range ran for a much shorter production time their value to collectors is correspondingly higher. During the period 1934 to 1940 a number of large boxed sets of Dinky aircraft were released, such as The R.A.F. Presentation Set, The Camouflaged Set and the Presentation Set. These items are highly sought after by collectors today.

Post War: Dinky resumed production late 1945 and by Christmas there was a range of twelve aeroplanes available. Most of these were reissues of pre-war items made from the same castings.

A completely new range introduced in 1946 reflected the many developments in the world of aviation and this was called the 70's series. Many Dinky models were dropped from the range in 1949 including the whole range of aeroplanes. Although production was taken up again in the 50's many of the favourites like the Spitfire and Hurricane were never to be produced in this way again.

Whilst Dinky are probably the best known die cast aeroplane model producers, there were other makes available. During the 50's and early 60's Mercury made a range of planes in Italy to the scale of between 1/150 and 1/220. They made very good castings of some unusual aeroplanes of the period but not a great deal is known about this range.

In Denmark Tekno were producing some nice aeroplanes, notably the Caravelle and DC7 Airliners which, boxed and in mint condition, fetch £30 to £40 each.

In France at this time Solido were making a popular range of die cast models to 1/150 scale. This range includes some not so well known French aeroplanes.

In the early 1970's a range of very finely detailed airliners and military planes were made by Aeromini Ltd. of Japan. Most of these models were made in Japan but a few were made in the U.S.A. where the main market was. The models are die cast and extremely well detailed. The range includes Boeing 747, 737, 727, DC9, DC8, VC10, Phantom F4's and F104 Star fighters. The 747 was produced in at least seven liveries including TWA PAN AM, Air Canada, JAI United Eastern and BOAC. These 747's now fetch between £40 and £50 and, in boxed and mint condition, are much sought after.

When you start collecting you will want to know how to identify models.

With the exception of the larger scale 1965 models, Dinky's do not have their number on them but most will have the name of the aeroplane they represent cast or stamped underneath. Only the older and smaller models are unmarked but there are a number of clues. When the models were first produced in 1934, aeroplanes generally had two bladed propellers and so did the Dinky models. As we moved towards the second world war, aeroplanes featured three bladed propellers, as did the Dinky models. If the model is boxed, this may display a number code. For example, 10-38 indicates the month and the year of production.

Pre-war items fetch high prices and you can expect to pay around £70 for a mint condition, boxed, 60 series model and only slightly less for a 62 series item. The camouflage models which ran for such a short period before the war are particularly sought after and, in good condition, may fetch over £100.

Rarest Dinky Aeroplanes: The Imperial Airways Liner, number 60a, was one of the first issued in 1934 and was based on the Imperial Airways Armstrong Whitworth Atlanta of the time. It is now quite scarce and can fetch over £100. The D.H. Flamingo was announced in the 1939-40 Dinky Catalogue and given the number 62F and a price of 6d. But to my knowledge it has never been seen and it is almost a certainty that none ever reached the shops. Yet, to have a price in the catalogue it must have been costed and it is likely that a few were cast so that the costing could be done. If one were found today it would be priceless to a Dinky collector.

Probably the most sought after model to any Dinky collector is number 992 Avro Vulcan. This model of the most famous of the R.A.F. V-Bombers, was produced between 1955 and 1956. The model is quite large and finished in silver. Although it was given the number 992 it carried the number 749. This Dinky Super Toy differed from others in that it was made of aluminium and not mazak. This model was not offered for sale in England and it is presumed that all of the production went to the North American market. It is listed in the catalogue at that time for One dollar 40 cents.

It is not known how many were produced and estimates range from 100 to 500. It is only in recent years that one or two examples have turned up. There are probably not more than about twenty-five examples in the U.K. and one of these can be seen in the Dinky Museum in London. An original mint and boxed Dinky Vulcan could reasonably be expected to fetch between £1,000 and £1,400 at auction. The original box is extremely rare and adds a great deal to its value.

JU89 Heavy Bomber, 67A, 1940-41, German markings. **£100**

Comet 4 Airliner No. 702, 1954-65. **£16**

The first Dinky boxed set, No. 60, issued in 1934 to 1940. **£300**

Avro Vulcan No. 992, issued 1955, (not issued in U.K., unknown number released in Canada). **£1,200**

BEA Viscount No. 708, 1957-65. **£25**

A pair of Fairey Battles, known as the Mirror Image Pair, 1939-40. **£100**

(Dave Sutton)

MODEL AIRCRAFT

A pre-war Empire Flying Boat No. 60R,
1937.   £45

French Meccano Mystere IUA, No. 60A,
1957-63.   £15

Mayo Composite Aircraft No. 63, 1939-41.
                                         £90

Shetland Flying Boat No. 701, 1947-49.
                                        £175

Imperial Airways Liner No. 60A, 1934-40.
                                         £75

French Meccano Sikorsky S.58 Helicopter
No. 60D, 1957-61.   £15

Frobisher Class Air Liner No. 62R, 1939-41.
                                         £45

Air France Viscount No. 706, 1956-57. £30

(Dave Sutton)

250

MODEL AIRCRAFT

Tempest II Fighter No. 70B, 1946-55. £8

Bristol Britannia No. 998, 1959-65. £45

JU90 Air Liner No. 62N, 1938-41. £70

Iomica (Japanese) F-14A Tomcat, 1978-80.
£15

Lockheed Constellation No. 60C, produced
by Meccano France, 1957-63.   £100

A pre-war Giant High Speed Monoplane No.
62Y, R/H Gree.   £45

Hawker Hunter No. 736, 1955-63. £7

Japanese Aeromini F-4 Phantom, 1973-77.
£30

(Dave Sutton)

251

MODEL AIRCRAFT

Post-war Spitfire No. 62A, 1945-49.   £10

60u Armstrong Whitworth Whitley No. 62T, Silver 1937-41.   £75

Shooting Star No. 70F, 1947-62.   £4

719 Dinky Spitfire, 1969-78.   £7

British 40-seat Air Liner No. 62X, 1939-41.   £50

726 Modern Dinky ME109, 1972-76.   £7

Four-engined Liner No. 62R, 1945-49.   £20

Dinky Viking No. 70c, 1947-62.   £7

Monospar No. 60E, 1934-41.   £75

(Dave Sutton)

MODEL AIRCRAFT

DM Comet Racer No. 60G,
1945-49.   £20

Hawker Hurricane No. 62H,
1939-41.   £35

Ensign Air Liner No. 62P,
1938-41.   £40

Flying Boat Clipper III,
No. 60W, 1938-41. £45

Seaplane No. 700, 1945-49.
                        £10

Auro York No. 70A &
704, 1946-59.   £20

Fairey Battle No. 60N,
1937-41.   £40

Twin-engined Fighter
No. 70D, 1946-55. £10

Spitfire No. 62E, 1940-
41.   £40

(Dave Sutton)

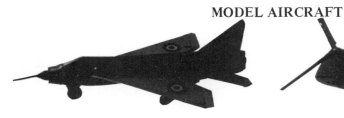

**P1B Lightning Fighter No. 737, 1959-68.
£8**

**Bristol 713 Helicopter No. 715, 1956-62.
£10**

Flying Fortress No. 62G, 1939-41. £50

A post-war Empire Flying Boat, 1949. £20

**Camouflaged Whitworth Ensign Liner No.
68A, 1940-41.   £55**

**Sea Vixen No. 738 Naval Fighter, 1960-65.
£14**

Modern Dinky Phantom 730, 1972-76. £7

Vickers Viking No. 70C, 1947-62. £7

(Dave Sutton)

MODEL AIRCRAFT

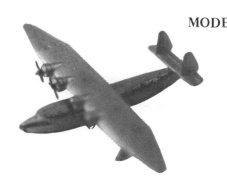

Four-engined Flying Boat, No. 60W, 1945-49. £15

French Meccano Air France Viscount No. 60E, 1957-60. £35

Westland Sikorsky S.51 Helicopter, 1957-62. £8

Gloster Javelin No. 735, 1956-66. £7

Ensign No. 62P, 1938-41. £40

Nord Noratlas No 804, 1960-64. £100

Vautoor No. 60B, French Issue, 1957-63. £20

Bloch 220, No. 64BZ, French made Dinky, sold in U.K., 1939-40. £45

(Dave Sutton)

255

Douglas Air Liner No. 60T, (supposed to be a DC3 by many, but is probably a DC2).   £55

DM Comet Racer No. 60G, 1935-41.   £35

A post-war Giant High Speed Monoplane No. 62Y, R/H Gree.   £25

French Meccano Farman 360, No. 61C, 1935-40.
£60

Japanese Aeromini 747, 1973 -77.   £50

Gladiator Fighter No. 60P, 1937-41. £40

Kings Aeroplane (Envoy) No. 62K, 1938-41. £45

Air France Caravelle No. 997 — £30 for an English one or £45 for one of French manufacture.

Amiot 370 No. 64AZ, French sold in U.K., 1939-40.   £25

(Dave Sutton)

MONEY BOXES

Most of the early money boxes we see today are made of metal. Many have a mechanical function and most still work. One of the earliest patents for a cast iron mechanical money bank was taken out by J. Hall on 21st December, 1869, for his 'Excelsior' bank.

Magic banks always have a mechanical function. A typical example is where a coin is placed under a magician's hat which, when lowered, causes the coin to disappear. The Trick Dog bank is activated by a lever which causes the dog to leap through a hoop and deposit the coin from its mouth into a barrel. These mechanical banks are fascinating but most are a bit pricey.

Special note: Look out for a mechanical bank featuring a young girl skipping. Only recently 'A Girl Skipping Rope' mechanical bank from the late 19th century, sold at auction for £8,250.

American late 19th century Speaking Dog cast-iron mechanical bank, 7in. long. £286

An unusual tin 'Combination Safe' money box. £20

A Pratt money box model-led as a chapel, inscribed Samuel Townsend 1848, 17cm. £418

An unusual wind-up drummer boy money box, 6in. high. £40

Oliver Hardy money box, late 1950's. £10

Late 19th century American cast-iron 'Santa Claus' mechanical bank, 6in. high. £495

(Paul G. Sheppard)

Late 19th century American cast-iron 'Trick Pony' mechanical bank, by Shepard Hardware Co., 7in. wide. £418

Late 19th century American cast-iron leap frog mechanical bank, by Shepard Hardware Co., 7½in. wide. £308

A 20th century English cast-iron 'Dinah' mechanical bank, by John Harper & Co. Ltd., 6½in. high. £104

Late 19th century American 'Uncle Sam' mechanical bank, by Shepard Hardware Co., 11½in. high. £220

Stevens cast-iron Indian and Bear mechanical bank, Conn., circa 1875, 10.9/16in. long. (Robt. W. Skinner Inc.) £799

Organ and Monkey mechanical bank, patented 1882, 7¼in. high. (Robt. W. Skinner Inc.) £227

'I always did 'spise a mule' mechanical bank, by J. & E. Stevens, patented 1879, 8in. high. (Robt. W. Skinner Inc.) £189

Late 19th century American cast-iron 'Punch & Judy' mechanical bank, by Shepard Hardware Co., 7½in. high. £462

Late 19th century American cast-iron 'Paddy and the Pig' mechanical bank, by J. & E. Stevens Co., 8in. high. £385

NUTCRACKERS

It was a Victorian tradition to serve fruit and nuts in their shells towards the end of a meal and predictably, these gadget conscious people had to have the proper tools for the job.

It was not however, considered sufficient to provide a simple and effective appliance, for, like the nutmeg grater and any other implement which had to be used in the presence of company, a pair of nutcrackers had to compliment the tableware and reflect the status of the household.

For practical purposes, nutcrackers had to be made from a fairly sturdy metal and the focus of attention centred on design. The handles were often decorated with ivory or bone and some were fitted with a scalpel shaped pick, designed to help winkle the kernel from the shell.

Finer examples in silver plated or gilt metal rarely survive intact.

A pair of finely carved Scandinavian treen nutcrackers, circa 1880, 6¼in. long. (Christopher Sykes)   £35

Pair of 19th century steel nutcrackers.   £3

An 18th century yewwood nutcracker of hinged form carved with a man's head, 6¾in.   £308

A 19th century pair of steel nut and also lobster shell crackers, circa 1870, 5in. long. (Christopher Sykes)   £15

A pair of cast brass 19th century nutcrackers, the top in the form of a cockerel's head, circa 1800, 5¾in. long. (Christopher Sykes)   £47

Finely engraved steel nutcrackers, circa 1850, 6½in. long. (Christopher Sykes)   £28

A pair of 19th century nut crackers, the handles with turned wood grips, circa 1860, 6¼in. long. (Christopher Sykes) £18

A cast-steel nut cracker in the form of a 7¼in. long alligator, circa 1925. (Christopher Sykes) £22

A pair of early 19th century steel nutcrackers. (Paul G. Sheppard) £6

An 18th/19th century walnut nut cracker in the form of an old woman seated, 7¾in. £110

A late 18th century wood figure of a sailor his mouth operating as a nutcracker, 9½in. high. (W. H. Lane & Son) £57

A 19th century walnut nut cracker of screw type, 8½in. £88

Wrought steel nutcrackers, circa 1820, 5½in. long. (Christopher Sykes) £15

A 17th/18th century boxwood nut cracker of hinged form, 6in. long. £264

Victorian steel nut crackers with 'barley sugar' handles, circa 1860, 6in. long. (Christopher Sykes) £18

As more and more people become aware of the power of advertising and the influence it has upon their lives, it becomes obvious that, by looking back at company images created at a time when the publicity men must have been more or less working in the dark, some got it right, Shell, Castrol and Mobiloil, and some were not so successful, B.P. and Pratts for example. So, as we move into the present day and take a look at these old pieces of functional advertising in the form of oil cans and pourers, it is the Shell and Castrol examples which are the most sought after and the High Performance Oil containers of these companies 'Aeroshell' and Castrol R' which are the most popular.

The Shell company used a variety of shaped enamel signs which now fetch a considerable amount of money.

The Castrol company passed through four distinct design periods. The first can be seen in the Castrol R tin, followed by the style used on the quart Oil Power. There are examples of a pourer in the first style having been re-painted and a transfer from the later style applied to bring the pourer up to date. The subsequent style which was employed up to the 1950's can be seen on the quarter and half pint pourers. It was at this time that the present style came into use with the loss of the lower arm on the logo. As time goes by, these modern pieces will almost certainly be collected but as yet they do not really interest collectors.

Remember, you will not be able to find any early Esso items for the Anglo-American Oil Company used the name of Pratts and, demonstrating the march of progress, all Esso stations are now Exxon in the U.S.A.

'Shell' motor oil enamel sign by Shell-Mex Ltd. £80

Mobiloil poster 'Give Me Mobiloil'. £15

(Mike Smith)

261

OILIANA

Aeroshell Lubricating oil pourer with winged Shell emblem.   £20

Castrol motor oil bottle.
£2

'Caltex' motor oil pourer.
£4

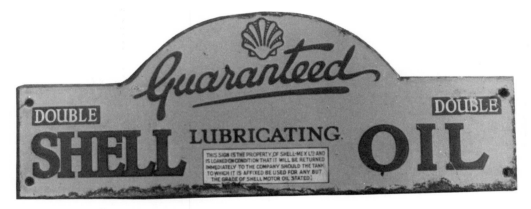

Shell Oil sign with guarantee for affixing to tanks.   £20

2nd World War 2 gallon Army jerry can.   £2

A pair of early Castrol pourers, ½ pint and quart.   £20

Castrol XL motor oil tin.
£10

(Mike Smith)

'Mobiloil' oil bottle with
screw top.   £3

'Shell' globe for surmount-
ing a petrol pump.   £25

'Motorine' motor oil pourer.
                                    £10

A 2 gallon Adcoids tin by
Alexander Duckham & Co.
                £20

Castrol 'D' Gear Oil tin with
screw top.   £8

N.B.C. Lubricants oil bottle.
                            £8

Castrol motor oil enamel sign.   £30

Duckham's Adcoids thermo-
meter.   £75

(Mike Smith)

Castrollo motor oil pourer with glass panel. £20

Shell X 100 motor oil bottle. £3

A pair of Castrol motor oil pourers, ¼ and ½ pint. £6

Moebius Challenge motor oil can with integral handle. £30

Delivery Certificate issued by Shell Mex Ltd. £10

Castrol 'R' motor oil can. £10

Castrol motor oil quart pourer. £20

'Filtrate' tin for Armstrong Siddeley self changing gear box. £20

W. B. Dick & Co. Ltd. oil pourer issued by the service department. £15

(Mike Smith)

Esso motor oil pourer. £4

Redex, the oil and fuel additive dispenser.　£5

Shell X 100 motor oil pourer of pint capacity.　£5

An unusual combined Shell motor oil and petrol can. £35

Texaco enamel sign made by The Texaco Company, U.S.A.　£20

Castrol one pint motor oil tin of conical form.　£15

Aeroshell lubricating oil tin of rounded triangular section.　£8

'Vitafilm' motor oil pourer with high film strength. £10

Mobiloil 'BB' motor oil tin by the Vacuum Oil Co. Ltd. £12

(Mike Smith)

A small all metal pump-action oil can. £1

Shell X-100 ½ gallon motor oil pourer. £5

A rare 'Shell' motor oil can, 9in. high overall. £4

B.P. Motor Spirit, 2 gallon can. £3

Delco-Lovejoy Shock Absorber Oil tin. £4

An old petrol pump with 'Super' illuminated globe. £50

Mobiloil 'B' motor oil tin by the Vacuum Oil Co. Ltd. £10

Brass oil spraying container with plastic handle. £14

Vigzol enamel sign 'Shut This Gate'. £5

(Mike Smith)

PADLOCKS

Although locks have been made since early antiquity in both China and Egypt it wasn't until much later that a European version of a locking device came into widespread use.

The Romans had a form of tubular padlock, probably used on shackles or restraining chains on slaves, and similar devices have been used for centuries on humans and animals alike. The principle was for a key to pass through a tube engaging spring loaded pegs, pressing them inward to release the hasp.

The tumbler lever was introduced at the end of the 18th century and padlocks from this period are generally heart-shaped and impressively large, possibly in a vain hope of fooling any passing footpad into thinking they were more secure than they actually were.

Although most of the 19th and 20th century padlocks are fairly uninspiring from an artistic point of view, those from the 18th century often sport fine decoration and have become works of art in their own right.

Steel ferret collar and lock, brass plaque with the number '1835' stamped on it, circa 1835 (no key). (Christopher Sykes)   £38

Nico brass padlock, Made in England.   75p

A small D7 Secure brass and steel padlock. £1.50

Duplo lock No. 107. 50p

Squire padlock and chain.   £1

G.W.R. (Railway) 4 lever padlock, all brass.   £8

Squire No. 24 ribbed padlock.   £1.50

English made Belfry brand 4 lever padlock with key cover.   £6

Hero, Hong Kong made padlock.   75p

(Paul G. Sheppard)

267

PADLOCKS

Early 19th century Spanish padlock and key. £14

Late 16th. century Spanish iron padlock, 17¾in. long. £550

A miniature Squire padlock. £1

A circular English made Anchor brass and steel padlock. £2

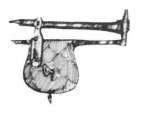

Late 17th century English bar padlock and key. £45

A Secure brass and steel padlock. £1.50

Early 19th century French padlock with key escutcheon cover. £18

British 'hand made' brass lever padlock. £2.50

Nico 'Clacton' steel and cast metal padlock. 75p

Nico steel and cast metal padlock. 75p

17th century Germanic or Central European padlock. £125

A German Abus all steel black painted padlock. £1.50

(Paul G. Sheppard)

268

PENCILS

The modern form of pencil with a graphite rod inserted into a wooden shaft was designed in 1565 by the German scientist Konrad Gresner.

Propelling pencils were invented by the firm of Mordan & Hawkins in 1822 and it is these which offer the greatest variety for collectors.

Made in gold, silver, enamel and EPNS most work by either sliding a knob up and down or turning the cap against the shaft.

Interesting examples incorporate a peeper in the shaft with views of a seaside resort, or even naughty pictures of Paris, while others incorporate a watch.

Many are rather small, up to 2½in. long, and were designed to be worn on the chatelaine or watch chain.

Makers to look for are Mordan, Berry, Hicks, Thornhill and Cartier.

Combined pen and pencil, circa 1920. £5

An embossed silver housekeeper's pencil, circa 1880. £6

EPNS propelling pen and pencil set, circa 1920. £6

Silver propelling pencil by Sampson Mordan. £25

Small EPNS pencil for attachment to chatelaine, with peeper, 2¼in. long. £6

Late 19th century silver pencil with chatelaine ring. £8

EPNS propelling pencil with peeper of Berwick. £7

A gold and enamel propelling pencil watch, dial signed Cartier, 10mm. diam., circa 1930. £1,320

Gold plated handbag pencil with leather case. £8

Late 19th century gold plated fob pencil. £6

Edwardian silver propelling pencil. £12

Set of early 19th century drawing instruments. £65

(Paul G. Sheppard)

PEN NIBS

The earliest steel nibs, made in 1828, were designed as a facsimile of the quill. It may be helpful in dating a nib to note that designs from around 1830 introduced a hole placed at the head of the existing slit and, a few years later, some nibs feature additional slits at each side of the point. The closer the resemblance to the quill — the earlier the nib is likely to be.

By 1900 there were many new patented 'wonder,nibs' on the market. Many writing nibs were produced in conjuction with a patented pen such as the Oriental, the Silver Wonder and the Rob Roy.

As a rule, gold and platignum nibs were designed for use with a fountain pen and were originally boxed. Gold plated and many other types were sold on a card. These cards add interest to a collection; often providing much useful information on the number of nibs in an original set, the sizes and some may give an indication of the original retail price.

Sheaffer 14ct. gold nib.   £6

Perry & Co., No. 120EF, London. £1.30

Perry & Co. Artletter pen nib, No. 613. £1

Myers & Son 'crow quill', No. 5062. 30p

G. Brandauer & Co. Mail pen nib, Birmingham, No. 139.   £2

Wm. Mitchell's Decro calligrapher's pen nib, No. 17.   75p

Osmeroid gold plated 18ct. fountain pen nib, No. 45.   £1.50

M. Myers & Son Ltd. Light Brigade pen nib, No. 600.   £1.20

Wm. Mitchell's Decro Series No. 5, Reg. No. 0999/5.   60p

Wm. Mitchell's Pedigree Round Hand nib, No. O.   50p

Wm. Mitchell's scroll writer, No. 60. 80p

Joseph Gillott's Warranted, No. 170. 40p

Heintze & Blanckertz, Berlin, No. 01. 45p

Wm. Mitchell's scroll writer, No. 40. 70p

C. Brancauer & Co. Oriental pen nib, No. 312.   90p

Perry & Co. Artletter pen nib, Series No. 613.   70p

Osmeroid gold plated 18ct. fountain pen nib, No. 45.   £1.50

Wm. Mitchell's Decro calligrapher's pen nib, No. 19.   75p

Gillott's 'crow quill' mapping pen nib, No. 65A.   30p

Macniven & Cameron Manifold 4 page nib, No. 383.   £1.50

(Paul G. Sheppard)

PEN NIBS

John Heath's solectet J. 70p

Decro No. 15 by Wm. Mitchell. 75p

Perry & Co. lance eraser, No. 4. 40p

M. Myers & Co. selected J., No. 3448. 40p

Wm. Mitchell's scroll writer, No. 50. 70p

Wm. Mitchell's Decro calligrapher's nib, No. 3B. 65p

Wm. Mitchell's Pedigree cup point, No. 0591F. 80p

Wm. Mitchell's Decro Series No. 4, Reg. No. 0999/4. 75p

Wm. Mitchell's Pedigree cup point nib, No. OS91E. £1.50

Joseph Gillott's artist's pen nib, No. 1950, blued steel. 70p

R. Esterbrook & Co., U.S.A., drawlet pen nib, No. 16. 50p

Osmeroid gold plated 18ct. fountain pen nib, No. 35. £2

Wm. Mitchell's scroll writer, No. 30, calligrapher's pen nib. 70p

G. W. Hughes spoon point Series No. 757EF. £1.40

S. O. Bak-Ein, Reg. No. 1M. 65p

Wm. Mitchell's scroll writer, No. 70. 70p

Reeves manuscript pen nib, No. 4. 60p

Map maker's pen nib. 30p

Joseph Gillots Warranted, LL No. 404. 40p

Wm. Mitchell's Pedigree Round Hand nib, No. 2½. 50p

R. Esterbrook & Co. drawlet pen nib, No. 10. 80p

Crawfords old reliable velvo pen nib, No. 208. £1.75

Wm. Mitchell's mapping quill, No. 0567. 40p

'M' Warranted first quality fountain pen nib. 50p

R. Esterbrook & Co., U.S.A., drawlet pen nib, No. 4. 50p

Osmeroid gold plated 18ct. fountain pen nib, No. 37. £2

Wm. Mitchell's skooter pen nib, No. OS68. £2.50

Heintze Blanckertz, No. 83½, Germany. £1.50

(Paul G. Sheppard)

271

PENKNIVES

Single bladed pocketknives were originally designed for the purpose of trimming and cutting the quill pen; thus the common name penknife. A knife with both a large and a small blade can usually be dated from about 1850 onwards.

Small silver bladed fruit knives, with bone or ivory handles, date from the 19th century. Traditionally used for peeling and cutting fruit, the silver blade left no nasty aftertaste and some better examples have a little silver fork attachment.

The Victorian capacity for invention was given full rein in developing gadgets for the popular multi-purpose knives with features such as scissor blades, button hooks, corkscrews and other gadgets; some exhibition pieces incorporate blades for hundreds of different functions.

Although many of these functions are obscure and difficult to identify one of the more obvious mechanisms is that for a boxlock percussion pistol, only 4in. long.

Late Victorian miniature knife with steel blade, 1in. long. £2

Miniature double bladed mother-of-pearl handled penknife, 2in. long. £3.50

Miniature bone handled knife, 1in. long. £3

A Belgian boxlock percussion combination knife pistol, barrel 4in., Liege proved, folding blade 4in. (Wallis & Wallis) £230

Unmarked gold miniature knife with one steel blade and one gold blade, 1½in. long closed. £12

A World War II O.S.S. Special Forces combination clasp knife. (Wallis & Wallis) £320

Late 19th century miniature penknife with mother-of-pearl handle, 1½in. long. £2.50

Victorian pocket fruit knife and patent orange peeler with mother-of-pearl handle. £100

Silver penknife with mother-of-pearl handle, dated 1897. £20

(Paul G. Sheppard)

272

PENS

A potted history of pens would take us from the stylus used in ancient times by scribes scratching away on tablets of wax, to the quill and stalk pens of the 6th century A.D.; from the nib and penholder, to the fountain pen invented in the 1880's; the ball point pen introduced in 1944, to the myriad designs on the market today.

The earliest type of fountain pen was the Vulcanite which was filled with ink from a glass tube fitted with a rubber bulb on the end. Many patented designs exist, but it was from the Vulcanite that we see the transition to the rubber ink holder, sometimes with a lever action, followed by the screw top plunger and eventually, the cartridge.

There are many fine examples for the collector and some are worth a considerable sum of money. It is worth looking out for pens which were either the property of a well known personality or used at the signing of significant documents. In either case, some authentication is necessary if the top price is to be achieved.

A good quality 1950's Parker pen with 14ct. gold nib.   £12

Early 20th century bone handled silver pen with chased barrel.   £3

A Swan fountain pen No. 4662, with gold plated nib.   £7

A silver cased Swan fountain pen with chatelaine attachment.   £15

1940's Sheaffer 'Snorkel' with 14ct. gold nib, in original box with instructions. £18

Early 1960's Parker 51 with 14ct. gold nib.   £7

A gold and enamel calendar fountain pen by Cartier, circa 1925, 10.5cm. long.   £1,331

1970's lady's gold plated pen with 14ct. gold nib.   £8

A Swan fountain pen in chased silver case.   £20

Late Victorian silver cased fountain pen by Swan of London.   £12

Indian silver quill pen.   £40

Swan pen with plated lapel clip, circa 1905.   £4

1930's desk pen mounted on an onyx base.   £8

Fountain pen used by King Edward VIII to sign the Abdication Document. (Phillips)   £2,000

Late 19th century silver cased housekeeper's fountain pen.   £20

Hallmarked silver ruler pen by Asprey, London.   £45

(Paul G. Sheppard)

273

PHOTOGRAPHIC EQUIPMENT

The Victorian passion for the art of photography has left us a legacy of fine quality cameras together with all the essential paraphernalia of the photographic studio.

Over the last ten or fifteen years, a lot of publicity has been given to the staggering sums of money paid for old brass and wood plate cameras. One of the rarest examples to come on the market was the Sutton Panoramic Wet Plate Camera which fetched £11,000 at auction, the resulting publicity bringing two more to light which also sold for about the same figure. Not so much attention has been focused on the less spectacular but thriving trade in equipment. Enlargers, dryers, darkroom lamps, viewers, cutters, tripods, all were made with precision and style. Most of this equipment is still in usable condition but perhaps more important still, it looks good, and is treasured for its fine quality rather than its utilitarian value.

A 35mm. hand-cranked cinematograph camera with Rodersdorf Roo Kino 5cm. f 2.5 lens. (Christie's S. Kensington)   £900

'The Trident' ceramic developing tray.   £3

35mm cinematograph machine complete with small paraffin burner.   £35

Conway camera de luxe model in leatherette case.   £5

Photographic darkroom lamp with three red glass slides, circa 1880.   £10

Wallace Heaton negative album with brass screw binding.   £5

(Paul G. Sheppard)

PHOTOGRAPHIC EQUIPMENT

An early Kodak film tin. £2

A Thomas Sutton's patent wet-plate panoramic camera by Ross, London, taking 5 x 10¾in. exposures. (Christie's S. Kensington) £6,000

The Paterson film developing tank, adjustable model. £5

Tin case containing numerous old 35mm films. £35

1950's Kodak film machine for 620, 120 and 127 film, obtainable with two 2/- pieces. £35

Ernemann Kinette 35mm. hand-cranked portable cine camera, and two film cassettes. (Christie's S. Kensington) £200

A mahogany stereoscopic tailboard camera by W. I. Chadwick, Manchester, with 3in. stereo lenses, 4¼ x 6¼cm. (Christie's S. Kensington) £240

A full plate tailboard camera of mahogany and brass construction by Ross of London. (Anderson & Garland) £280

An early combined photographic darkroom lamp and contrast printer with inbuilt burner, light refraction hood and red and yellow glass slides, circa 1900. £20

PIPES

The earliest European pipes were made of clay and, because tobacco was so expensive, fitted with a small bowl. The stem of the early pipe was short in length, as in the Cutty, which was followed by a longer stemmed pipe known as the Churchwarden. During the reign of George I the Churchwarden pipe was adapted to accommodate a red wax tip to the mouthpiece and was then referred to as the Alderman.

The best English pipes were made at Winchester and Bronseley. Brier pipes made fom the root of the brier shrub are well collected, but the most popular of all is still the Meerschaum. Meerschaum is a material ideally suited to carving and has the added attraction of turning the most beautiful mellow colour with use.

One of the most important, but lesser known pipemakers was Gambier of Paris. His work includes pipes in the form of stylised animals, satirical caricatures of prominent figures and some quite macabre subjects.

Carved burl Civil War pipe bowl, American, circa 1862-63. (Robt. W. Skinner Inc.) £591

Late 19th century German Meerschaum figural pipe with amber stem, 12¼in. long. (Robt. W. Skinner Inc.) £500

Silver mounted cast iron pipe bowl, probably German, circa 1840, 3¾in. high. £286

Late 19th century Meerschaum pipe, carved with a lion's head, 7½in. long. (Robt. W. Skinner Inc.) £250

A 19th century Meerschaum pipe, modelled with a figure of a bearded gentleman, 19cm. long. (H. Spencer & Sons) £240

Plain Meerschaum pipe with curved bowl and white metal mounts, carved in high relief with coat of arms. (Christie's S. Kensington) £100

A 17th century Dutch fruit-wood pipe, 3.3/8in. long. £1,980

A Staffordshire pottery curled pipe painted with blue and yellow dashes. £220

Indian brass pocket 'Hashish' pipe, circa 1960. £6

PLAYING CARDS

The origin of playing cards is still a subject for speculation, the most widely held view being that they probably originated both in the East and the West independently and simultaneously. The earliest record in Europe is a decree of 23rd May 1376, issued in the City of Florence, prohibiting their use.

The earliest decks, now of course out of reach of most collectors and to be found only in museums, were hand-drawn and painted packs commissioned by Royalty and the wealthy aristocracy of the period. The earliest pack a collector can hope to possess dates to the end of the 17th Century when a series of playing cards in England were used as general information for the public. These early engraved packs are priced at around £500 and above. The range for the collector is otherwise very wide indeed. Cards of the last century can vary dramatically in price range with rarer packs fetching as much as £1,000 whereas some of the common ones are priced at below £10. There also is a very wide range of modern cards with unusual designs produced in the past decade which are priced well below £5 per deck and are undoubtedly the collectors pieces of the future.

Collectors will only be interested in 'non-standard' decks, that is ones that have unusual designs, mainly of the Court card and in game packs which are card decks without suit signs. The English suit signs of spades, hearts, diamonds and clubs (which are derived from the French packs) are not universally in use and even today, the Germanic countries still use the hearts, leaves, dumb-bells and acorns and the Spaniards and Italians still use the coins, cups, swords and sticks. The subject matter of Tarot and fortune-telling cards is an additional and effectively separate branch within the overall picture of playing cards.

Italy — 18th century 'Cucu' deck 38/38.
£300

England — A deck to honour the marriage of The Duke of Edinburgh, published by De Larue 1874, Courts depict the allies of the period, including Queen Victoria, President Grant, the Russian Czar and the German Emperor.
£195

(Yasha Beresiner)

277

Spain — standard deck of 1920, 48/48. £18

Italy — Playing cards by E. Dotti, Milan, circa 1870, hand-coloured.   £160

England — Victoria Diamond Jubilee deck by Goodall & Son, London 1897, all portraits of British Royalty.   £85

Spain — Non-standard design by J. L. Picardo, published by Fournier 1959.   £14

(Yasha Beresiner)

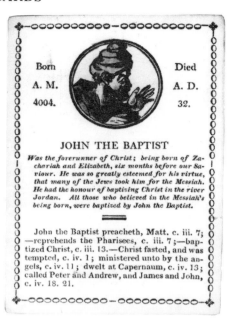

Italy — A single-suited French deck produced by Viassone in Turin, circa 1820, 52/52.   £80

England — Biblical educational cards by J. Wallis, circa 1800, 32/32.   £85

France — The 'Four Seasons' designed by J. P. Le Doux, published by Draeger, Paris 1961.   £25

Iran — Persian 'Asnas' deck, circa 1860, 25/25, hand-painted and lacquered.   £280

(Yasha Beresiner)

India — Mogul Ganjifa cards from Hyderabad, hand-painted on ivory, circa 1850, 96/96, usually in hand-painted box.   £850

France — Standard Marseille Tarot, circa 1850, 78/78, by N. Conver.   £250

Spain — Standard Spanish pattern, published in Madrid 1877.   £45

Japan — 'Unsun Karuta' pack, 75/75, by an unknown maker, circa 1970, limited edition produced every year.   £110

(Yasha Beresiner)

Russia — A Slavic costume deck unknown
maker, circa 1935.   £60

Popish Plot 1679 by R. Walton, London.
                                      £800

Italy — Pack designed by D. Baroni and N.
Pazzaglia, published by Mondadori, 1973.
                                      £10

England — Transformation pack by Maclure,
Macdonald and Macgregor, Manchester,
circa 1870.   £220

(Yasha Beresiner)

England — Count & Sons — successors to Gibson, standard English deck 1805, single courts.   £135

Spain — The Don Quixote non-standard design by A. Bruzon, published by Fournier 1964.   £18

England — The game of Khanhoo by W. H. Wilkinson, published by Goodall & Son, 1895, double pack, 31 in deck.   £45

France — 'Cartes a Rire' — transformation pack attributed to Baron Louis Atthalin 1819 (Courts represent Paris newspapers).   £950

(Yasha Beresiner)

PLAYING CARDS

Belgium — The 'Dilkhus' playing cards, makers unknown, circa 1920, Indian ethnic pack. £35

Netherlands — A non-standard deck by V. Vermoeyen, maker unknown, circa 1938. £12

Austria — 'The Residenz — whist number 147', by Piatnik of Vienna, circa 1910. £45

Hungary — The Four Seasons pattern, circa 1880, 32/32, by Elso Magyar, Budapest. £40

(Yasha Beresiner)

POST BOXES

The first, experimental, roadside post box was introduced in Jersey in 1852. The second was erected at Botchergate, Carlisle, in 1853 — the rest is history.

The postal system was, at this time, in its infancy but, as the idea caught on, demand for the facility increased until boxes were distributed throughout the land — even introduced to hotel lobbies for the convenience of the guests.

The standard pillar box used by the British Postal Service from 1857 to 1859 was designed by the Department of Science & Art and was made by Smith & Hawkes. Boxes were either free standing or set into a wall. They were made of cast iron and, as time went on, the basic design was modified and adapted to achieve the best possible weatherproofing and security for the contents.

Good examples of early designs may be found in local museums and the changing features are of great interest to the collector.

19th century official wall post box, 2ft.4in. high. £80

A George III mahogany house letter box with lattice sides and hinged lid, 7in. wide.   £132

Oak, country house letter box formed as a miniature pillar box, 16in. high.£160

George VI official internal post box with brass lock and key.   £12

Victorian six-sided post box.   £850

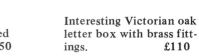

Interesting Victorian oak letter box with brass fittings.   £110

(Paul G. Sheppard)

The familiar picture post card as we know it today, was first granted permission for use in Britain on 1st October, 1894 but the history of the post card goes back beyond that date and offers an area rich in interest for the collector.

The first ever post card, known as an official stationery card, was issued in Austria in 1869.

The British version followed one year later and was issued measuring 121mm x 88mm. This size proved to be unwieldy in handling along with other mail and the size was duly reduced to 121mm x 74mm. These cards issued in late 1870 carried a pre-printed, pre-paid ½d. stamp and were intended for inland use only. Government permission was granted on June 17th, 1872 for privately produced and printed cards to be used but these first had to be taken to the Post Office for the official pink/orange stamp to be impressed. These early cards were so thin and flimsy that the politician Gladstone, who was much in favour of the use of the post card, voiced a public complaint as to their poor quality. On 1st February, 1875 the Post Office issued a sturdier version which consisted of a centre thick card with a covering layer of paper compressed to both sides forming a very stiff finished card. Others followed suit. This modified version is referred to by collectors as 'The Gladstone'. It is worth noting that any picture post card sent through the postal system prior to permission being granted in 1894 would have done so illegally and would therefore command a high price. An exception to this would be a card issued legally by a private company and bearing an illustration of sorts, and this clearly does not constitute a picture post card. Post marks on early cards can also be of great interest to the collector and may add a considerable amount to the value of the card.

Chromo Litho 'vignette' picture post card Sept. 20th, 1900, reverse Bathing Scene. £5

Thin postal stationery card, 25th March 1875, Manchester to London, nice duplex mark and receiving mark from J. Wooley Sons & Co. £5

Court size private postal stationery card, orange halfpenny stamp, Nov. 9th, 1897, message on reverse 'Sorry I cannot come and have a romp with you this morning'.£6

Universal Postal Union official postal stationery card, 20th August 1902, arrival cancellations. £2.40

(Paul G. Sheppard)

Gladstone type 'private' postal stationery card with legal interest, Jan. 6th, 1880. £1.75

Thin type postal stationery, January 8th, 1874, London–Brighton. £3

Early thin 'official' postal stationery card sent from Exeter to Cornwall in 1874. Duplex postmark over purple halfpenny printed stamp. £8

Gladstone type postal stationery card, 1891, reverse advertising Metropolitan School of Shorthand Ltd. £6

Blue Letter Card, London to Birmingham 1894, perforations still complete. Experimental London squared circle postmark (four arcs). £8.50

Official British Empire Exhibition postal stationery card, sent out by Stamp Dealer, 1st September, 1924. £10

Gladstone type postal stationery card, Torquay to Leominster, March 21st, 1878, nice duplex cancellation mark. £3.50

Thin type postal stationery card, good clear postmark 1877, Printed Rehearsal Notice for Herefordshire Philharmonic on reverse. £15

(Paul G. Sheppard)

Gladstone type postal stationery card Salisbury local, Dec. 9th, 1878, duplex postmark message on reverse 'Will you please send at once to the house 2 tons of coal'. £3

Gladstone type postal stationery card, April 1st, 1894, signed on reverse F. Pigon. £6

Gladstone type postal stationery official card London local, red receiving cancellation, 1885, reverse requesting Mr Hughes to accompany him to Wool Warehouse. £4

Thin type postal stationery card, September 7th, 1879, St. Albans to Birmingham from Cooper Box & Co. Wholesale Hat Manufs. £4

Official postal stationery card, green halfpenny stamp, March 15th, 1906 postmark. 65p

Universal Postal Union 'official' card, 29th July 1901, with hooded circle station postmark and 'too late for G.P.O.'. £18

Gladstone type postal stationery card, May 13th, 1897, to arrange lecture for students in Knightsbridge. £2.30

Early thin postal stationery card, London to Birmingham, October 21st, 1873, referring to eccentric buckle pattern. £8

(Paul G. Sheppard)

Gladstone type postal stationery card, Hereford to Newcastle, January 17th, 1892, nice clear duplex cancellation. £2.60

Gladstone type postal stationery card, printed confirmation of letter receipt on reverse from Lingham Bros. (Jewellery Quater) of Birmingham 1896. £2.50

Gladstone type postal stationery card, Chester to Bury St. Edmunds, April 12th, 1879. £3.20

Gladstone type postal stationery card 1894, requesting catalogue from International Stores Ltd. £3.25

American 'Private Mailing Card' (authorised to be used by Act of Congress from May 19th 1898), this example has fishing scene on reverse. £2

Reverse of picture postcard of King Charles Tower, posted from Chester, July 24th 1901. £3.50

Thin type postal stationery card Oxford to Bath, March 14th, 1885, clear duplex postmark. £3.50

Gladstone type postal stationery card, London to Salisbury, February 1st, 1878, early advertising on reverse 'Annual Winter Clearance Sale of Optics, Clocks, Bronzes, Musical Boxes etc.'. £8

(Paul G. Sheppard)

Gladstone type 'private' postal stationery card from R. Davenport Vernon Ironmonger, nice duplex postmark 1877.   £3

Gladstone type postal stationery postcard Grimsby to Wakefield, February 15th, 1877.   £2

Court size 'official' postal stationery card, May 12th, 1902, sent by author G. B. Howes (b. 1853) 'Many thanks for reprint of pamphlets, on reverse.   £4.50

'Private' postal stationery postcard, embossed pink stamp, Manchester local, September 27th, 1883.   £3

Australian 'illustrated official', 1893, sent from Sydney to Germany.   £6

Dutch 'official' postcard, 5th May, 1892.   £1

'Order Return' postal stationery postcard, unused.   £3.75

Early advertising postal stationery Gladstone type postcard, unused.   £2.50

(Paul G. Sheppard)

Thin type postal stationery card, August 25th, 1875, reverse 'printed in red', Notice of Removal of Albert Gibbs, carrier and leather seller to new address. £6.50

Novelty letter card, French 1907, opens up to reveal velvet applied fish and two ribbons and 'J'ai peche le poisson dans le fieuve de l'affection'. (I am fishing in the river of your affection'). £10

Thin type postal stationery card, London to Birmingham, August 21st, 1875. (Damaged). £2

Gladstone type postal stationery card August 1893, Pearson Hill parallel motion machine cancellation NW3 sent to piano maker. £3.75

French 'official' postal stationery postcard, Paris to London 1895, scroll hooded, receiving postmark in red on reverse. £4

'Court' size, 115 x 89mm., postal stationery postcard. Printed appointment message on reverse from The Winterbottom Bookcloth Co. Ltd., 25.8.1900. £4.50

'Court' size postal stationery card, Kensington to Birmingham, January 8th, 1903. £1.40

Field Service 'official' postal stationery postcard, crossout sentences on reverse 'if anything else is added the postcard will be destroyed'. £1

(Paul G. Sheppard)

October 23rd, 1871, postal stationery 'thin' card to Wholesale Ironmonger requesting samples and prices of bottom spindles. £8

Thin 'official' postal stationery card, Wednesbury to Derby, January 1st, 1875, duplex postmark. £4

Thin type postal stationery card, memo from Cooper Box. & Co., St. Albans to London, 17th March, 1880. £2.40

Oriental postal stationery 'official' card, many marks on reverse. £3.50

Universal Postal Union 'official' postal stationery card, unused brown penny printed stamp. £1.60

'Mint' South African 'official' postcard overprinted 'VRI'. 75p

Cape of Good Hope 'official' Gladstone type postal stationery card, unused. £2

Thin type postal stationery card, 27th Sept. 1877, memorandum from Ermen & Roby apologising for error. £3.50

(Paul G. Sheppard)

POSTCARDS, UNUSUAL

Amongst the assorted debris collected throughout ones own, or some other persons life-time, we are almost certain to come across a few old postcards which have been kept as souvenirs of an excursion to the country or a happy day at the seaside.

Throw these away at your peril — for you will certainly upset the Cartologists and you may even be chucking five pound notes into the dustbin.

A Cartologist collects postcards on an infinite variety of themes and this is indeed, a fast growing market.

Collections are invariably sorted into specific groups but there are always some which defy classification and these are listed here under the heading 'Unusual'.

This must be one of the most fascinating categories for collectors providing a rich source of interesting material and always a great deal of speculation as to the value of any card.

Postcard with aviation interest, 'For the Homeland', issued by the French National War Fund Committee 1914-18 War. £1.50

'The only girl I ever loved', Rotary photo by Gale & Polden No. 6776C. £1.50

'Hold to light' four funnel liner and sailing ship. Moon, sea and portholes illuminate when held to light. £8

Italian postcard sent from Morecambe to Dukinfield on 14th April 1922 with message written in shorthand for privacy. £2

'A curious house near Wolverhampton'. The top storey of the cottage consists of an old broad gauge railway carriage converted into three bedrooms. £8

'Die Fahrt ins Weisse', carved ice car, Swiss card, real photograph. £1

(Paul G. Sheppard)

Unusual 'Hold to Light' postcard (artwork by W. H. Elliam), when held up to light this card reveals a girl bathing. £9

'Hippo' in Africa by S. J. Moore, Nairobi, this card would also have shooting and photographic interest for the camera and gun. £3.50

Betancourt the French Cuban chair balancing act. Card was produced in aid of the parcel and tobacco fund for the brave men at the front (1914-18 War). £4

Novelty Christmas card, undivided back, applied 'babies'. £2

The Knight Series No. 579 Map of the True-love River. £2.25

'Lightning' by Judges Hastings (time exposure shot) photographic card. £2

'Hindu Cremation' photographic card by D. Macropole, Calcutta. The pyre consists of wood, cow dung and ghee (butter) and gives off an odour 'not easily forgotten'. £4

Mr Gladstone and Family at Hawarden, photo by Elliot & Fry. This one was posted after his death, referring to him as a 'grand old man'. £2.50

(Paul G. Sheppard)

POSTCARDS, UNUSUAL

Arab beggar in Haifa,
photographic postcard.
£1.75

Real photo postcard of
the clock 'Greenwich
Observatory'.   £2

I. Benghiat & Son, Aden,
A real mermaid?   £5

Belgian Soldiers Fund official
card 1916, 'The Late Nurse
Cavell', shot by a German
firing squad.   £2

'The biggest wager on record',
he wins the amount shown
if he walks round the world,
He has to marry on the way
and conceal his identity
throughout by wearing the
helmet.   £6

Camden Graphics post-
card No. 477, 'Blue Collar'
Compliments of Staples
& Griffin cash grocers',
modern card.   25p

Nancy's Lawn Sale by Art
Strader, 1982. Comic caricature of the president's
wife.   £1.25

Real photo postcard of
'The Stocks at Aldboro'.
£3

(Paul G. Sheppard)

'The Pygmies' J. Beagles
(London), illustrating the
chief and the princess. £2

Unusual personality 'Kubelik' the violinist, Rotary photo 1904. Czech violinist and composer naturalised Hungarian citizen 1903 — (1880-1940). £4

WBSS Series No. 196 'Come on Hertz, beloved sweetheart all the way to my bosom'. £2.50

Pondichery 'A smoker of opium'. £3

The violin maker at work, German card, notice his old tools and mug of tea! £3

'Rationed' news photo reproduction postcard by Camden Graphics. 30p

'Madame Gulliver' by J. Lagarrigue, Nugeron Series No. H4. £1

Raphael Tuck's 'oilette' 'Coon Kids' Series No. 9092, 'We'se out sportin''. £2

'Hold to Light' card, applique type with red celluloid windows and applied glitter and fabric for leaves, Giesen Bros. Series, London, No. 124. £6

Much sought after cards, real photos of theatre, this one the Palace Theatre Doncaster in 1915, by J. S. & S.) No. 434. £12

(Paul G. Sheppard)

Real photograph of 'Beute' The Fasting Man, circa 1910. £3

Cut-out mask, circa 1928, it is rare for post-cards such as this to survive intact.   £17

A promotional card for 'Cheeky the Dwarf'.   £1.50

'President Sadate, Mr. Begin and President Carter' meet to sign a peace treaty. £1.50

Victory Day Souvenir card May 8th 1945.   £3

(Paul G. Sheppard)

POSTCARDS, UNUSUAL

Real photograph of Hitler by Hopemann of Munchen 1935.   £5

East Wolverhampton Election, Liberal majority of eight won by G. Thorne in 1908.   £8

'Donkey and Cart' put-up for auction 316 times to raise £253 at Red Cross Jumble Sale.   £12

'The World renowned Willy Pantzer and his wonderful midgets'.   £2

Real photograph of 'The Girls Friendly Society' motor caravan, circa 1910.   £7

(Paul G. Sheppard)

Nurse of Negus of Abyssinia, purchased from the Turkish Shop Hotel l'Europe, Aden. £6

Novelty card from Swansea, purse opens up to reveal multi-view, Valentine Series 'mailing novelty', shape passed by G.P.O. for ½d stamp, 1910. £2.50

'World's Champion Woman Hater', Albion, L. Clough, photographic. £3.50

'Hello Elizabeth' by Jean Lagarrigue, Nugeron Series cards, French, caricature of HRH The Queen, modern card. £2

'Harry the Rag', age 78, challenges England for the 60 yards. £4

'Pre-War Joy', news photo reproduction by Camden Graphics, modern. 30p

'Fun on stilts', teddy bear card by W. H. Ellam, Faulkner Series No. 918. £3.25

Germanic Humour/Fantasy chromo litho card SB Series, notice mouse in mouth. £8

'Hold to Light' card, illuminates holly, berries, moon and windows when held to light, 'Tobogganing in the snow'. £4

(Paul G. Sheppard)

'Fancy Dress' costume made from parcel wrappings. £2

Embossed 'frog' New Year card 1906/07, artist drawn Erika Series. £6

Germanic Fantasy/Humour chromo litho SB Series card, 'One way to keep her quiet'. £9

'Margaret Thatcher' by Oscar da Costa, Athena series, England, modern card but this sort is certain to increase in value. 50p

Shuttering carpenter Paul Kaunda Mc Makachia, Nairobi 1980, photo by Mike Wells, Cotswold Collotype Series. 50p

Prevent Street Crime, photomontage by Cath Tabe, Leeds postcards. 50p

Mr. Attrill's shell house at Cowes, I.O.W., it took ten years to complete, photographic card by White & Sons, Cowes. £4

Embossed chromo litho postcard with real velvet applied to figures' clothes, Novelty 'Applique' card. £4

Broncho Billy, official film co. issue, made by the Garraway Co., Rutherford, New Jersey. £4

(Paul G. Sheppard)

French card of the remains of a gentleman's aeroplane 'After the Race'. Caption on reverse 'How do you like the turn out?', aviation interest. £7

'Witty Series' comic card by Tempest, published by Bamforth & Co. Ltd. £1

Photographic card of early horse-drawn transport at Sydenham by Reade Photopress, Parkstone. £14

Souvenir of The Rt. Hon. Joseph Chamberlain MP, on his 70th birthday. £7

London County Council Volunteer Ambulance drivers, real photograph November 1939. £3

(Paul G. Sheppard)

Russian Communist Party official card 1919.　£15

'The Disastrous fire at Mr Somervelle's house, Harrow School, April 3rd 1908'.　£8

'Vote for Clive and speed the plough', local publicity for national elections, 1908.　£5

'Consul' a trained chimpanzee, pupil of Frank C. Bostock, the animal king.　£3

Inspection of Horses for the War Office at Newent, August 5th, 1914.　£10

(Paul G. Sheppard)

'Dainty Doris Grahame', comedienne and clever dancer, real photograph. £1.50

'Sooty's Garage. published by J. Salmon Ltd., Sevenoaks. 50p

'Dare Devil Peggy', England's greatest high diver, real photograph. £2

Hospital Fund Raising Day, 'Bruce' at Swindon, collected £400, 1908. £6

The Rt. Hon. A. J. Balfour (Wolverhampton), Lafayette photograph autographed on reverse. £9

Harold Pyott 'The English Midget', 23in. high at age 39. £3

Mr. Jan Van Albert, 9ft. 3½in., Mrs. Jan Van Albert and Peppetoni, 2ft.6in. high. £1.50

Wilfred Westwood, tallest, heaviest boy in the world, aged 11 years, weight 20st. 6lb. £1.50

Mariedl, The Tyrolean Giantess, aged 27 years, weight 360lb. £1.50

(Paul G. Sheppard)

Helen Coulthard, The Girl Preacher, 'Isaiah 55-6'.50p

Anita 'The Living Doll' aged 30 years, the smallest adult the world has ever seen (signed postcard).   £6

Marshal J. Stalin, real photograph.   £3

Germanic humour, Tramps, 'Devil is that all', WBSS Series No. 163.   £3.50

The Prime Minister, Winston Churchill, photographed in Canada.   £4.50

'Heartiest Congratulations' may your troubles be little ones.   £1.50

'Lady Little' the Doll Lady published by Lilywhite, Halifax.   £1

Ruby Westwood, aged 13 years, weight 17st.4lb.   £1.50

Raphael Tuck's oilette 'Be patriotic and reduce your dress bill'.   £2

(Paul G. Sheppard)

Albert Morrow art card of scene from 'Two Little Vagabonds' 1906. £6.50

German Nazi propaganda postcard 1938 by Franz Schilcher. 'To reprint is forbidden' on reverse, rare item. £12.50

Mining 'Rescue Team', real photo postcard by Chapman, Swansea. £10

The old tumble-down stile 'Charlecote' real photo card. 75p

Mr Tony Benn, Labour MP 1979, printed by Expression Printers, London. 40p

'3D' (three dimensional) novelty card 'Woodland Animals' £2.50

Raphael Tuck 'oilette' Series No. 9793 'Teddy Bears at the Seaside', artist Wm. Henry Ellam. £3

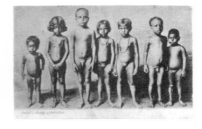

India's rising generation, described on reverse as 'street urchins' with further comments as 'no doubt they would cause a sensation in Piccadilly and adults of the region's villages walk around in similar attire!' £2

(Paul G. Sheppard)

PRAMS

The earliest known baby carriage in Britain was made in 1730 (for the children of The 3rd Duke of Devonshire), and designed to be pulled along by a small animal. The first of the baby carriages manufactured for public use was made in 1840. This was a three wheeled version with iron tyres and it still had to be pulled along. About the mid 19th century, a handle was fitted to the back so that the pram could be pushed and this version was called the perambulator. The three wheeled perambulator remained in popular use until about 1880 when it was displaced by the new four wheeled bassinette. The early four wheeled prams were, at first, categorised by the authorities as road vehicles but as they became more popular, this was rescinded.

The pram has always been something of a status symbol and the early prams were no exception. They were coachbuilt with bodies made of wood, sometimes of leather, and dressed with fittings of brass. They were lavishly trimmed and the interiors were often upholstered in soft skins or a leatherette, some deep-buttoned for effect. Safety features such as brakes and strappings were not introduced until after 1900.

An early safety feature perhaps worth noting, is the pram fitted with two handles, one at each end. This was not merely a fashionable 'extra' but a necessity for the safe-keeping of the infants who were trundled around the treacherous roads of the early perambulating days. Pavements were either very narrow or non existent and traffic regulations for coaches and carriages still a bit sketchy, which made turning a pram for the return journey, a hazardous business. With a handle fitted at both ends, the prampusher only had to pass alongside the pram to reverse direction in safety.

1930's simulated leather doll's pram with folding hood and brake. £35.

An early Star Manufacturing Co. round-head pram with leather trim and porcelain handle. £250

Tan-Sad wartime Cot-Kar pram, No. 3214, with wooden body and leatherette hood. £85

(Min Lewis)

A large 1960's Silver Cross pram with metal body and fabric and leatherette upholstery.
£35

Doll's pram with scroll and lattice wicker-work body, 30in. long.
£55

Country style oak framed back to back twin pram with brass hubs.
£180

A metal bodied Leeway pram with plastic interior.
£45

1920's Acme pram with wooden body and 'C' springs, reg. no. 465485.
£80

A rare Bassinett two handled double pram with painted leather body, circa 1860. £250

(Min Lewis)

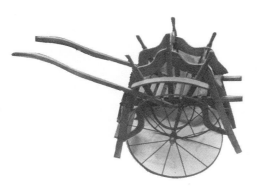

Country style 'mail cart' pushchair with iron wheels. £100

The 'London' baby coach with wooden body and fabric cover. £55

1930's Stella doll's pram with plywood body, leatherette hood and umbrella holder. £40

Wooden bodied doll's pram with vinyl interior and fabric hood. £30

Wooden 'mail cart' pram with carved sides, leather hood and brass trim. £300

A rare T. Trotmans patent 1854 folding pram with carpet back seating and wood and brass wheels. £400

(Min Lewis)

1930's 'Pedigree' pram by A. J. Dale & Son, Warminster. £55

Tri-ang doll's pram with metal body and plastic and fabric hood, 1960's. £25

1930's German wickerwork pram with alloy wheel arches and bumpers. £60

Silver Cross 1930's twin hood doll's pram with metal and wood body and leatherette and fabric hood. £50

1950's Royal' pram with plywood body. £35

1950's doll's pram with tin body and fabric hood. £30

(Min Lewis)

PURSES & HANDBAGS

Apart from any natural deterioration resulting from the passage of time, an attack of moths or storage in a damp place, evening bags and purses are generally found to be in fair condition; used mainly on special occasions they were rarely subjected to the rigors of everyday use.

The body of the pouch was produced in a number of materials including leather, beadwork, tapestry, embroidered silks and a chain mail of gold, silver or steel links. The clasps, and mounts too, were sometimes made of precious metals inset with gem-stones, gilt, silver or silver filigree but more commonly of tortoiseshell.

All types of old handbags are now being appreciated for their 'period' styling and this includes handbags produced up until the 50's and, in cases like the Cartier, to the present day.

A fine late 19th century beadwork purse with plated mounts. £22

String crochet bag with metal Art Nouveau fittings. £15

Black pigskin handbag with metal clasp, circa 1940. £15

Edwardian snakeskin clutch bag with silver mounts. £100

A 19th century beadwork and mother-of-pearl button decorated purse. £7

Edwardian brown leather bag with brass fittings. £8

A 9ct. gold mesh evening bag, by S. Blanckensee & Son Ltd., Birmingham 1838. (Lawrence Fine Art) £605

Early 19th century Palais Royale purse, 6½in. wide. £648

A Victorian floral beaded bag with sterling top, made in Greece, 10in. long. £33

(Paul G. Sheppard)

A small 1930's leather purse with brass fastener. £1

Mid 18th century Louis XV gold mounted black leather purse from the collection of Madame de Pompadour, 11cm. £1,261

A small soft leather purse decorated with fleurs de lys and with a fake sovereign clasp. £6

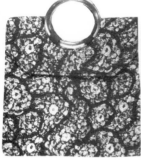

1940's floral fabric hand-bag with silk lining. £5

Pigskin bag with fitted compartment by Davis, Picca-dilly. £12

A 20th century French hall-marked 18ct. gold mesh evening bag, 192.8gr. (Robt. W. Skinner Inc.) £1,068

Art Nouveau sterling silver mesh purse with matching belt hook. (Robt. W. Skinner Inc.) £75

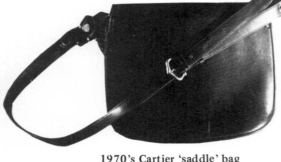

1970's Cartier 'saddle' bag with gold plated fittings. £150

Ojibwa beaded bandolier bag with floral motif, 35in. long. (Robt. W. Skinner Inc.) £255

Plains beaded buckskin tipi bag, 20 x 13in. (Robt. W. Skinner Inc.) £600

An Art Deco suede evening bag encased in a mesh of pearls with an onyx and diamond set frame. (Phillips) £3,500
(Paul G. Sheppard)

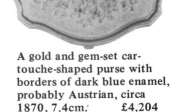

A gold and gem-set car-touche-shaped purse with borders of dark blue enamel, probably Austrian, circa 1870, 7.4cm. £4,204

RAILWAYANA

It would seem that the fascination for all aspects of railway transport has been with us since the first locomotive, Trevithicks Tram Engine, hauled a train of trucks at Merthyr Tydfil in 1804.

The first public railway, Stockton & Darlington, opened on 27th September 1825, to be followed by the Liverpool & Manchester on 15th September 1830.

The first broad gauge engine, the 'North Star', was built at Newcastle upon Tyne for overseas railway but was sold to G.W.R. in 1836 — the first broad gauge railway opened on 4th June 1838.

The field is vast, for absolutely everything connected with the railway is collectible, from whole trains to station signs, lamps, clocks, tickets and even the locks of the lavatory doors.

Cast iron railway sign 'Weight in train'. £20

Cast iron sign for Sellafield.   £80

An original Pullman transfer from the Orient Express.   £32

British Rail sign 'Caution, to be shunted with care'.   £75

An enamel on tin sign 'Omnibuses Stop Here'.   £15

Cast brass steam engine plate 'W. G. Bagnall Ltd.'   £60

(Steamtown Railway Museum)

British Rail tin for explosive fog signal.   £3

Railway porter's hat in mint condition.   £4

British Rail galvanised tin guard's lamp.   £30

British Rail all brass windproof lamp. £20

British Rail 'Sway Gauge' in original box.   £30

Late 19th century brass train whistle.   £45

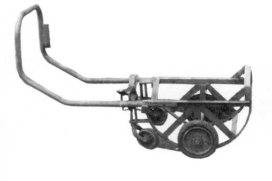

British Rail signal indicator.   £30

British Rail porter's trolley.   £15

British Rail tie with insignia 'Forward'.   £4

(Steamtown Railway Museum)

Lancashire & Yorkshire Railway original transfer. £30

British Rail steel ticket clipper. £10

Original British Rail transfer. £25

British Rail guard's hat. £8

Original transfer from the London Midland and Scottish Railway Co. £28

N.E.R. painted metal string tin. £12

A fine large British Rail metal lamp with brass fittings. £40

Cast metal sign 'Beware of Trains'. £20

Painted metal tail-light with red glass shade. £18

(Steamtown Railway Museum)

RAILWAYANA

Cast iron railway plate 'Max Speed 45 m.p.h.'.
£30

British Rail sign 'Spring Relieving Screws'.
£25

Child's white china potty, all part of British Rail's Sleeper Service. £4

Great Western Railway, envelope label. 25p

G.W.R. label for 'Passenger Rated Traffic'. 50p

British Rail employee's peaked hat bearing the B.R. logo. £5

G.W.R. wagon label for perishables. 50p

'Andrew Barclay Sons & Co., Kilmarnock, 1942', original cast brass train plate. £85

Six G.W.R. luggage labels. £3

G.W.R. Parcels Way Bill, Mitcheldean to Hereford, 1867. £1

L.M. & S.R. wagon label 'Perishable'. 50p

(Steamtown Railway Museum)

RAILWAY POSTCARDS

Now that the recent passion for Railwayana has sent the price of all appliances, fixtures and fittings, indeed all the apparatus of railway transport to such a very high level, collectors are turning their attention towards ephemera.

Around 1900, there were over two hundred companies operational throughout the giant networks of the land and they all issued Official Postcards. These cards are keenly collected today and the price range is wide. Official view cards range from 50p. to £5, Locomotive £1 to £5, Stations £3 to £15, Map Cards £8 to £35 and poster type cards can fetch as much as £100 depending upon the condition, subject matter and the company of issue.

It is worth looking out for some of the better official cards such as Barry, Caledonian, Callander & Oban, Cambrian, Cheshire Lines, London Chatham & Dover, London & South Western and Midland & Great Northern.

Many independent postcard companies published individual cards and sets of cards depicting rolling stock, steamers and railway buildings. Some of these are well executed, artist drawn cards and range in price from £1 to £20 according to the scarcity of the subject. Trains usually fetch around £2 and transport (buses etc.) up to £20

Many local publishers issued, in fairly limited numbers, the real photo type cards depicting various aspects of railway business and events; some illustrated railway disasters. Good examples of these cards may fetch upwards of £50 each. There is a shortage of material in this area and good examples are usually snapped up as soon as they come on the market. The most desirable real photo cards should be well animated with lots of activity and detail.

LNWR real photo postcard of rear of Brownhills route bus BM 2598 with close-up of conductor.   £12

LNW Railway real photo postcard of railway guard outside his van.   £9

(Paul G. Sheppard)

HOLYHEAD STATION, DEPARTURE OF BOAT EXPRESS
(L. & N.W. RAILWAY.)

Holyhead Station L & NW Railway official postcard showing interior of station and departure of boat express; 'L & NW is noted for punctuality, speed, smooth riding and dustless tracks, safety and comfort', on reverse.
£10

LNWR Additional series January 1905, Gantry signals at Rugby.   £3.50

Swiss printed postcard, A. Trub & Co., of the Caledonian Railway Co's. Central Station Hotel in Glasgow.   £6

LNWR Turbine steamship 'Princess Maud', Stranraer & Larne Service, real photo post-card.   £4

The 'Micheline', the first train on pneumatic tyres, card advertising that a 'Micheline' will arrive at Wolverhampton LMS Station on Sunday 10th April, issued by Micheline Tyre Co. Ltd., Stoke on Trent.   £5

(Paul G. Sheppard)

GWR S.S. St. Patrick steamship, Weymouth-Channel Islands Service, real photo postcard.
£4

LNWR multi-view 'miscellaneous' postcard, locomotives, landing stage and station. £5

R. Tuck's 'Wide Wide World Famous Expresses', postcard No. 9329 'Orient Express', Paris to Constantinople. £3

LNWR official postcard 1905 'A load of fish empties', Haydon Square Station. £9

An LMS Holiday Caravan, postally used in 1937, interesting photographic postcard. £3.50

(Paul G. Sheppard)

LNWR 'Three horse brake bus, Lime St. Station and Landing Stage Liverpool', official postcard 1905.   £15

Real photo postcard of team of railway workmen building barriers.   £4

Tuck's 'Famous Expresses' Series postcard No. 9662 GNR 'Flying Scotsman'. (Raphael Tuck's oilette).   £3

Southern Railway Paddle Steamer 'Shanklin', real photo postcard.   £3

Real photographic postcard showing three LNW Railway buses with conductors, garage staff and drivers of Brownhills, Chase Terrace and Hednesford routes.   £30

(Paul G. Sheppard)

L & NW Railway official postcard, Additional Series January 1905, 'Single Horse Family Omnibus'.   £18

Real photo postcard No. H76 by W. Shaw Burslem 'Interior of Stoke Station'.   £9

LNWR official postcard, four cylinder compound express goods engine, coupled wheels, built in 1903.   £3

The Star Series, painted photo, Paddington Station, London GWR.   £4

'A load of hops' official LNWR postcard, horse-drawn transport.   £10

(Paul G. Sheppard)

LNWR official postcard 1905, Parcel Collecting Van, 'A train leaves Euston every night for the North so that delivery next morning is assured'. £12

LNWR official postcard 'Their Majesties Royal Saloons, built 1903'. £2

Real photo postcard LNWR Motor bus No. 2598 'on route to Norton Canes' £25

LNWR official postcard 'Six wheels coupled side tank passenger loco, built 1896'. £3

LNWR McCorquodale postcard S.S. Scotia running between England and Ireland, colour. £3

LNWR official postcard 1905, 'Pair Horse Family Omnibus with rubber tyres'. £14

'Push n' pull', Jane Spooner locomotive at Festiniog. £2

Station approach Ealing, Wyndhorn Series No. 7077, postally used in 1904, GWR signs in distance, hand-tinted printed photocard. £2

(Paul G. Sheppard)

RATTLES

Since the beginning of time is has been a tradition to present a young child with a rattle of sorts. Examples exist from the simplest dried gourd with rattling seeds to the most elegant of Georgian rattles crafted by leading silversmiths and decorated with coral. Coral rattles were the most highly prized for the substance was thought to contain medicinal properties beneficial to the child.

As a rule, Georgian rattles are plain and Victorian rattles fussier; having bunnies, elves and other sentimental characters introduced into their design.

One of the most attractive designs was created for the older child. It is known as a poupard and consists of a doll's head and body placed upon an ivory stick incorporating a whistle. When the stick is turned a small musical box within the body of the doll plays a melody.

Rattles of ivory or wood and even the celluloid Art Nouveau type are less expensive and will form the foundation of an interesting collection.

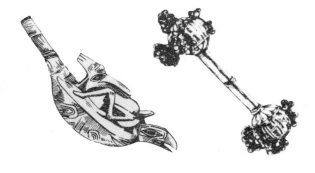 

Georgian silver baby's rattle and comforter, maker's mark GU on whistle mouthpiece, Sheffield, 1818, 5in. long. £125

North American Indian carved wood rattle, 1ft. long. £3,400

17th century child's rattle bearing the Edinburgh date letter for 1681. £1,250

An Edwardian plated baby's rattle. £4

Sterling silver baby rattle with sliding monkey, Birmingham, circa 1905, 6½in. long. £316

1960's plastic rabbit rattle. 30p

Victorian silver rattle with ivory teether and whistle. £90

A 20th century baby's plated rattle. £10

ROBOTS

Toyland was first invaded by robots in the 1950's and, as you might have guessed, over 90% were made in Japan.

These colourful tinplate mechanical men and other related space toys with their numerous battery operated talents were an immediate success. They were able to perform hitherto undreamed of feats, many combining more than one action i.e., walking, talking, turning, shooting, flashing lights while rotating at a dizzying speed and so on.

Demand was high in the 1960's and the manufacturers entered a 'golden age' of production. In 1970 however, production of the well-loved tinplate models was abandoned in favour of the use of plastics but these were not nearly as pleasing, nor as popular.

As an indication of the current interest in collecting robots of the 50's and 60's, note that Mr. Atomic Robot, made in the early 1960's, is now valued at over £400.

1960's Japanese flying saucer with robot operator. £15-£20

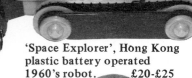

'Space Explorer', Hong Kong plastic battery operated 1960's robot. £20-£25

1960's Japanese space explorer vehicle with robot operator. £15-£20

'Dino Robot', 1970, Japanese tin and plastic robot whose head opens to reveal a dinosaur's head. £80-£100

Japanese made 1960's flying saucer, X15, complete with robot operator. £15-£20

'Last in Space Robot', 1970 American, plastic battery operated robot. £60-£80

'Planet Robot', 1960's Japanese plastic. £40-£60

'Astronaut', Japanese 1960, battery operated robot. £40-£60

(Andrew Clark)

ROMANTIC POSTCARDS

Collectors of postcards really are spoiled for choice with themes too numerous to be listed here. None however, seems more popular than the cards depicting romantic scenes. These have been popular ever since the main period of their production which was during the first World War.

Anyone who has ever owned a few romantic cards will confirm that there is always a great reluctance to part with them.

Apart from ephemera collections they find their way into all sorts of general collections and none is more favoured than examples from the Art Nouveau and Art Deco periods.

Continental cards of the early periods tend to be very colourful and these can be collected as a category and further split into sub division of the many themes illustrated such as 'Kissing', 'Classical', 'Comic', 'Satirical', etc.

Cards of good artistic merit and fine examples of chromolitho are always popular.

E.M.M. series 'Forget-Me-Not', by Toby 1919. £2.60

'The Last Waltz', by M. Munk, romantic dancing. £2.75

'Ein kub in ahren', (A kiss on the ear), by M. A. Lerisch, kissing romance. £3.25

'Happy Dreamers', a Degi postcard, romance. £2

Heckscher series 'The Joys of Spring', A. von Riesen. £2.75

'The flame of love' by J. Hansen, kissing. £4

(Paul G. Sheppard)

G.K.V. Romantic series, 'Please Forgive Me', by E. Lang. £2.50

Serenade 'Leibesklange', Asco card. £1.50

'After Dinner Dessert', by A. Jongh, sensual romance. £4

Hermann Wolff series 'As Evening Dies', by R. Borrmeister 1918. £3

'Goodbye Again', MMB series by Kunstler, romance. £2

Asco 'Danish Art' series, 'The Vow' by A. Bjordk. £3

'Say Yes', by Prof. E. Doubet, E.M.M. series. £3.25

'Friede' (Peaceful), by Hans R. Schutze, statue and swans. 60p

(Paul G. Sheppard)

ROYAL POSTCARDS

Cards of Queen Victoria and King Edward VIII are in demand, as are some of the lesser known royal families. Mourning cards fetch good prices and in particular the card produced by Faulkners within fifteen hours of the death of Queen Victoria. This card will fetch upwards of £15.

Foreign royalty cards are well liked with Russian royalty probably leading the field in popularity and price.

Woven silk portraits can obtain as much as £30 each and, even quite recently produced cards such as that issued by the P.O. for the wedding of H.R.H. Princess Anne and Captain Mark Phillips (P.H.Q.3) is in demand at £8 or more.

The range is vast and collectors are keen enough to have formed their own society. The Royalty Postcard Collectors Club is based at Kidderminster.

Naval Review at Spithead 1937 by H.M. King George VI, multi-view card by Wright & Logan, Southsea, showing 15 named naval warships. £5

Souvenir of The Silver Jubilee of their Most Gracious Majesties 1910-35, Excel Series real photo postcard. £4

King Edward VII mourning card, Faulkner Series No. 942. £3

Investiture of H.R.H. The Prince of Wales, Caernarvon 1911, Williams real photo postcard. £3

Valentines postcard (colour) No. XT53R, H.R.H. Prince Charles Philip Arthur George, Prince of Wales, Earl of Chester, Duke of Cornwall, Duke of Rothesay, Earl of Carrick, created Prince of Wales and Earl of Chester 26th July 1958. £3

T.R.H. The Duke and Duchess of York with Princess Elizabeth, portrait by Marcus Adams. Raphael Tuck's Royal Portrait Series 3976A. Princess Elizabeth born 21st April 1926, real photo postcard. £2

(Paul G. Sheppard)

Her Majesty The Queen, H.M. Queen Mary crowned June 22nd 1911. Raphael Tuck's Royal Portrait Series No. 3936F, real photo postcard. £1.50

Their Majesties King George V & Queen Mary, Rotary Series No. 9577R¹, real photo postcard. £1.75

H.R.H. Princess Elizabeth of York, R. Tuck's Royal Portrait Series 3948, from a portrait by Marcus Adams. £2.50

H.M. Queen Alexandra, Rotary Opalette Series, patented 1908, real photo postcard. £2

H.R.H. The Prince of Wales at Caernarvon Castle, published by Her Majesty's Printers Eyre & Spottiswoode Ltd., Portsmouth. £2

H.R.H. The Duchess of York & Princess Elizabeth, R. Tuck's Royal Portrait Series No. 3976B, from a portrait by Marcus Adams. £1.75

H.R.H. The Prince of Wales, Rotary Series No. 500C, real photo postcard. £1.50

Lady Curzon, Rapid Photo Co. Series No. 1191, real photo postcard, 1904. £2

H.R.H. The Duke of Kent, Raphael Tucks's Royal Portrait Series No. GM1. £2.50

(Paul G. Sheppard)

His Majesty King George
VI, Valentine's Series K
8, Bertram Park photo.
£1.75

Lady Curzon in Durbar Dress,
F.H.L. Series No. 1891, printed photo.   £1.50

H.R.H. Prince Albert, Rotary
Series No. 37K, real photo
postcard. Message on back
reads 'How do you like
Prince Albert's quiff?'.   £3

H.R.H. Princess Marina of
Greece who became H.R.H.
The Duchess of Kent, R.
Tuck's Royal Portrait
Series No. GM2, real photo
postcard.   £2.50

Caricature of Prince
Charles, Dervish Paris
Series No. 3. Modern
French, nice card.   £1

H.M. King George V,
Rotary Series No. 40,
real photo postcard.
£1.50

H.M. Queen Elizabeth,
Beagles Series No. 280,
real photo postcard.
£1.75

H.M. Queen Victoria,
Rotary real photo post-
card, undivided back, no
Series No.   £8

The Queen of Spain, Prin-
cess Ena of Battenberg,
Rotary Series No. 281F,
real photo postcard. £4

(Paul G. Sheppard)

H.R.H. The Duchess of York, Elizabeth Angela Marguerite Bowes-Lyon, born in 1900, photo Hay Wrightson real photo postcard. £2

H.R.H. Prince Edward of Wales, Rotary real photo postcard, Series No. 6B, 1904. £3.50

Her Majesty Queen Elizabeth II, Raphael Tuck Series No. DW2, 1953.£2

Their Majesties The King & Queen. Raphael Tuck's, Series No. 540S portrait by D. Wilding, real photo postcard. £2

Her Majesty Queen Elizabeth II, John Hinde original postcard No. 2/1001. £1

The Gun Carriage entering Paddington Station, King Edward VII's death, photo by Underwood & Underwood. £1.40

H.R.H. The Princess of Wales. Rotary real photo postcard. Postally used May 1904. £2.50

Lying in State of the late King Edward VII. Rotary Series No. 9476, real photo postcard. £1.75

National Relief Fund card, Treasurer H.R.H. The Prince of Wales, Earl Kitchener, Patriotic postcard 1st Series. £1

(Paul G. Sheppard)

To commemorate the visit to Wolverhampton of H.M. Queen Elizabeth II, 24th May 1962, colour, portrait by Pietro Annigoni. £3

H.M. King Edward VII, by Rotophot Series No. 7380, real photo postcard. £2.50

H.M. Alexandra 'The Queen Mother', Beagles Series No. 855A, real photo postcard. £1.50

H.R.H. Princess Mary, Viscountess Lascelles with her sons George & Gerald. Photo by Speaight, London, Beagles Series No. 528C. £2.50

H.M. The Queen at Balmoral with corgi's, photo by Lichfield, published by Whiteholme, Dundee, No. 254, 1978. £1.25

The Duchess of Sutherland and Daughter, Rotary postcard Series No. 901, real photo. £3

H.M. King Edward VII, Philco Series No. 3294 E, real photo postcard. £1.50

The Princess Elizabeth, Beagles Series No. 26C, real photo postcard. £2

National Relief Fund, H.R.H. The Prince of Wales. £1

(Paul G. Sheppard)

H.M. Queen Mary, Valentines XL Series, real photo postcard. £1.50

King & Queen of Spain and Infant Prince. Rotary Series real photo postcard. £3

H.M. Queen Alexandra, Beagles Series No. 1384, real photo postcard. £2

'Four Generations', Her Late Majesty Queen Victoria, His Late Majesty King Edward VII, H.M. King George V, Duke of Cornwall & Rothesay, Beagles Series No. 396, real photo postcard. £3

Queen Alexandra's letter to the Nation May 10th 1910, Faulkner Series postcard. £2

'A Joyous Reunion', The Duke & Duchess of York with baby Princess Elizabeth, Beagles Series No. 248P, real photo postcard. £1.75

The Hon. George Henry Hubert Lascelles, H.R.H. Princess Mary's little son, Beagles Series No. 525A, real photo postcard. £1.75

The King & Queen of Portugal, Rotary Series No. 100A, real photo postcard. £4

H.M. King Edward VII, Rapid Photo Series No. 4483, real photo postcard. £1.75

(Paul G. Sheppard)

Marchioness of Headfort, Philco Series No. 3005F, real photo.   £2.50

Her Late Majesty Queen Victoria, Rotary Series No. 10, real photo postcard.£7

H.R.H. Princess Mary 'Latest Portrait', Beagles Series No. 1264, Ernest Brooks photo.   £1.50

'Four Generations', Rotary Series No. 7111F, real photo postcard.   £3

King Edward VII in memoriam card, Faulkner Series No. 943.   £3

King George & Queen Mary & H.R.H. Princess Mary, 'happy moments with the little ones', Beagles Series No. 1016C, real photo postcard.   £2

Z. M. Boudewijn I, King of Belgium, printed photo card.   £3.50

Prince Oscar of Sweden and Princess Margaret of Connaught, Rotary Series No. 252C, real photo postcard.   £4

H.R.H. Princess Mary, Rotary Series No. 486A.   £1.50

(Paul G. Sheppard)

RUGS

Traditionally, in the east, Oriental carpets have always performed a dual role:
Firstly, as furnishings they have been used not only as floor coverings but also wall hangings, divan covers, and in decoration generally. In Turkey and Iran in particular they satisfy an aesthetic need which, in the west, paintings have fulfilled.
Secondly, in countries where governments and currencies were unstable they performed the function which stocks and shares perform here — a reserve of wealth to fall back upon in bad times.
As an investment in present day Europe and America they similarly should fill both roles — for those who take household furnishings seriously they may combine profit and pleasure.
Remember that, unlike paintings, the value of a rug is more in proportion to its size and type. This is because the intrinsic value of a rug depends upon months or even years of hand knotting.

A tufted wool rug designed by Marion Dorn, 1930's, 195 x 140cm.   £825

Kazakh prayer rug with central ivory panel, 6ft. 5in. x 3ft.9in.   £528

A Modernist rug in shades of brown and beige, 231 x 173cm.   £297

Early 20th century Kirman rug, 6ft.8in. x 4ft.4½in. (Robt. W. Skinner Inc.)   £325

Early 20th century American calico cat hooked rug, 15½ x 32in. (Robt. W. Skinner Inc.)   £224

A Hamadan rug with dark blue field, second quarter 20th century, 4ft. x 6ft. 8in. (Robt. W. Skinner Inc.)   £310

Late 19th century Anatolian Village rug with ivory field, 3ft.11in. x 2ft.10in. (Robt. W. Skinner Inc.) £586

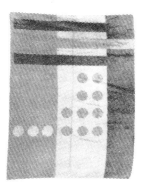

An Art Deco hand-made tufted wool carpet by Terence Prentis, 363 x 263cm. (Christie's) £1,080

Early 20th century Persian Kelim rug, 10ft.3in. x 5ft. 3in. (Robt. W. Skinner Inc.) £216

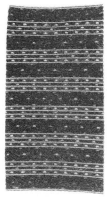

Turkman Gelim, madder ground with white and brown bands, 5ft.10in. x 4ft.11in., circa 1880. £418

Early 20th century Persian village rug, 6ft.2in. x 4ft. 6in. (Robt. W. Skinner Inc.) £342

A Shiraz rug, the blue-black field woven with a blue lozenge pole medallion, 5ft. 11in. x 4ft.5in. (Lawrence Fine Art) £462

20th century Trans-Caucasian rug, the abrashed dark blue field featuring three Lesghi stars. (Robt. W. Skinner Inc.) £123

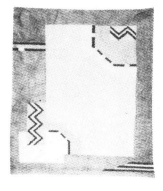

A Modernist carpet, 327 x 267cm., 1930's. £715

Late 19th century shirred rug, New England, 2ft.11in. x 4ft.4in. (Robt. W. Skinner Inc.) £800

SCISSORS

Scissors at first took the form of sheep shears with no central pivot, the cutting action being performed by compressing together the naturally sprung open arms.

Examples found in mediaeval graves are pivoted, but have finger loops set centrally on the arms. It wasn't until the 18th century that the finger loops generally became set on the outside edge of the arms much in the style of modern scissors.

As with many tools, scissors have been adapted for the specific tasks demanded from an individual trade or need and a fascinating collection can be built up of just grape scissors or those for surgeons, hairdressers or dressmakers.

Most 19th century examples found today were made in Sheffield and few made today can compete with them for quality.

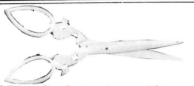

Pair of Edwardian bone scissors with peacock handles, circa 1910.   £3

A pair of early 20th century steel folding scissors, 3½in. long.   £4

A pair of French silver gilt grape scissors, by Alexandre Lefranc, Paris, 1819-38, 6oz. 7dwt. (Christie's)   £248

19th century steel wick trimmers.   £8

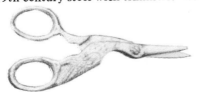

Pair of miniature scissors, 1¾in. long. £2.50

A large pair of shears for cutting sheet metal, 18in. long.   £17

An unusual pair of 19th century steel scissors.   £6

Tang silver gilt scissors, 7½in. long. £8,000

Combination scissors incorporating a file, screwdriver, wire cutters, glass cutter and glass snapper, 4in. long.   £5

Late 18th. century pair of Spanish engraved steel tailor's shears, dated 1791, 14in. long. £495

(Paul G. Sheppard)

SEWING ITEMS

Sewing tables and workboxes in papier mache or richly polished woods, sewing chairs with expertly executed needlework covers, even some rare sewing machines all have the potential to reach high prices these days. The baskets of bits and bobs however, are often overlooked and they may provide a rich source of interest to the really keen collector.

Apart from their aesthetic appeal as props in a room already kitted out with some of the choice pieces already mentioned, many of the tools are still usable and, in fact, some do a better job than their modern counterparts. A little cased set, called a lady's companion, usually contains a tool for every need and, depending on the quality and presentation, can be worth around £10 to £15. Individually, odd tools rarely cost more than a pound or two, early cotton reels — not much more, though some early paper wrapped or card mounted goods with names and dates on the packaging may be worth a bit more.

Look out for bobbin or reel stands as these are now fetching keen prices at auction.

Crewel needles by E. J. Arnold, Leeds.   25p

19th century weaver's bone shuttle.   £1

'Newey's hooks and eyes 'By Appointment to Her Majesty Queen Mary'. £3

Victorian walnut bobbin stand with pin cushion top. (Reeds Rains) £125

Dorcas Dressmaker's Steel Pins tin.   £1

Edwardian fabric sewing basket.   £5

Sewing glasses case of leather with plated fittings and clip for attaching to waist chain.   £5

An early 19th century oak and rosewood reel stand, 13in. high.   £286

Late 19th century embroidery stilletto with mother-of-pearl handle.   £1

(Paul G. Sheppard)

335

SEWING ITEMS

Victorian bone needle case and holder, 3in. long. £4

Six wooden cotton reels. £3

Sharps egg-eyed best quality needles. 25p

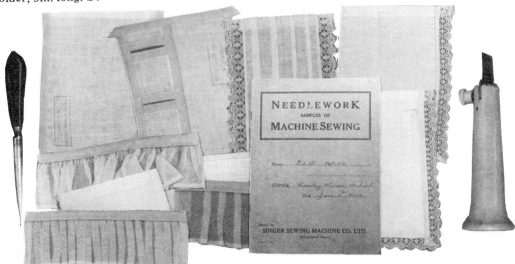

Victorian embroidery stilletto with ebony handle. £1

Needlework samples of Machine Sewing, school book belonging to Edith Webb 1936, issued by Singer Sewing Machine Co. Ltd. £16

1960's plastic handled buttonhole cutter. 75p

John Lewis spun silk mending thread. 25p

Paragon Snap Fasteners card. 50p

Wooden sewing mushroom. £1

(Paul G. Sheppard)

SHOP FRONTS

Collectors who have always taken a keen interest in material of a social or historical value have in recent years been turning their attention to the old photographs which can provide a most pictorially stimulating and fascinating glimpse into the daily life of the times.

This applies particularly to the busy studies of old shop fronts. In many of these lovely old photographs we can see at a glance exactly the type of goods held in stock together with fine examples of contemporary advertising and in those featuring people we may observe the fashions of the day.

The best examples should be well photographed and will include lots of animation showing people, animals or transport, and above all, in order to fetch the very best price the shot should have been taken at a location which has been identified. A good photograph will usually obtain a higher price when sold in its place of origin.

L. Tydeman, Pork Butcher, Ham & Bacon Curer, actual photograph,
size 158 x 206mm., circa 1875, Stowmarket.   £55

(Paul G. Sheppard)

Hatton & Co. decorated watchmaker's shop and antique shop in Commercial
St., Hereford, 1918, and Victory Celebrations, real photograph.   £10

Mitchell 'Florist and Fruiterer' at Fore Street, Edmonton, real photograph. £7

(Tim Ward)

An interesting sweet shop front with proud owner, real photograph, circa 1908.   £7

Colesworthy staff pose outside their clothes and shoe shop, circa 1908, real photograph.   £6.50

(Tim Ward)

Mary's Tea Shop, Ashford, Middlesex, 'Tea & Jam'. £5

Confectionary shop in Hall Lane, Walsall, with proud manageress and assistant. £6.50

Patisserie Bruxelloise, Belgium, proprietor Emile Dassy, 'Cakes and Teas', English spoken. £3

L. Tydeman, Family Butcher, with fine display of meat, actual photograph, size 160 x 205mm., circa 1870, Stowmarket. £65

(Paul G. Sheppard)

Millinery, Lingerie and Hose Shop in Perth, Scotland, 1920's photograph.
£7.50

Osman's General Stores, Port Said, 'The house that gives you a square deal — try one today'.
£12

Garsides, Baker and Confectionary Shop, with interesting enamel signs.   £9

A. R. Bennett, General Stores, Gloucester Street, photographic.   £7.50

The Woolworth Building, Piccadilly, Manchester.   £6

(Paul G. Sheppard)

Hunters' Tea Stores with a fine display of general produce, real photograph, circa 1910.   £8

Hardick Bros., Ironmongers, Cutlers and Sanitary Engineeers, real photograph, circa 1910.   £9

(Tim Ward)

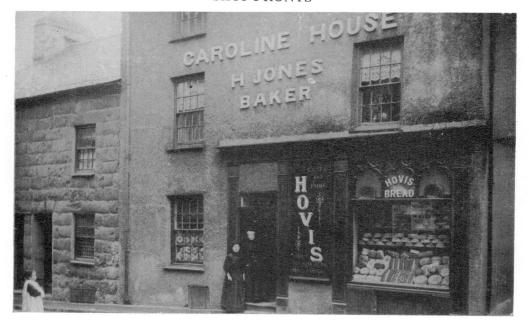

H. Jones Baker, with good Hovis sign and fine display of bread.   £5

International Stores, Newent, real photograph of staff and delivery motor-
cycle, circa 1920.   £20

(Tim Ward)

SIGNS

All types of old advertising signs are now appreciated to an extent which would bring smiles of amused pride to the faces of the old signwriters who made them.

Unfortunately, most artists of merit consider it beneath them to devote their talents to such commercial subjects, which is a great pity, considering that such notables as Toulouse Lautrec and Alphonse Mucha regarded signs and playbills as worthy fields for their not inconsiderable talents.

There was a time when enamel advertising signs could be found pinned to every available wall surface. With the revival of interest, good signs can now rarely be begged from the demolition men but some excellent work is still to be found on the market.

The art of designing a good sign lay in the ability of the artist to create a composition which would be visually arresting from a distance, even though it hung twenty feet in the air, and which was painstakingly researched and attractively rendered.

'Flea Circus' stained glass window, circa 1900, 5ft. long. (Robt. W. Skinner Inc.)
£387

A leaded glass pharmacy sign, America, 64½in. wide. (Robt. W. Skinner Inc.)
£484

Ogdens St. Julien Tobacco, enamel sign showing two blends of tobacco against green brick background, 18 x 60in., circa 1900.
£100

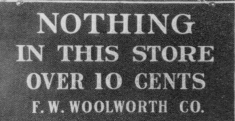

19th century gilt copper apothecary's sign. (Bonham's)
£200

Reverse on glass Woolworth's sign, circa 1900, 20 x 36in. (Robt. W. Skinner Inc.)
£368

Late 19th century wood advertising trade sign. (Robt. W. Skinner Inc.)
£930

Essolube enamel sign. £25

A painted metal roadsign
'Cattle'. £10

Morse's Distemper, enamel
sign by Hassall, 60 x 40in.
£385

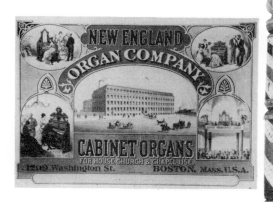

'New England Organ Company'
advertising sign, 24 x 34in.
(Robt. W. Skinner Inc.)
£348

'August Wolf Milling' advertising sign, circa 1890, 21½
x 31½in. (Robt. W. Skinner
Inc.) £387

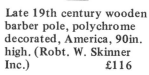

Late 19th century wooden
barber pole, polychrome
decorated, America, 90in.
high. (Robt. W. Skinner
Inc.) £116

'Selo Film' enamel sign in
yellow, red and black, 14in.
wide. £200

19th century cast iron police
station sign. £38

Enamel newspaper sign
'Hush!! He's Busy'. £75

RAC Parking Road enamel
sign. £7

Garage sign for 'Air' with
illuminated globe. £20

A Mayer Prattware plaque
made for Huntley &
Palmer's. £850

A very large enamel sign 'Player's Bachelor
Tipped', 8ft. long. £50

SPEED NOT TO EXCEED 15 MILES PER HOUR

WEST MALVERN RD.

Painted alloy roadsign.
£8

Cast iron sign 'Speed not to exceed 15 miles
per hour'. £10

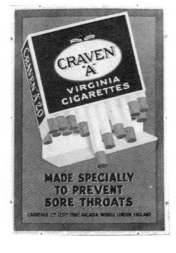

An enamel sign for Phillips
Bicycles. £45

Craven 'A' Virginia cigarettes.
£45

A solid slate advertising sign
'Bass in Bottle, 12in. wide.
(Christopher Sykes) £87

SIGNED PHOTOGRAPHS

Collecting signed photographs on a limited budget is still possible and may even prove to be a profitable experience.

A new collector would be well advised to start at the lower end of the market, buying and selling in a comparitively safe area until he has made a few contacts, acquired some knowledge of the subject and learned to identify the mass produced machine signed copies circulating within the market. Many stars of the early cinema, music hall performers, even some of yesterdays' pop idols signed photographs which now change hands at between £1 and £10. This is an interesting area and valuable experience may be gained before moving up into a league where a fine photograph of Tchaikovsky, signed and inscribed by the composer, will fetch over £1,000.

'Sincerely Yours, Hetty King, 1/7/07', male impersonator.   £30

'To Madge, Cheers! Benny Hill'.   £2

'My Best Wishes to you, Gertrude Lawrence'. £8

'Dennis Eadie'.   £2.20

'To Paul, I only do 'me'', Bernard Hill'.   75p

'Geo. Robey', Mr & Mrs G. Robey and children. £2.75

(Paul G. Sheppard)

'Sincerely yours Agnes Ayres'.   £4

'To Irene, Sincerely Rex Ramon, 1946'.
£8

'Faithfully yours Clark Gable'. (Facsimile)
£3

'All Good Wishes, Billy & Dolly'.   £7

(Paul G. Sheppard),

Mary Pickford in 'Rosita'.
£7

'With best wishes Ben Lyon'.   £7

'With Good Wishes, From Zona Vevey,
1916'.   £4

'To Miss Irene Jones, With kindest regards,
Sincerely Lee Donn, Sept. 11th, 1937'. £6

(Paul G. Sheppard)

SIGNED PHOTOGRAPHS

'Yours very truly, Herbert Cave'.   50p

'Sybil Thorndike'.   £4.25

'Mirthfully Yours, Tommy Gover', 1924, 'Ginger the Clown'.   £8

'Yours sincerely, Violet Vanbrugh'.   £2.50

'Anton Lang', Prologus.   £2.50

'To Madge, Sincerely Tessie O'Shea'.   £3.50

'Marie Studholme, 1908', Miss Hook of Holland.   £2.50

'Oscar Asche'. £3.25

(Paul G. Sheppard)

Celia Franca as 'Myrtha, Queen of the Willis Giselle'.   £14

SIGNED PHOTOGRAPHS

'Lily Brayton'.   £2

'Yours sincerely, Thomas E. A. Quinney'.   50p

'Vesta Tilley', male impersonator.   £6

Greta Gynt, Norwegian leading lady.   £3

'Best Wishes, Guy Mitchell'.   £1

'Yours sincerely, Billie Burke'.   £3.25

Alexis Rassine in 'Le Lac des Cygnes Pas de Trois' (Act III).   £8

'Tommy Trinder'. £3

(Paul G. Sheppard)

'Yours sincerely, Ada Reeve'.   £3

'Sincerely Yours Dolly Hylton'.   £4

'Nelson Eddy', signed photograph together with original envelope.   £15

'To Irene Jones, My best wishes, Ben Lyon, Bebe Daniels'.   £12

'With My Kind Regards, Max Erard, 1916'.   £4

(Paul G. Sheppard)

SIGNED PHOTOGRAPHS

'Cyril Maude', signed Miniature Post Card.
£2

'To Miss Rene Jones, Best Wishes from Florie Forde, 1936'. £10

'Sincerely Jack Pickford'.
£6

'Henry Ainley', signed Midget Post Card.
£2

'Good Wishes, The 5 Sherry Brothers, April 1935'. £15

'Joan Morgan'. £3

(Paul G. Sheppard)

SIGNED PHOTOGRAPHS

'Alice Delefrie'. £2.50

'Yours Carl Brisson'.
£5

'Sincerely Yours, Rene Ray'.
£3

'Sincerely Yours, Camille
Clifford', the original
Gibson Girl.   £4

'Elenore'.   £1

'Phyllis Dare'.   £2.50

'Mabel Love', 1908. £2.50

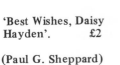

'Best Wishes, Daisy
Hayden'.   £2

(Paul G. Sheppard)

'Sincerely, Zena Dare', as
Victoria Siddons in 'The
Gay Gordons'.   £2.50

354

SIGNED PHOTOGRAPHS

'Fay Compton'. £3

'To Marge, Best Wishes, Chico Marx'.   £8

'Best Wishes, Sonia Holm'.   30p

'Yours sincerely Owen Nares'.   £4

'Tommy Steele'.   £1

'Good Wishes, Lilian Braithwaite'.   £2.25

'Shirley Temple'.   35p

'Sincerely, Gladys Arch-butt', and 'Sincerely Yours, George Mudie'.   £4.75

'Merrily Yours, Kitty Hay'.   40p

(Paul G. Sheppard)

355

'Faithfully Yours, G. P. Huntley'. £3.40

'John Mills'. 45p

'To Elizabeth, Love Russ Conway'. £1.80

'Emile Ford'. £4

'Clifford Jones'. £1.25

'Yours truly, Willie Edouin'. £3

'E. Maitland'. £1.50

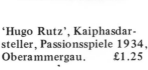
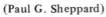

'Hugo Rutz', Kaiphasdar-steller, Passionsspiele 1934, Oberammergau. £1.25

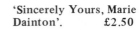

'Sincerely Yours, Marie Dainton'. £2.50

(Paul G. Sheppard)

SODA SIPHONS

The soda-water siphon was invented in 1813 by Charles Plynth who named it 'the portable fountain'. It was activated by depressing a lever which released gas under pressure, forcing the aerated water to be discharged through the siphon tube.

The soda siphon was an immediate success and is still popular today. Many old siphons are still perfectly usable and can be refilled for a nominal charge.

Early siphons were fashioned in attractive shapes and made from blue, green, amber or ruby glass. Coloured glass siphons are more expensive than the clear type.

The 'sparklets' siphon which can be refilled at home using a small gas canister, has also been popular for many years. Early examples are most attractively wire bound and these too come in a variety of shapes and colours and a progression of body materials from glass, to metal then alloy.

Some old glass siphon bottles have company names etched into the body.

An early Sparklets wire-bound soda siphon. £10

Blue glass soda siphon inscribed Job. Wragg Ltd., with acid etching on front, dated 1902.   £12

T. Mason & Sons, Manufacturers of High Class Table Waters, Smethwick, fluted blue glass siphon.   £8

Spaco Ltd. Royal Leamington Spa blue glass soda siphon with silver plated top.   £12

Table siphon by J. Burgess, 12in. tall.   £6

Greenock Apothecaries & Lawsons Ltd. soda siphon, circa 1902.   £6

(Paul G. Sheppard)

357

SOUVENIRS

Although people travelled to a limited degree it was not until about 1880, when trains and paddlesteamers made the journey easier, that people started flocking to the seaside.

Wages and working conditions had improved greatly during the previous decade, and with sea bathing being made respectable, nay beneficial by Victoria, the resorts were packed throughout the summer. Added to this were the daytrippers, all seeking some little momento to take home for their friends, which meant a massive growth in the souvenir business.

Although they had been made on a commercial scale since the opening of the Thames Tunnel in 1843, and given a boost by the Great Exhibition of 1851, it was W. H. Goss, with his little porcelain urns and vases bearing Coats-of-Arms, who really took advantage of the market.

Early 20th century brass caddy spoon with figure handle. £1

A creamware cylindrical mug with loop handle, inscribed George Selby, 1804, 13.5cm. high. (Christie's) £648

Weston-super-Mare brass caddy spoon. £1

1950's souvenir cushion cover from Jamaica. £2

A Lowestoft 'trifle' mug with scrolling handle, 3½in. high, circa 1795. £935

Souvenir plate from Lerwick with a pierced edge. £8

(Paul G. Sheppard)

SOUVENIRS

Souvenir shaving mug by W. H. Goss, 4in. tall. £36

Paper knife of bone with deer foot handle inscribed 'A Present from New Brighton', circa 1890.   £8

Souvenir ashtray by W. H. Goss.   £10

Empire Exhibition commemorative brass caddy spoon. £1.50

Black Forest souvenir three dimensional kitchen scene.   £7

Carlton china figure 'Son of the Sea' from Westcliff on Sea.   £20

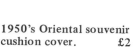

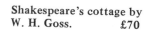

Souvenir Pixie jug from 'St. Columb Minor'. £1

1950's Oriental souvenir cushion cover.   £2

Shakespeare's cottage by W. H. Goss.   £70

(Paul G. Sheppard)

SOUVENIRS

Souvenir printed tray Vancouver, B.C., Canada. £1

An unusual six-sided brass seal depicting views of London, circa 1845, ¾in. sq. £25

Seaside souvenir picture of The Esplanade Western-super- Mare. £5

Souvenir match holder from Brentford. £7

A small 1953 Coronation souvenir, 1in. tall. £1

A Welsh souvenir inkwell with coat-of-arms. £8

A small souvenir basket with a print of London on the base. £1

Leather souvenir jewellery box, 'Anstey's Cove Torquay'. £4

Commemorative Stafford-shire plate 'The War Time Bread and Butter Plate' 1917. £14

Souvenir toby jug 'A Present from Ludlow', 6in. high. £2

1950's wooden three dimensional wooden souvenir, Bavarian livingroom scene. £5

Souvenir of Wales tea towel 'Welcome in the Hillsides'. £2

(Paul G. Sheppard)

SPECTACLES

Before 1880, spectacles were usually made of gold or steel, and later, of rolled gold or gold filled. Gold was preferred because it was acknowledged that it was the material less likely to cause any skin irritation.

Until recently, old spectacles were bought up for the scrap value of the gold content but now they are being collected out of an interest in their history and the development of the many different styles.

Written evidence dates 'eye glasses' to as far back as 1289.

Temple spectacles, with side pieces, were introduced by E. Scarlett in 1727 and, bi-focal lenses by Benjamin Franklin in 1785.

Sunglasses date from the 1880's.

Contact lenses were devised in 1887.

Expanding type spectacles with 9ct gold chain and ear loop, circa 1905, complete with case.   £5

Silver mounted shagreen triple spectacle case, early 19th century, 13cm. high, complete with spectacles.   £475

A fine pair of early sunglasses with blue steel frames complete with velvet case, circa 1875.   £30

Tortoiseshell framed spectacles with simulated crocodile case.   £7

A pair of binocular spectacles with adjustable lenses.   £10

A pair of Victorian silver spectacles in a beechwood case, circa 1850, case 6½in. long. (Christopher Sykes)   £28

Gold plated spectacles with green lenses by Chave & Jackson.   £6

9ct. gold 'nose grip' spectacles and case.   £14

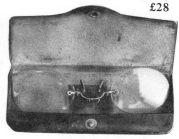

14ct. gold 'nose grip' spectacles and case.   £8

(Paul G. Sheppard)

SPOONS

Although it is doubtful if the luck of a Devon farmer will be repeated when he found a 16th century silver spoon worth thousands while rethatching his cottage roof, there are still plenty of prizes to be found in old cutlery drawers.

Most sought after are the early seal top and apostle spoons which have a cast finial joined to the flattened stem with a 'V' joint. Of more unusual form are moat spoons, for scooping the floating debris from the surface of a cup of tea, moustache spoons which have a barrier on the leading edge of the bowl and castor oil spoons designed to administer the beneficial elixir with as little hardship as possible.

The most likely prize to be found however are caddy spoons which generally have a large ornate bowl and very short handle, find one of these in the form of an eagle and we are talking about over £1,000.

A Liberty & Co. 'cymric' silver and enamel spoon, designed by A. Knox, Birmingham, 1902, 12.25cm.   £594

An apostle spoon, marked on bowl and stem, Thomas Dare Sn., Taunton, circa 1632.   £605

Silver mustard spoon made from a silver coin.   £1.50

A William IV caddy spoon, the bowl formed as a limpet shell, 1830, maker's mark WT. (Christie's)   £702

An 18th century beechwood basting spoon with narrow bowl and turned handle, 13½in. long.   £27

A George IV caddy spoon by C. Reily and G. Storer, 1828. (Christie's) £302

19th century African carved wood spoon, 9in. long.   £8

A West Country spoon with Buddha finial, circa 1640, 7½in. long. (W. H. Lane & Son)   £700

Bright cut caddy spoon, Birmingham, 1798. (Dreweatt Watson & Barton)   £55

A Charles II trefid basting spoon, by Samuel Pantaine, Cork, circa 1680, 3oz. 17dwt.   £1,540

Sioux horn spoon with plaited quill wrapped handle, 9¾in. long. (Robt. W. Skinner Inc.)   £362

19th century African carved wood spoon, 9in. long.   £8

SPORTING POSTCARDS

All artefacts designed with a sporting theme hold a particular interest for the collector and postcards are no exception to this rule.

Sporting cards are usually real photographs with postcard backs. They may illustrate well-known personalities, teams, special events, trophies won or lost and many have the added attraction of some very quippish comments printed on the reverse side.

Postcards linked to any sport will be of interest but a personal association will often lead to a specific area. Football supporters in particular, find it interesting to record the historical background of their favourite club, etc.

Golfing cards are much sought after and all of the better quality or slightly unusual cards are keenly collected. There is a growing interest in all track and field events.

Signed cards usually fetch a good price and a really rare card will fall into the 'price by negotiation' category.

Cricket — M. A. Noble (Australia N.S.W.), Ralph Dunn & Co. photographic No. 1000.   £5

W. G. Grace, one of the most famous cricketers, Rotophot Series No. 7685.   £7

A. Cotter (N.S. Wales), real photo, R. Dunn & Co., No. 1012, photographer Thiele.   £5

C. B. Fry, Sussex, Rotophot Series No. 7256.   £5

Cricket— E. Humphreys, Kent, real photo by Mockford, Tonbridge.   £4

S. Gregory (N.S. Wales), real photo, R. Dunn & Co., No. 1004.   £5

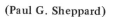

(Paul G. Sheppard)

Billiard Room B.E.L.C. Cologne, real photo
card.   £3.50

Motor Cycle Scrambling/Racing, R. Sneath,
Sheffield, real photo, facsimile signature,
R. Barrowclough riding a Douglas.   £6

Cricket — South African Cricket Team pre
1910, G. Alsop, Manager, printed photo.£4

Old Wulfrunians Football Club winners of
the Chattrian Cup 1905-6, Bennet Clark
real photo postcard.   £7

Chelsea Football Club 1907-8, real photo by Durrett & Martin, Upper
Tooting, posted from West Ealing to Wolverhampton, December 16th 1907,
message reads 'The Old Wulfrunians seem to be doing well? In both their
cups'. Team list as per foot of card.   £6

(Paul G. Sheppard)

Ladies' v. Gents' Cricket Match at Bosbury, June 17th, 1909.

Ladies Cricket Team, Bosbury 1909, published by Tilley & Son, Ledbury.
£10

Leeds City A.F.C. photo by R. Scott & Co.,
pre 1910?, Broad, Trainer, G. Gillies, Mana-
ger.   £3

Motor Cycle Scrambling/Racing, R. Sneath,
Sheffield, real photo, facsimile signature,
E. Elder riding a Douglas.   £5

Boxing Club at Wolverhampton, real photo
by G. Whitfield.   £4.50

Wolverhampton Wanderers in 1906-7, real
photo by Guggenheim.   £5

(Paul G. Sheppard)

Wolverhampton Wanderers, Old Wulfrunians Football Club, in 1904,
photographic postcard, posted locally March 1st 1904, message reads
'Some local 'actors' for your collection'.   £6

Straw hatted young men playing croquet,
circa 1918.   £2.50

Real photograph of 'Top Green', Clacton-
on-Sea, Bowling Club, circa 1960.   £2

Real photograph of Sir Henry Segrave and
Miss England II.   £6

Winning Polo Team of the W.S. Senior Cup,
Dunster.   £5

(Tim Ward)

The Village Blacksmith, 'The Great Wrestling Match'.   £1

'Dorando', The Marathon Race 1908, published by Davidson Bros.   £5

Mickey Walker, Famous Boxer Series, published by J. Beagles & Co. Ltd.£4

The Mighty Young Apollon, World Famous strength and muscle builder, signed 1932.£3

(Tim Ward)

STAFFORDSHIRE

If you stand in the car park in the centre of Stoke and turn full circle, you will be confronted by numerous chimneys emblazoned with the household names of the most famous potteries. Drive a few miles and the road signs tell of Fenton, Longton, Hanley, Burslem, Tunstall and Burmantofts, all familiar names to collectors of Staffordshire pottery. At one time there were over four hundred factories going full blast to meet the insatiable demand of the Victorians to have a pottery figure covering every available surface.

Most are press moulded and decorated in underglaze blue and black with touches of colour in overglaze enamel and gilding. Early examples have closed bases or sport a small hole in the base, while 20th century pieces are usually slip cast in Plaster of Paris moulds and are open ended.

Rare bust of Plato after a model by Enoch Wood, late 18th century, 13¼in. high. £253

Early 19th century Staffordshire pearlware mantel ornament of the Royal Coat-of-Arms, 22.5cm. high. £858

Staffordshire figure of Eliza Cook, 1860's, some crazing, 10¼in. high. £110

Rare Thomas Parr figure of Archbishop Cranmer, tied to a stake, circa 1850, 9in. high. £682

A Staffordshire model of Palmer's house, circa 1856, with moulded title. £220

Large Staffordshire pearlware figure of a dog, 42cm. high, circa 1830. £968

One of a pair of gaudily painted mid 19th century 'Fenton' jugs. (Ambrose) £250

One of a pair of Staffordshire lion and lamb groups, circa 1850, 4¾in. £1,100

A Staffordshire silver resist lustre jug of quatrefoil ribbed form, circa 1815, 6in. high. (Christie's) £278

Mid 19th century tobacco jar and cover, modelled as the head of a spotted dog, 6¾in. high. £264

A Staffordshire pottery mug commemorating the Coronation of Queen Victoria, circa 1838, 8.5cm. high. £374

A 19th century pottery 'Village Group' 19cm. £154

A Staffordshire portrait bust of General Booth wearing Salvation Army cap, circa 1900, 13in. high. £330

Amusing Staffordshire group of 'Education', circa 1825, 6in. high, restored. £330

Early 19th century English figure of Britannia, with a lion at her side, 6¼in. high. £242

A Staffordshire group of lovers beneath an arbour, 9½in. (Woolley & Wallis) £65

Staffordshire canary yellow pottery jug, printed with two portrait busts, 1820's, 14.5cm. high. £143

A Staffordshire pottery figure of Samson and the Lion, 12¼in. (Dreweatt Watson & Barton) £80

A Staffordshire saltglaze polychrome jug, the baluster body finely painted, circa 1755, 7in. high. (Christie's) £550

Pair of Staffordshire figures of George Parr and Julius Caesar, All England XI, 13¼in. high. (Christie's S. Kensington) £580

A Staffordshire saltglaze bear jug and cover, circa 1740, 23.5cm. high. (Christie's) £702

Staffordshire figure of Lady Isabelle Burton, 8¾in. high. (Christie's S. Kensington) £140

A Staffordshire pearlware mug, printed with execution of Louis XVI picked out in enamels, 8.5cm. high, 1790's. £240

A Staffordshire pottery figure of Tom King, the highwayman, 11½in. high. (Dreweatt Watson & Barton) £75

STANDS

If you are one of those happy souls whose habit it is to arrive home late on rainy evenings with muddy boots, library book in one hand, a walking stick in the other, rubber plant and fruitcake clutched to your chest and umbrella held aloft in a vain attempt to keep your new hat dry; and if, when you do arrive home so encumbered, you find that the power workers have called a lightning blackout and you have to grope your way about in candle-light — just relax. All you need is a collection of appropriate stands and your problems are over.

There are candlestands, plant stands, reading and music stands, cake stands, kettle stands, umbrella stands, hat stands, boot stands, shaving stands, even wig stands. Such was the ingenuity of past craftsmen and designers that there is a purpose built stand for just about everything from whips to cricket bats.

A 1930's 'pop up' drum bar, 76cm. diam. £60

One of a pair of 19th century rosewood adjustable candlestands, by E. Nye, Tunbridge Wells. (Dreweatt Watson & Barton) £460

An 18th century mahogany adjustable knee rest, 13¼in. £242

J. & J. Kohn bentwood coat stand, designed by Josef Hoffmann, circa 1905, 202cm. high. £352

Oriental carved teakwood stand, 16in. diam. (Stalker & Boos) £300

Unusual Victorian music stand with papier-mache top inlaid with mother-of-pearl, circa 1850. £660

A late 19th century beech-wood smoker's companion, 35in. high. £209

An early 19th century mahogany boot jack, 33½in. high. £253

Late 18th century George III mahogany three-tier stand, 42in. high. (Robt. W. Skinner Inc.) £666

A mahogany marquetry etagere by Louis Majorelle. (Christie's) £918

A Swiss carved pine umbrella stand in the form of a standing bear, 4ft.9in. high, circa 1900. £462

Gustav Stickley oak plant stand, circa 1903, 28in. high. (Robt. W. Skinner Inc.) £500

Victorian oak and cast-iron reading bracket and circular table. (Butler & Hatch Waterman) £95

A 19th century mahogany whip and boot rack, 39½in. £110

William IV cue stand. (Ambrose) £550

TAXIDERMY

Taxidermy was not perfected technically until the beginning of the 19th century. The interest in collecting and preserving birds and animals increased as the century progressed, coinciding with a general awakening of interest in natural history until, by the 1880's, almost every town and village in the country had its own taxidermist. The interest began to wane shortly before the Great War, and did not return until the 1960's, since which time cased taxidermy has become steadily more collectible.

The quality of the work produced during the heyday of taxidermy (1860-1914) varied enormously, but it is only the top quality work which has any real value today, and this represents perhaps less than 5% of all that was actually produced. Although it is not essential, it is a good idea to look for the taxidermist's label which is usually placed inside or on the back the case. Variations include Peter Spicer of Leamington who, for example, incorporated a signed pebble into the groundwork of his cases. Condition is of prime importance: taxidermy specimens are notoriously susceptible to attacks from moths and beetles. The quality of the taxidermy and case setting is equally important: the bird or mammal must be mounted in a lifelike manner and be set in an artistic but appropriate simulation of its natural habitat. Within these limits, each taxidermist evolved his own particular and distinctive style, and the very best cases are today recognised as works of art.

The photographs chosen are mostly items from the top end of the market, and the prices, which are considered to be the current market values for each case, reflect this.

An example of a typical case label, that of Pratt of Brighton, circa 1890.

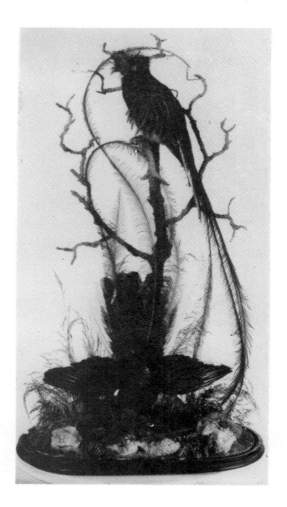

Two quetzals in oval dome, circa 1890.
£200

(Christopher Frost)

373

Domestic pigeon in dome, 1922. £50

Three lapwings in case by T. E. Gunn of Norwich, circa 1890. £100

Pair of trout by J. Cooper of London, (who specialised in fish), in a bow-fronted case, 1920. £150

Fox mask on shield by Peter Spicer & Sons, circa 1920. £50

Group of wading birds by S. Hibbs of Ollerton, circa 1890. £175

Pair of red grouse by Peter Spicer & Sons of Leamington, circa 1905. £150

(Christopher Frost)

Badger by J. Gardner of London, circa 1880.　£125

Pair of Arctic hares by J. Hutchings of Aberystwyth, circa 1905.　　　£125

Pair of lesser birds of paradise, taxidermist unknown, circa 1880.　£120

Pair of little bustards by Saunders of Great Yarmouth, circa 1910.　　　£175

Peregrine falcon by Rowland Ward of London, circa 1900.　　　£200

(Christopher Frost)

Pair of pochard by Peter Spicer & Sons of Leamington, circa 1910.   £200

Smew drake by Peter Spicer & Sons of Leamington, 1929.   £150

Golden eagle by Macpherson of Inverness, circa 1900.   £300

Pair of grey squirrels by Rowland Ward of London, circa 1900. £100

Barn owl by Allen of York, circa 1890.   £100

Pair of albino pheasants by G. White of Salisbury, circa 1900.   £100

Pair of great bitterns by T. E. Gunn of Norwich, circa 1890.   £250

(Christopher Frost)

A pike, 26lb., mounted in a bow-front display cabinet, 131 x 45 x 29cm. (Osmond Tricks) £200

A fishing trophy of a stuffed brown trout by J. Cooper & Sons, caught in 1912, the case 77.5cm. (Lawrence Fine Art) £143

Late 19th century stuffed stag's head on shield-shaped mount. £25

Victorian case of stuffed birds in mahogany glazed case. (Reeds Rains) £54

A stuffed sea-trout, 20¼in., mounted in a bow-fronted case, 27¼ x 6¼ x 13½in. £176

Fox and weasel in naturalistic setting contained in a glazed case. £100

A Victorian ram's head snuff mull. £1,500

TEA BOXES & CADDIES

Ever since Samuel Pepys recorded his first cup of tea on the 25th September, 1660, tea caddies and boxes have been made in all shapes, sizes and decorations. They are to be found in a number of materials including wood, ivory, papier mache, silver, copper, tortoiseshell, china, straw work, Tunbridgeware and with painted decoration.

When tea was a valuable commodity, it was kept safely under lock and key, in a caddy, which was usually displayed in one of the main rooms of the house. Because it was a custom for the mistress of the house to dispense tea at the tea table, a great deal of attention was focused on the appearance of the caddy.

During the last fifteen years or so, the price of these fine quality caddies has rocketed upwards and, anyone who was clever enough to get a collection together as early as the late 60's, should be very well pleased with himself.

When tea became cheaper and more plentiful, it was adopted as the national beverage and, thereafter, it was generally stored in the kitchen. The colourfully decorated painted tin tea boxes of the early 20's and onwards are now collectible.

A small 19th century Sheffield plate tea box with lid.
£15

A pair of tea caddies, one in applewood , the other in pearwood, 4¼in. and 6½in. high.
£3,960

Brass topped tea box with pokerwork 'Tea', 4in. high.
£1

Chromium plated tea box, circa 1950.   £2

Walnut tea caddy of hexagonal shape, each side with oval shell inlaid panel. (Butler & Hatch Waterman)£320

A white bakelite tea box, 1940's.   £3

A George III satinwood tea caddy with inlaid strapwork borders, 7½in. wide. (Dreweatt Watson & Barton) £360

A Whieldon square tea caddy, the tall sides with arched shoulder, circa 1760, 7in. high. (Christie's) £308

Regency penwork tea caddy with domed lid, circa 1805, 1ft.2in. wide. £935

George III walnut brass mounted tea caddy, late 18th century, on brass scallop feet, 9in. wide. (Christie's) £293

Three-colour Wedgwood tea caddy, circa 1895, with domed lid, 6in. high. (Robt. W. Skinner Inc.) £310

George III rectangular inlaid tea caddy on a brass edged base on bracket feet, 10in. wide. (Christie's) £308

Art Deco style brass tea box, circa 1930. £6

Late 1930's Army & Navy Stores type tea box. £2

An 18th/19th century tea caddy in the form of a boxwood toadstool, 5in. high. £748

A late Georgian tortoiseshell tea caddy on four silver plated ball feet, 7in. (Lawrence Fine Art)   £330

George III mahogany and rosewood crossbanded octagonal tea caddy , circa 1790, 5in. wide.   £120

A rosewood single division tea caddy, 5½in. wide.   £143

A Staffordshire saltglaze rectangular tea caddy, circa 1755, 9.5cm. high. (Christie's)   £518

George III tea caddy, 9¾in. wide.   £1,210

Festival of Britain plated tea box, 1951.   £3

1930's wooden tea box with plated fittings.   £5

George III rolled paperwork tea caddy, dated 1799, panels inset with mezzotints, 7¼in. wide.   £935

An 18th century tea caddy in the form of a canteloupe melon, 5in. high.   £1,540

TEDDY BEARS

President Reagan has one, so has Princess Anne, together with Enoch Powell and Pope John Paul, although his stays in the Vatican. Mrs. Thatcher's is called Humphrey and he often raises money for charity and Lord Bath's friend called Clarence wears spectacles.

Arctophily is the name of the game — they all have bears.

Margaret Steiss, a crippled dressmaker, is credited with making the first bear about 1900, but it wasn't until Teddy Roosevelt refused to shoot a bear on an organised hunt (it was, after all, tied to a stake by someone eager to please) that the Teddy Bear really took off in popularity.

Early bears have a hump on the back, jointed arms, head and legs and are generally stuffed with straw. The best have glass or button eyes and come complete with a growl.

Most early bears are often described as 'well loved' which is why those in good condition will always command a premium.

An orange plush teddy bear with smiling mouth, small hump back and swivel joints, 16in. high, circa 1930. £88

Two teddy bears, one 14in. high, the other 8¼in. high, German, circa 1930. £187

Tan mohair teddy bear with shoe button eyes, circa 1910, 12¾in. high. (Robt. W. Skinner Inc.) £133

A dual-coloured teddy bear, with black and beige tufted mohair plush, circa 1950, 25in. high. £22

A blonde mohair plush teddy bear with voice box, circa 1910, 18½in. high. £264

A tan mohair bear with wired limbs, blonde plush ears, snout and feet and glass eyes, Germany, circa 1930, 11in. high. (Robt. W. Skinner Inc.) £38

TEDDY BEARS

Pre-war fur fabric teddy bear, 15in. high. (Reeds Rains) £20

Early white mohair teddy bear, Germany, circa 1906, 13½in. high. (Robt. W. Skinner Inc.) £533

A chubby long blonde mohair teddy bear, fully jointed with glass eyes, 20in. high. (Robt. W. Skinner Inc.) £134

Late 19th century clockwork brown bear, real fur pelt, possibly France, 7in. high. (Robt. W. Skinner Inc.) £114

German teddy bear by Steiss of pale plush colour, renewed pads, snout and nose, circa 1909. (Phillips) £1,100

An R.D. France drinking bear, dark brown and white rabbit fur, glass eyes, electrical, 1930's, 14½in. high. (Robt. W. Skinner Inc.) £461

A straw filled ginger teddy-bear, with ball and socket joints, 74cm. high. (H. Spencer & Sons) £50

Early amber plush teddy bear and accessories, circa 1910, 15in. tall. (Theriault's) £126

A Steiss Centennial teddy bear, for the German market, golden mohair, black button eyes and ear button, 17in. high, 1980. (Robt. W. Skinner Inc.) £269

THERMOMETERS

Quite a lad was our Galileo, for he also found the time to invent the thermometer when not peering at the heavens through his telescope. The original consisted of a glass tube ending in a bulb, with the open end immersed in water. After being heated it was noted that the water ran up the inside of the tube as the air cooled.

The most common type to be found today are the alcohol thermometer, with red liquid, the mercury and the circular diaphragm type.

Although the simple task of taking one's temperature is the most common use to which thermometers are put, they have been adapted for numerous tasks such as brewing, cookery, photography and hatching.

Some of the most interesting are those taken up by the souvenir trade, for in the past when purchase tax was not applicable on medical items, the thermometer was stuck onto numerous inappropriate articles in order to market them cheaply.

Brass cased incubator mercury thermometer with inbuilt hook.   £3

A thermometer stand by H. Hollanby, 4½in. high.   £93

1960's desk thermometer in pewter frame.   £6

Red Indian novelty spirit thermometer.   £2

An oak cased thermometer with ivory dial engraved with maker's name 'Kemp & Co. Ltd, Bombay', 4¾in. long, circa 1850.   £85

Late 19th century brass framed thermometer, 10in. high.   £6

(Paul G. Sheppard)

TILES

Following the strong revival in the fashion for decorative tiles in the 19th century, many of the leading porcelain manufacturers came into production.

They produced single tiles to be arranged according to individual taste and sets of tiles composed of intricate patterns and extensive scenes. Indeed, some sets were produced to decorate and face whole shop fronts with appropriate illustrations.

There were tiles depicting representations of the four seasons, famous characters in literature or well known plays, landscapes, seascapes, classical interiors and so on ad infinitum. Tiles were used in dairies, kitchens, fireplace surrounds and as wall decorations.

A new collector would be wise to seek out some background information on the manufacturers, dates and styles, for tiles have been produced and reproduced, in such huge quantities over the years and a little knowledge may help to establish authenticity.

Liverpool delft shipping tile, signed Sadler, 5in. square, circa 1760. £175

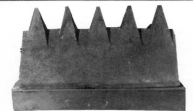

Early 19th century ridge tile.   £4

Liverpool delft tile printed in black, circa 1760.   £75

One of twelve Minton pottery tiles decorated with classical scenes.   £75

A Wedgwood pottery tile picture by W. Nunn, 46 x 77cm.   £418

Bristol delft polychrome tile, circa 1760, 13cm. square, slightly chipped.   £135

A De Morgan tile panel comprising three tiles, 1882-8, 51 x 20.6cm.   £330

Chinese 18th century pottery Foo lion roof tile, 10¼in. high. (Robt. W. Skinner Inc.)   £216

Four mid 18th. century Dutch Delft polychrome tiles.   £150

TIN OPENERS

Chocolate was one of the first foodstuffs to be manufactured on a commercial scale, from a factory opened in England in 1728, but it was a long time before other products were introduced. At first it was mainly sauces and pickles which were taken up by the house-keepers for they were time consuming to make, but they continued to preserve their own food for most of the 19th century.

The first mass produced tinned food was 'Bully Beef', for Her Majesty's troops, which is why the first tin openers often took the form of a bull's head.

When the manufacturers really got going, soup was by far the most popular product, but it was very expensive and only had a limited market among the wealthy households.

Tin openers, of course, developed in tandem with tinned food, the Victorian inventors vying with each other to introduce new patented designs.

Sheffield made tin opener with piercer. £9

All metal Sheffield made tin opener. £6

Knights Patent tin opener with beechwood handle.   £3

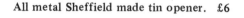

British made tin opener with elm handle.
£3

An unusual Sheffield made tin opener with shaped wooden handle.   £4

Rare sardine tin opener by Edward Preston.
£27

Early 20th century beech handled tin opener.
£3

Early 20th century cast iron bull's head tin opener, the rail is curled to form the handle, 6¼in. long. (Christopher Sykes)   £15

(Paul G. Sheppard)

TIN OPENERS

All metal American made tin opener. £2

Combined all metal bottle and can opener. 50p

Heavy all metal Sheffield made tin opener. £9

British made tin opener with beechwood handle. £2

An unusual sardine can opener with spring arms. £16

Metal corkscrew and tin opener by Henry Squire & Sons. 75p

Patented tin opener with wooden handle. £1

All metal combined bottle opener, lid priser and twist key can opener. £1

New Erie British made tin opener with shaped handle. £4

(Paul G. Sheppard)

TINS

From mid to late Victorian times it was quite common practise for manufacturers of perishable goods to package their wares in decorative tins. Fierce competition led to the production of a vast array of styles and a most inventive selection of shapes.

Although at the time of their manufacture these tins had little or no monetary value, a great many have survived in excellent condition to this day, for they were both useful and attractive and most were kept and put to some use in the household.

Confectioners and biscuit companies made the most attractive tins and examples produced before about 1914 are the most collectible of all.

Most tins bearing advertising material are collected today and the market is continually expanding to embrace even the most modern examples.

Brompton Hospital 'Lozenges' tin, by Ernest Jackson & Co. 50p

Player's 'No Name' tobacco tin. £2

Cohen, Weener & Co. Ltd. 'Afrikander Smoking Mixture' tin, 3 x 4in. £2

Prilect travelling iron tin, 1950's. £2

Walter's 'Medium Navy Cut' cigarette tin. £2

Hignett's 'Pilot Flake' tobacco tin, 6in. long. £3

Cook's Standard 'Ring Travellers' tin, 6 x 4in. £4

Boots 'Head and Stomach Pills' tin. £1

'His Master's Voice' half tone needles. £3.50

(Paul G. Sheppard)

'His Master's Voice' half tone needle tin. £2.50

Yardley's Old English, Lavender Solidified Brillantine tin, 3in. high. £5

Edward Sharp & Sons 'Golden Toffee' tin. £2

Victorian display tin for a Gnat clock by the British United Clock Co., Birmingham, 2½in. diam. £4

'Cuticura' talcum powder tin, 6in. high. £1

'His Master's Voice' fibre needles tin. £2.50

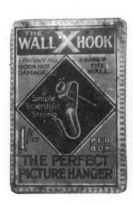

The wall X hook, tin, 3in. tall. £2

C.W.S. biscuit tin by Crumpsall and Cardiff. £5

'X Rays Burning Oil' for cycle lamps by The Elephant Chemical Co. £5

(Paul G. Sheppard)

TINS

J. & H. Wilson Ltd. 'Celebrated Snuff' tin.   30p

'Bisodol' Antacid Digestant sample tin.   £2

'Nigroids' tin for throat and voice by Nigroid Ferris Ltd.   30p

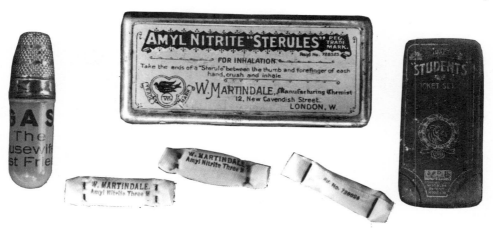

'Gas, The Housewife's Best Friend' thimble set.   £1

Amyl Nitrite 'Sterules' tin complete with contents.   £3

Container for 'The Students' Pocket Set of Mathematical Instruments.   £3

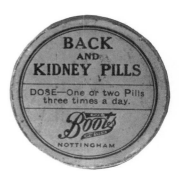

'Radiospares' tin reel complete with wire, 2in.   £1

'Everyman Cycle Oil' by C. C. Wakefield & Co.   £1

Boots 'Back and Kidney Pills' tin.   £1

.(Paul G. Sheppard)

TINS

Gray Dunn & Co., Glasgow, chocolate tin with pictorial lid. £20

Stothert's 'Foot Paste' tin. 50p

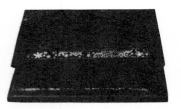

Rowntree & Co. chocolate tin of Oriental design. £7

Cadbury's Dairy Milk chocolate churn. £10

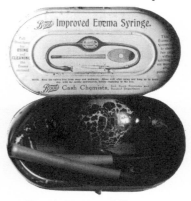

Boot's Improved Enema Syringe in a decorative tin container, guaranteed for six months. £7

Slippery Elm infant's food tin. £3

Mackintosh's Nurseryland toffee tin. £6

The 'Greys' Silk Cut Virginia tobacco tin. £2

Marshall's Reel Fly Catcher tin. £1

Wilkinson's Pontefract cakes tin. £2.50

Mackintosh's Sampler chocolate tin. £8

Packet of Thermogene Curative Wadding for treatment of Rheumatism, 6in. wide. £2

(Paul G. Sheppard)

TOOLS

Although the great, important pieces maintain their places, the mass of antiques is subject to the fluctuations of fashionable taste. The constantly growing demand for antiques has resulted in new fields being explored and new tastes created.

Just such a new field has been created with the current interest in old tools, specifically old woodworking tools.

Certain items, of course, have been moving upwards in price for some time and this applies in particular to the wood plane. There are over fifty different types of plane, ranging from the 3in. plane used by violin makers to the 17in. jack plane, and nowadays, some of the early 'named' examples can fetch hundreds rather than tens of pounds.

Another popular item is the brace and bit. This tool has been in use since the Middle Ages but, while there are some very old ones around, a brace fitted with an interchangeable bit can be dated as coming after the first quarter of the nineteenth century.

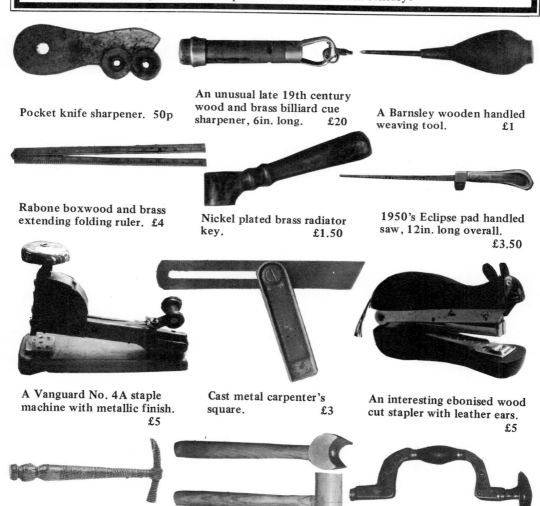

Pocket knife sharpener. 50p

An unusual late 19th century wood and brass billiard cue sharpener, 6in. long. £20

A Barnsley wooden handled weaving tool. £1

Rabone boxwood and brass extending folding ruler. £4

Nickel plated brass radiator key. £1.50

1950's Eclipse pad handled saw, 12in. long overall. £3.50

A Vanguard No. 4A staple machine with metallic finish. £5

Cast metal carpenter's square. £3

An interesting ebonised wood cut stapler with leather ears. £5

An early 18th century lignum vitae and steel upholsterer's hammer, inscribed J. Sarney and 1716, 9½in. long. £605

A Naval serving mallet of boxwood for serving shipped ropes. £15

A superb Marples ultimatum ebony and brass brace. £300

(Peter R. Ware)

TOOLS

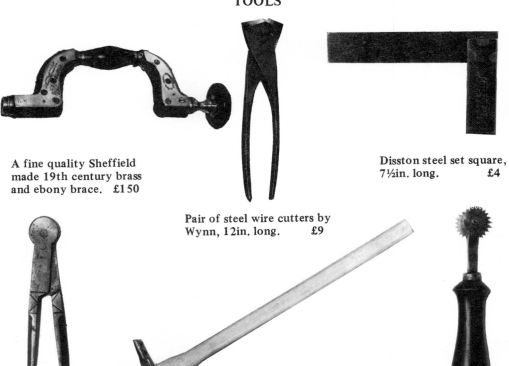

A fine quality Sheffield made 19th century brass and ebony brace.   £150

Pair of steel wire cutters by Wynn, 12in. long.   £9

Disston steel set square, 7½in. long.   £4

Pair of late 18th century steel callipers.   £12

Early 20th century pole axe.   £45

Early stamp perforator with twin wheels and beechwood handle.   £3.50

Button chuck wooden brace, circa 1850.   £24

A small late 19th century iron pick, 9in. long.   £5

An early all metal side valve lifter.   £14

(Peter R. Ware)

TOOLS

Late 19th century wooden framed fret saw.   £15

19th century short handled adze.   £8

1930's steel side valve extractor.   £8

Shaping plane axe with beech-wood handle, 9in. long.   £6

Iron wood jack for rope attachment after hammering into wood.   £6

19th century wire gauge tool with wooden handle.   £1

19th century wooden shaft cooper's mallet.   £7

British Army trenching tool, circa 1885.   £80

A cooper's (barrel makers) hatchet with short handle.   £40

(Peter R. Ware)

393

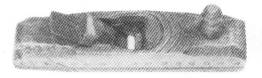

A 19th century beechwood cooper's plane with turned handle, 10¾in. long.   £55

A 19th century beechwood try plane carved with the name T. Hale, 28in. long.   £60

A fine quality plane with wooden handle, 9in. long, by Norriss.   £85

A mid 18th century Dutch beechwood plane dated 1766, blade stamped Robt. Moor, 8in. long.   £825

A large good quality plane by Robert Sorby, Sheffield.   £154

Late 19th century wooden moulding plane, 8in. long.   £18

A fine wood and brass jack plane. £75

A fine 19th century Scottish bronze plane.   £80

(Peter R. Ware)

Mid 19th century mitre plane with brass box-shaped body, stamped G. Snelling and C. Keate, 7.1/8in. long.   £176

A small all metal Stanley plane.   £7

A small cast metal plane with wooden knob.
                                                      £8

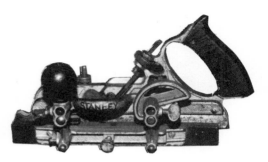

Stanley plane No. 45 with wooden handles and original box.   £70

Stanley plane for positive and negative curves.   £45

Metal plane by Record of Birmingham. £18

Stanley plane No. 78, made in U.S.A., with wooden handles.   £22

British made wood and metal plane by Bailey.   £18

(Peter R. Ware)

TOOLS

Large forged steel adjustable spanner, 1960's.
£4

An interesting sterling silver slide rule. £8

A Sunbeam multi-functional car tool. £1.50

Italian made hairdresser's thinning scissors. £2

Terry's 'hedgehog' pipe reamer, 2in. long. £2

19th century iron brace with wooden handle.
£15

Late 19th century bentwood carpet beater.
£3

Marine tool of ebony and brass for attaching ship's log.
£26

19th century iron candlesnuffers. £10

Steel handled rubber mallet, 12in long. £3

Late Victorian cast-iron tobacco cutter on
a beechwood baseboard.   £28

A Forgan brass die stamp with stained
baluster handle, circa 1870, 4½in. long.
(Christie's)   £97

(Paul G. Sheppard)

396

TOOLS

All metal wrench by Mossberg, U.S.A.,
1931.   £6

Victorian ebony and brass cigar cutter and
pipe scraper.   £12

A brass and steel Barson hammer drift.
£3.50

Pair of 19th century brass candlesnuffers.
£12

A Jaguar tool kit in a fitted case. £50

Vanguard stapler No. 6, 9in. long. £5

Swiss brass circular glass cutter. £3.50

Small spirit level with brass top, 4in. long.
£3.50

19th century hand plane with beechwood
handle.   £12

A late 19th century cast iron Kenrick No. 1
cork press.   £38

1960's Rapid 41 stapler, 5in. long. £1

A combined cigar cutter and pipe scraper
with leather case.   £14

(Paul G. Sheppard)

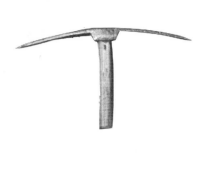

Victorian blacksmith's swage hammer, 18in. long. £12

Paver's hammer with elm handle. £20

A large stonemason's hammer, 22in. long. £10

A small stonemason's hammer with iron head. £9

Nicely shaped brick hammer, 14in. long. £12

Victorian scaffolder's hammer for tightening lashings in pinewood pole scaffolding. £20

Lead dressing hammer with lignum vitae head. £8

Chipping hammer with elm handle. £6

19th century upholsterer's hammer, 14in. long. £12

(Peter R. Ware)

TOOLS

Small universal hammer
with elm handle.   £4

Combined plough, hammer
and spanner by Ottis &
Sons.   £10

Coal hammer with elm handle.
                    £6

Late 19th century raking
hammer.   £10

Brick hammer with elm
handle.   £10

Panel beater's hammer, 14in.
long.   £5

Coal hammer with bulbous
head.   £6

Panel beating hammer with
iron head.   £12

Roof tiler's hammer with
elm handle.   £4

(Peter R. Ware)

399

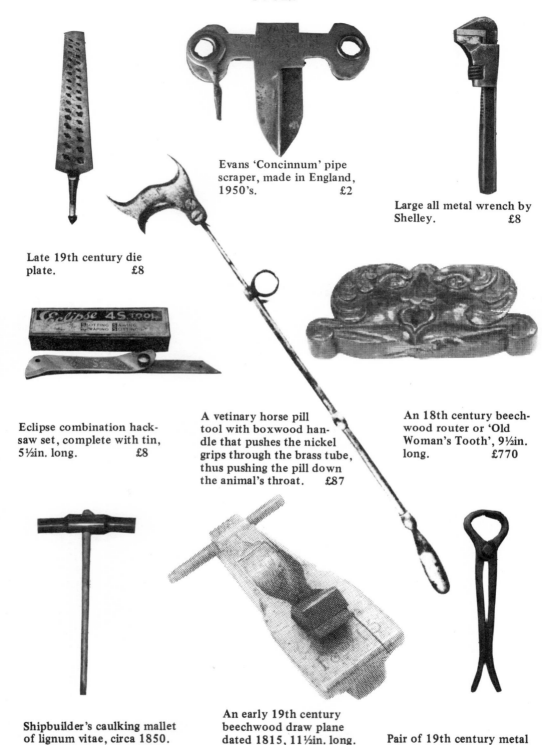

Evans 'Concinnum' pipe scraper, made in England, 1950's.   £2

Large all metal wrench by Shelley.   £8

Late 19th century die plate.   £8

Eclipse combination hacksaw set, complete with tin, 5½in. long.   £8

A vetinary horse pill tool with boxwood handle that pushes the nickel grips through the brass tube, thus pushing the pill down the animal's throat.   £87

An 18th century beechwood router or 'Old Woman's Tooth', 9½in. long.   £770

Shipbuilder's caulking mallet of lignum vitae, circa 1850.   £25

An early 19th century beechwood draw plane dated 1815, 11½in. long.   £176

Pair of 19th century metal pincers, 12in. long.   £6

(Peter R. Ware)

TORCHES

The first torch, 1891, was a square two candle power bull's eye lantern. It weighed 2lbs. and the battery was made by the Bristol Electric Lamp Co. The first batch of forty produced were supplied to the Bristol Omnibus Company.

The Ever Ready No. 1 torch was introduced to England in 1900 at a selling price of one shilling and sixpence.

Ever Ready and Lucas produced the World War II service issues including those issued to Air Raid Precaution and Civil Defence units. These wartime torches usually incorporate a 'blackout' guard.

Although it is difficult, in some cases impossible, to find suitable batteries for the early torches, they can be converted to take a modern version.

An early battery torch by Oralnx with magnifying lens and leather case.   £10

Early 20th century wooden framed torch with carrying handle.   £15

Early 50's battery torch with magnifying lens.   £6

S.S.S. chromium plated torch, made in China. £1

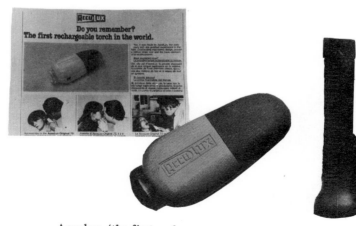

Acculux, 'the first rechargeable torch in the world' together with instructions.   £3.50

Ever Ready rubber cased torch.   £2.50

(Paul G. Sheppard)

TOYS

If every child treated his toys with the utmost care, didn't bang them into the skirting board, and carefully packed them away in their original boxes after use, it would have left a legacy of toys for future generations, but we would not be seeing some of the astronomical prices certain toys sell for at auction now.

A tin plate car by Carette sold for £6,700, a doll by A. Marque £24,000, a 1953 Vulcan Bomber by Dinky over £1,000 and a set of lead soldiers for nearly £3,000.
It is all to do with supply and demand for suddenly old toys are big business, well out of the reach of the children they were designed for.

Age is not the criteria, for even the Japanese plastic space toys of the 50's and 60's are now eagerly sought after and are starting to make good money.

A Wells tinplate ambulance, clockwork mechanism driving rear axle, 6½in. long, English, circa 1935, sold with another.
£143

A Distler tinplate and clockwork fire engine, 37.5cm. long overall. £209

A printed tinplate clockwork model of Sir M. Campbell's land speed record car 'Bluebird', circa 1930, 10¾in. long. (Christie's S. Kensington) £130

A Lehmann tinplate Anxious Bride, No. 470, German, circa 1910. £495

French early 20th century Decamps chamois-covered walking pig, 15in. long. £572

A Lehmann 'Kadi' tinplate toy, No. 723, German, circa 1920, 7in. long. £418

TOYS

An early Mettoy wind-up racing car.   £75

1930's wooden railway booking office, Brighton & South Coast Railway.   £18

A hand-made wooden toy train, 18in. long.   £15

A large and impressive Karl Bub tinplate and clockwork limousine, circa 1932, German, 50cm. long.   £968

A Gunthermann double-decker bus clockwork activated, German, circa 1930. £308

A Gunthermann tinplate and clockwork six-wheeled general double-decker bus, 35cm. long.   £165

German clockwork racing car with original tyres.   £90

A Chad Valley games van with clockwork mechanism, English, circa 1930.   £121

A small Victorian musical box, the top decorated with children playing, 6 x 4in. £45

German plush pull toy of a baby elephant by Steiff, 14in. overall. (Theriault's) £205

Early 20th century ventriloquist's dummy in a military coat. £200

German cloth character doll by Kathe Kruse, circa 1915, 17in. high. (Theriault's) £241

Wooden and paper toy theatre, manufactured for F. A. O. Schwartz Toys, circa 1885, 25 x 25in. (Theriault's) £66

German character doll in amber-tinted bisque by Kestner, circa 1915, 13in. high. (Theriault's) £1,305

A walking Felix the cat soft toy, circa 1928, 33½in. long. £1,210

German bisque character baby by Kammer & Reinhardt, circa 1915, 12in. high. (Theriault's) £325

A. G. Vichy bisque-headed tri-cyclist automaton, French, circa 1880, 10½in. long. £495

A small late 19th century musical box decorated with children playing on the outside rim, 2½in. diam. £40

Belgian doll's house, modelled as a detached town villa with three bays, 1870's. (Christie's S. Kensington) £2,400

Unique Art tin wind-up L'il Abner and his Dogpatch Band, American, 1946, 8½in. high. (Robt. W. Skinner Inc.) £150

American wooden character doll of Felix, by Schoenhut, 9in. high. (Theriault's) £279

Wooden character doll by Schoenhut, Philadelphia, 12in. high, circa 1915. (Theriault's) £230

French bisque child doll by Emile Jumeau, circa 1885, 15in. high. (Theriault's) £1,000

A Lehmann tinplate 'Oh My' dancer No. 690, German, circa 1912, in original cardboard box. £308

American cloth character doll, by Marjorie H. Buell, circa 1944, 14in. high. (Theriault's) £244

American wooden doll's house by the Bliss Toy Co., Rhode Island, circa 1900, 18 x 12 x 9in. (Theriault's) £383

TOYS

A 1930's leather 'Disappearing Banknote' pocket novelty. £1

A rare tin plate beetle by Lehmann, Germany, which walks and flaps its wings. £90

A Victorian Christmas cracker house. £20

Victorian pictorial play block, 4in. square. £3

Monkey on a string by Lehmann, 6in. long. £40

A metal framed child's mangle with wooden rollers. £10

A small 19th century musical box, 2½in. diam. £45

Dummy cigar box in which a hand and head pop out when a concealed button is pressed. £25

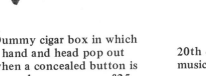

20th century 'Jiving Jigger' musical drum, 4in. diam. £40

(Paul G. Sheppard)

TRANSPORT POSTCARDS

In recent years postcard collectors have shown a growing enthusiasm for cards illustrating transport of all kinds.

The most collectible items are those real photograph cards which show lots of close-up detail and animation thus contributing to the value of a collection as a record of the changes taking place in our road transport system. As a rule, the more people the better, for they are likely to add to the nostalgia potential of any card.

While it is generally agreed that horse drawn vehicles are the most valuable cards, it is well worth looking at each individual card and judging it on its own merit with regard for potential scarcity and, of course, condition.

The Austin A30 Seven — 'You can depend on it', colour card No. 1002.   £3.50

Nice early motor car and driver, real photo postcard.   £4.50

17/18 seater Plaxtons 'consort', Bedford chassis coach.   £3

The Morris Oxford traveller, 'combines the comfort and performance of a saloon with the capacity of a small van', colour. £2.50

Royal blue charabanc, Bournemouth, notice the step-ladder.   £3

The Austin A40 Somerset, 'A sparkling comfortable car', No. 1003.   £3.50

(Paul G. Sheppard)

Early Cornish horse-drawn charabanc, real photo, postcard from 'Truro'.
£25

The Austin A10S saloon 'being an Austin you can depend on it', colour.   £3.50

Early horse-drawn coach full of railwaymen.
£12

3442c.c. 'D' type Jaguar with Mike Hawthorne at the wheel during the silverstone meeting May 1955. Posted to racing driver David Norton in Birmingham.   £6

Charabanc in Ilfracombe 1919, real photo.
£2.50

(Paul G. Sheppard)

The Standard Vanguard official colour postcard, Standard/Triumph. £2.50

H. Wilkinson & Son of Liverpool, tipping lorry, circa 1930. £12

Midland Red CL3 type luxury coach specially designed for cruises. £1.75

Nice photographic charabanc postcard. £3

The White Rose at Dyserth, better than average photographic charabanc postcard. £4

(Paul G. Sheppard)

E. Davies & Son, Maesllyn, delivery lorry with family and staff, published
by J. Jones.   £22

30 H.P. six cylinder Napier with good Michelin tyre advertisement, circa
1920.   £10

(Tim Ward)

His Majesty's Mail, donkey cart, photographed outside 'The Good Intent', Westbourne. £22

Sandwich & Deal horse-drawn bus full-up with passengers, real photograph.
£25

(Tim Ward)

Star Baby Cars delivery van.   £8

London Transport trolley bus on its way to Battersea, real photograph.   £5

The Standard Ten official colour postcard.
£2.50

'Jacksons Faces' Series, real photo of chara-banc in Garleston on Sea.   £2.50

Good early motor car and motor cycle, real photo postcard, well animated. £12.50

(Paul G. Sheppard)

New Hudson motor cycles with sidecars, nice photo. £7.50

E. Swallow, Hauling Contractor in G.W.R. coal yard, circa 1910.   £15

Seaside excursion open-top charabus, unidentified, real photo postcard.   £1.50

Monaco to Monte Carlo 1938, nice early coach.   £3.50

North Western coach, real photo. £3.50

(Paul G. Sheppard)

Real photograph of steam engine with winch for land draining, circa 1910.
£30

Real photograph of Walker's of Warrington wine delivery motor van, circa 1935.   £10

Benjamin Harper's licenced hawker's horse-drawn van in Gloucester, 1907, real photograph.   £22

Real photograph of a Foden steam lorry, circa 1930.   £18

Real photograph of a new style hay sweep mounted on a 1925 Irish Standard Fordson tractor.   £18

(Tim Ward)

Real photograph of W. Webb motor bus at
South Yardley, Birmingham, circa 1910.£20

The new Vauxhall 12-four, on sale at £189,
a 1939 advertisement card. £10

Real photograph of a Minerva motor cycle,
circa 1910. £6

Bailey & Turners Albion lorry advertising
daily services between Worcester and London,
circa 1950. £8.50

Real photograph of a Marshall ploughing engine belonging to Morvington
& Ray, East Harling, Norfolk, circa 1910. £35

(Tim Ward)

TRAYS

Early trays were made of wood, pewter or occasionally silver, but it was not until 'the cuppa' was taken up as the national beverage around 1750, that trays were made in any respectable quantities.

Early 18th century examples were usually japanned, though occasionally made of walnut, but later examples by such as Chippendale or Vile were of mahogany, often with high lattice work sides. The most commonly found today are those in the Hepplewhite and Sheraton styles, both of whom favoured oval mahogany trays inlaid with a shell, with vertical wooden rims and brass scroll carrying handles.

Trays from the Victorian period are, as a rule, of rectangular shape and can usually be bought quite cheaply. The exceptions are those of japanned metal decorated with domestic scenes and the superbly decorated papier mache examples.

More modern trays also have a popular following and this is definitely a good growth area.

British Rail Inter-City Sleeper tray. £1.50

1960's drinks' tray. £2

19th century papier-mache tray, stamped Clay, London, with cricketing scene. (Phillips)   £750

A painted tray by Duncan Grant, circa 1920, 35.3cm. diam.   £286

1930's oak tray with moulded edge.   £3

Regency papier-mache tray, stamped Howard, London, with gilt metal loop handles, circa 1810, 2ft.1¼in. wide.   £418

A Russian Art Nouveau rectangular pen tray, by O. Kurlyukov, 26cm. wide. (Christie's) £648

A rosewood visiting card tray of rectangular shape, 10¾in. wide. £187

A 19th century Chinese hardwood tray-top panel, having engraved brass corners, 23¾ x 32.5/8in. (Geering & Colyer) £420

Danish white metal plain circular tray, circa 1930, by Georg Jensen, 16in. diam., 68oz. (Christie's) £1,080

A papier-mache tray fixed to a folding wooden stand, 31½in. (Lawrence Fine Art) £1,540

An enamelled pub tray Dunville's Whisky. £12

George III satinwood oval tray with waved gallery and brass handles, 31in. wide. (Christie's) £2,268

A lacquered papier-mache oval tray with raised and gilt border, 29 x 24in. (Capes, Dunn & Co.) £340

TREEN

Treen is one of those collective terms which embrace a disjointed array of articles with the common factor being that they are all made of wood, and all have been produced on a lathe either in part or whole.

The majority are functional household articles, many originating in the kitchen, made from finely grained hardwoods such as yew, lignum vitae, sycamore and olivewood, which acquire a fine warm patina over the years.

Largely ignored little more than a decade ago, prices for good quality treen can now be measured in hundreds of pounds rather than tens.

Early 18th century American treen is particularly desirable and it is not unknown for a single bowl to fetch over £1,000.

A Scandinavian beechwood washing bat, dated 1842, 15in. long.   £253

An early 19th century mahogany cheese board, 10in. diam.   £264

A 19th century lignum vitae paperweight in the form of a pear, 5¼in.   £264

A late 18th/early 19th century mahogany artist's palette, 18in. long.   £38

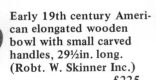

Early 19th century American elongated wooden bowl with small carved handles, 29½in. long. (Robt. W. Skinner Inc.)   £225

An 18th century yewwood double love spoon, 9in. long.   £396

A lignum vitae mortar and boxwood pestle, mortar 6½in., pestle 9½in.   £93

A 19th century mahogany egg cup stand, 7½in. high.   £418

A 19th century olivewood tobacco barrel with ring-turning and acorn finial lid, 4½in. high.   £110

TRENCH ART

Trench Art is a term embracing all those curious oddities made by our fighting troops from spent bullet and shell cases when they were not winging off mortars towards the enemy lines.

Most take the form of ashtrays or cigarette lighters, often sporting cryptic messages with names and dates, which give an added interest, while other pieces are quite ambitious and take the form of aeroplanes, tanks and field guns.

Polished brass shell cases can make a useful addition to the hearth for housing spills and fireirons as can souvenir shells complete with the business end, when buffed and polished.

Beware though, for it has been known for a First World War trophy to sit quite contentedly for decades by a roaring fire in a live condition — never assume they are harmless.

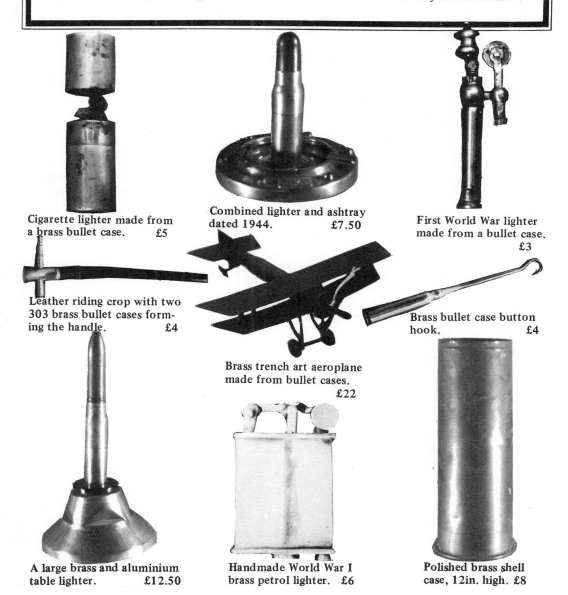

Cigarette lighter made from a brass bullet case. £5

Combined lighter and ashtray dated 1944. £7.50

First World War lighter made from a bullet case. £3

Leather riding crop with two 303 brass bullet cases forming the handle. £4

Brass bullet case button hook. £4

Brass trench art aeroplane made from bullet cases. £22

A large brass and aluminium table lighter. £12.50

Handmade World War I brass petrol lighter. £6

Polished brass shell case, 12in. high. £8

UNIFORM BUTTONS

Uniform buttons can be placed into the following general categories with a certain amount of overlap in each area. Military: Land Transport: Maritime: Hunt & Sporting Clubs: Fire Brigade & Ambulance: Police: Company & Family Livery.

Military:- After 1750 British Regiments of the Line were given numbers and this number became a feature on uniform buttons after 1767. Manufactured from silver plated or gilded metal for officers and lead or pewter for other ranks, these buttons are scarce and are prized by collectors. Values ranging between £15-£25. Between 1770-1810, Militia, Local Militia, Volunteers & Fencible Units were raised to defend Britain against the threat of French invasion. Many of these Regiments had their own design of buttons either in silver plate or gilt. Some are difficult to identify but all are sought by collectors and fetch prices between £12-£30. Irish units are particularly popular.

Many volunteer units were disbanded after 1815 but were reformed in the 1860's and with the advent of the Tunic new designs of buttons were introduced. These are generally larger than the previous Coatee type and are of a two piece or closed back design. Values range from £5-£10. Line Regiment Tunic buttons continued to be numbered until 1881 and are a favourite amongst military button collectors who try to obtain the full set of numbers from 1 to 109. Values range from £7-£12 although some of the more difficult numbers to find such as 18, 106, 107, 108 & 109 may command prices up to £25 for a mint specimen. Other military buttons collected include Line Regiment post 1881: Cavalry: Yeomanry Cavalry: Yeomanry: Imperial Yeomanry: Territorial: Officers Training Corps: Mess Waiters: Mess Dress & Blazer Buttons. Values vary from 25p.-£15.

Maritime:- Included in this category are buttons from Yacht Clubs, Boat & Rowing Clubs, Inland Waterways, Docks, Canals, Harbours, Customs, Coast Guards and Shipping Lines.

As many of the latter designs include a representation of the companies houseflag, identification may be possible by reference to books on this subject e.g. Brown's Houseflags & Funnels. Particularly sought after buttons are those of early Steam Ship companies or Clipper Ship Lines. Values vary between 25p. and £10.

Police:- Generally easy to identify for most buttons include the name of the Force on them. Prices for Kings or Queens Crown buttons rarely exceed 50p. though some of the early Victorian examples may be valued at £3-£4.

Fire Brigade & Ambulance:- Buttons in this category have gained in popularity amongst collectors over the last few years particularly items ascribed to private Fire Assurance Companies or early Town Fire Brigades. Modern Chrome plated buttons are plentiful and rarely cost more than 25p.

Transport:- Most popular transport buttons are without doubt those worn by employees of the many Railway companies that existed prior to the 1923 grouping. Prices in excess of £40 have been asked for some of the rare, small companies buttons of the mid 19th century. Bus Companies and Corporation Transport on the other hand rarely exceed 50p. in value although Tramway can sometimes fetch as much as £2-£3.

Hunt & Sporting Club:- Whilst providing a very attractive display, Hunt buttons have not proved to be particularly popular and prices rarely exceed £1 per button. Considering that many Hunts have been given up prices do not at this moment reflect the rarity of some buttons and interest in this subject may well increase in the years to come.

Company & Family Livery:- Company Livery buttons have not proved to be of great interest to collectors as many are virtually impossible to identify. Prices range between 10p.-50p. Livery buttons worn by servants of landed or titled gentry are increasing in popularity and whilst being difficult to identify with any degree of real accuracy, the designs in many cases reflect the zenith of the mid Victorian die-sinkers art and could well be collected purely for their aesthetic value. Prices vary from 50p. up to £3.

Information on the identification of many types of uniform buttons is in rather short supply as books on the subject are difficult to find and much original work is still to be done. This situation offers the collector an ideal opportunity to be 'First in the Field'.

UNIFORM BUTTONS

Cornwall County Ambulance Service, chrome plate, post 1948.   25p

Territorial Battalion of The Gordon Highlanders (blank scrolls), gilt, post 1908. £6

Staffordshire Militia, white metal, circa 1860.   £8

Royal|Scots Fusiliers, gilt, 1881-1901.   £4

Black Ball Line, gilt, circa 1870.   £5

15th Foot, gilt, 1855-81.   £9

Parachute Regiment, gilt, 1942-51.   £1.50

Royal Army Veterinary Corps, gilt, post 1918.   £1.50

Glasgow Imperial Yeomanry, brass, circa 1900.   £4

Huntingdonshire Cyclists Corps., gilt, circa 1914.   £6

Guards Machine Gun Regt., gilt, 1918.   £6

Motor Volunteer Corps. — white metal, 1903-1912.   £7

(Ian Scott)

UNIFORM BUTTONS

Bedfordshire Constabulary,
white metal, circa 1890. £3

Caledonia Golf Club, gilt,
circa 1905.   £2

Great Northern Railway,
brass, pre 1924.   £4

Spring Valley Hunt (U.S.A.),
gilt.   £1

Loretto School Officer's
Training Corps., gilt. £2

Leicester Yeomanry Cavalry,
Coatee, silver plate, 1850.
                         £8

Alexander, Earl of Caledon,
gilt, circa 1890.   £2

London & North Western
Railway Marine Dept., gilt,
pre 1920.   £4

Bourne & Hollingsworth
Ltd., white metal.   £1

4th Royal Irish Dragoon
Guards, gilt, 1855-1904.
                         £3

Beverley Police, white metal,
circa 1910.   £2

York & Ainsty Hunt, gilt.
                         £1

(Ian Scott)

UNIFORM BUTTONS

Midland Railway, white metal, circa 1920. £2

Brighton Police, white metal, circa 1900. £4

3rd Lanarkshire Rifle Vols., white metal, circa 1860. £7.50

Stamford School Officer's Training Corps., brass. £3

Officer's general pattern, Georgian, gilt, circa 1820. £10

Imperial Yeomanry, gilt, 1899-1902. £3

Tyzack & Brantfoots 'Well Line', gilt, circa 1890. £5

Co-operative Wholesale Socy. Fire Brigade, brass. £2

Wetherby Fire Brigade, brass, circa 1900. £5

Southern General Omnibus Co. Ltd., chrome plate, 1950's. 25p

Southern Vectis Omnibus Co., chrome plate, late 1940's. 50p

London & North Eastern Railway, brass, 1924-36. 50p

(Ian Scott)

423

UNIFORM BUTTONS

First Aid Nursing Yeomanry, brass, 1909-33.   £2

Border Otter Hounds, pearl, black inlay.   £2

Fermanagh Militia, 1795-1810, gilt.   £20

Dundee Clipper Line, gilt, circa 1880.   £5

Special Air Service, silver plate, 1940's onwards. £3

North of Europe Steam Navigation Co., gilt, circa 1850.   £10

Parsons, Earl of Rosse, gilt, circa 1890.   £2

Erskine, Earl of Buchan, gilt, circa 1900.   £2

West Yorkshire Road Car Co. Ltd., brass, circa 1935.   £1

Compania 'Peruana' De Vapores, Peru, gilt, circa 1930.   £2

The Anglo-Egyptian Bank Ltd., gilt.   £1

Duncan Dunbar, gilt, circa 1880.   £4

(Ian Scott)

VALENTINE CARDS

On St. Valentine's Eve, it was a custom for young people to meet and draw by lot, one of a number of names of persons of the opposite sex. Once two names were paired, the gentle-man was then bound to the service of his Valentine for the period of one year. This practice was adapted to form the custom we observe today; that of sending an anonymous greeting to a sweetheart. Valentine cards from about the 1850's were romantic with lash-ings of frills, lace, ribbons and flowers. Many survive, but not so many survive in perfect condition.

The Valentine postcard came into use around 1900 and, for twenty years or so, enjoyed a period of great popularity. The better examples in this category are good artist drawn, chromo litho cards by publishers such as Ettinger, Tuck, Hildesheimer, Wildt & Kray, Schwerdtfeger etc. Unfortunately, although many well known artists illustrated these cards, very few were ever signed.

True Love's Greeting, Royal Series by Max Ettinger, Series No. V90, chromo litho, embossed umbrella.
£4

Max Ettinger Series No. V125, 'Asylum for Lunatics'.   £5

'To My Love', Royal Series by Max Ettinger, printed in Germany, Series No. V87.   £3

'My Love to You', Royal Series by Max Ettinger Series No. V86, printed in Germany.   £3

'Faith, Hope and Charity', four in set, sometimes three in set. G. B. & Co. Series, embossed chromo litho with gold leaf applique. £2 each

Dove, heart and flowers, 'To My Valentine', Max Ettinger Series No. V75.
£3

(Paul G. Sheppard)

Max Ettinger Series V93, chromo embossed envelope 'My Valentine Thinks Of Me'. £4

Max Ettinger Series No. V82, chromo embossed hearts and flowers 'St. Valentine's Greeting'.   £4

Max Ettinger Royal Series No. V98, chromo embossed envelope 'A Message of True Love'.   £4.50

Max Ettinger Series Cowboys and Indians chromo embossed Royal Series No. V77, 'Wah-ha-hoo! I've found my Valentine'.   £6

Max Ettinger Royal Series No. V102, 'A Greeting of Love'.   £4

Max Ettinger Cowboys and Indians chromo embossed Royal Series No. V76, 'This is the strenuous life sure'.   £6

Max Ettinger Series chromo embossed hearts and flowers No. V83, 'My Heart's Best Gift'.   £4

Max Ettinger Series V95, chromo embossed envelope 'Fond Greeting to my Valentine'.   £4

(Paul G. Sheppard)

VALENTINE CARDS

Max Ettinger Royal Series No. V97, chromo embossed envelope 'To My Love'.　£4.50

Max Ettinger Royal Series No. V104, embossed chromo hearts and flowers 'With Love's Greeting'.　£3.50

Max Ettinger Series chromo embossed hearts and flowers No. V81, 'Love's Greeting to my Valentine'.　£4

Max Ettinger Royal Series No. V96, chromo embossed envelope 'My Valentine', 'Think of Me'.　£4.50

Max Ettinger Series V92, chromo embossed envelope 'Love's Greeting to My Valentine'.　£4

Max Ettinger Royal Series No. V100, cupid's arrow, heart, children, chromo embossed, 'To My Sweetheart'.　£4

Max Ettinger Series Cowboys and Indians, chromo embossed Royal Series No. V79, 'Heap Much Love'.　£6

Max Ettinger Series chromo embossed hearts and flowers No. V80, 'With Love's Greeting'.　£4

(Paul G. Sheppard)

Royal Series by Max Ettinger Series No. V85, chromo litho, embossed, 'To the one I love'. £3

'Fortune' card, Fortune Series No. 37 by J. Marks, New York, embossed, circa 1910. £3

'To the one I love', Royal Series by Max Ettinger Series No. V91, chromo litho embossed. £4

Max Ettinger Series No. V12, 'St. Valentine Greets You and wishes to say she has noticed with pleasure how well you play' £5

American floral valentine/ romantic card, chromo embossed. £2

Max Ettinger Series No. V24, 'Oh What A Mug U.R.' £5

'My Love To You', Royal Series by Max Ettinger Series No. V88, chromo litho embossed. £4

'My Heart's Gift', Royal Series by Max Ettinger, printed in Germany, No. V84, chromo litho, embossed. £3

'To My Valentine', Royal Series by Max Ettinger Series No. V89, chromo litho, embossed, umbrella. £4

(Paul G. Sheppard)

VANITY FAIR CARICATURES

An assemblage of Vanity Fair lithographs provides both a fascinating pictorial history of the latter half of the nineteenth century and an authentic collection of great charm.

A collection of original prints also offers an opportunity for great investment potential for many are irreplaceable with plates no longer in existence.

What kind of magazine was Vanity Fair? It could best be described as a combination of three magazines; 'Town & Country' 'New Yorker' and 'Harpers Bazaar'.

Published weekly from 1869 until 1914 Vanity Fair brought to the reader the eagerly awaited details of important society functions, the comings and goings of the Royal family, great satire, news of the week and up to date information on the fashions of the day. The undisputed highlight of each issue was the caricature, in colour, of a well known personage.

These lithographs of extremely fine quality came in plate size for a single page of approximately 7.3/4in. x 12.7/8in. and double page size of approximately 19¼in. x 13¼in. and were published complete with a biography. A lithograph complete with this historical background material will have greater value as a collectors' item.

Lithographs were published in a series from one upwards and, as a very general rule of thumb, the earlier the series the better, tho' this may be influenced in some cases by the rarity of the subject and condition of the print.

Quite apart from any possible market value the vast majority of people who collect these prints do so for the pleasure they give — and I can think of no better reason.

Mr. Charles R. Darwin, No. 33, 3rd series, September 30, 1871. £65

HRH The Prince of Wales, No. 1, 5th series, November 8, 1873. £30

(J. J. Binns)

Mr. Maguire, No. 109, 4th series, March 23, 1872. £80

Mr. Charles Francis Adams, No. 126, 4th series, October 5, 1872. £35

The King of Prussia, No. 8, 3rd series, January 7, 1871. £48

Pius IX, No. 6, 2nd series. £22

(J. J. Binns)

Henri Rochefort, No. 4, 2nd series, January 22, 1870.   £40

Alfred Tennyson, No. 28, 3rd series, July 22, 1871.   £45

The Nawab Nazim of Bengal, Behar and Orissa, No. 8, 2nd series, April 16, 1870.   £85

Victor Emanuel I, No. 7, 2nd series, January 29, 1870.   £30

(J. J. Binns)

The Honourable Hamilton Fish, American Secretary of State for Foreign Affairs, No. 112, 4th series, May 18, 1872.   £80

Mr. William Powell Frith, RA, No. 63, 5th series, May 10, 1873.   £38

The Honourable Sir James Bacon, Vice Chancellor and Chief Judge of Bankruptcy, No. 6, 5th series, February 8, 1873.   £95

Lord Skelmersdale, No. 88, 3rd series, July 15, 1871.   £22

(J. J. Binns)

Mr. Horace Greeley, candidate for the Presidency of the United States, No. 118, 4th series, July 20, 1872.   £85

Sir Richard Costa, No. 47, 4th series, July 6, 1872.   £42

Sir Arthur Richard Wellesley, Duke of Wellington, KG, PC, No. 116, 4th series, June 22, 1872.   £28

The Honourable Charles Sumner, Member of the United States Senate, No. 113, 4th series, May 25, 1872.   £35

(J. J. Binns)

Abdul Aziz, Sultan of Turkey, No. 5, 1st Series, October 30, 1869.   £100

The Right Honourable William E. Gladstone, No. 14, 1st series, February 6, 1869.   £95

HRH The Duke of Edinburgh, No. 2, 6th series, January 10, 1874.   £75

Napoleon III, Emperor of the French, No. 1, 1st series, September 4, 1869.   £200

(J. J. Binns)

Viscount Bury, PC, KCMG, No. 103, 7th series, May 1, 1875.   £26

Alexander II, Emperor of Russia, No. 4, 1st series, October 16, 1869.   £60

Isabella II, Queen of Spain, No. 2, 1st series, September 18, 1869.   £85

Signor Tommaso Salvini, No. 104, 7th series, May 22, 1875.   £75

(J. J. Binns)

The Duke of Buccleuch and Queensbury, No. 137, 5th series, January 25, 1873.   £28

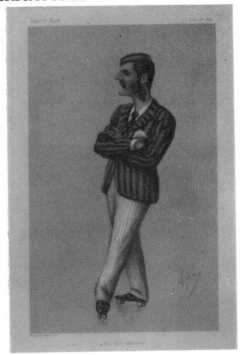

Mr. Herbert Praed, MP, No. 179, 6th series, July 18, 1874.   £80

Sir Garnet J. Wolseley, Bart., KCB, No. 83, 6th series, April 18, 1874.   £75

Mr. Henry Irving, 6th series, December 19, 1874.   £40

(J. J. Binns)

WALKING STICKS

Walking sticks have been collected for a very long time and a survey of the current market shows no decline in their popularity as collector's items.

Relevant factors to consider when starting any collection must be availability, variety and of course, space available to display the chosen objects. The walking stick seems to fulfil all of these requirements with ease.

A good collection will include examples on an international scale which in turn leads to a healthy exchange of information and objects in a field where everyone involved can indulge their own individual taste while selecting from the great variety of items available.

Some collectors will prefer walking sticks with handles of carved ivory, silver, hardstone or gold while others favour the simpler animal handles or the more humble and very individual 'country stick' which is usually made from a piece of wood selected from a hedgerow or special tree and carved according to the skill of the craftsman.

Walking sticks are often designed to serve a dual purpose, the shaft cleverly concealing the mechanism for a variety of functions. Since sticks were 'worn' as part of the 17th/18th century gentleman's dress the inclusion of such accessories as a watch, telescope or drinking flask seemed a very sensible idea. A typical example is the sword stick with a slender steel blade attached to the cane handle and concealed within the shaft of the stick.

This category has always had great appeal for collectors but anyone can join in and the chance of finding a unique interior fitting is always a possibility.

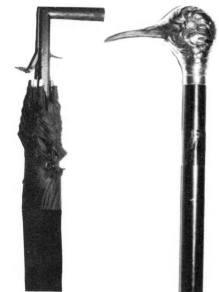

Rare percussion muzzle loading umbrella gun with Birmingham proof stamps, the brolly being ornamental, 35in. long, circa 1840. £600

Victorian lady's cane with silver snipe handle and ebonised shaft, 34in. long, circa 1880. £120

Mid 19th century carved whalebone stick, the handle carved in the form of hand grasping a scroll, 32in. long. £400

The 'Ben Akiba' camera cane invented by E. Kronke, Berlin 1903, and manufactured by A. Leh, with 24 exposures and ten spare rolls of film carried in the shaft, 35in. long. £4,000

(Michael C. German)

437

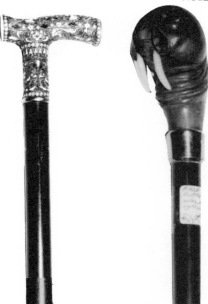

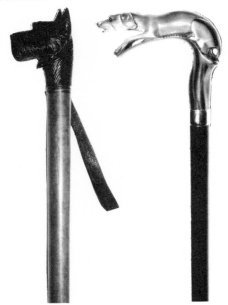

A rare silver and enamel walking stick with tau-shaped handle and ebonised shaft, 33in. long, circa 1880. £650

Rosewood cane with carved wood walrus head handle with ivory tusks and gilt metal collar, circa 1880, 35in. long. £130

A Malacca shaft walking stick with carved wood dog handle the jaw hinged for holding silk gloves, 34in. long, circa 1870. £90

English stick with rosewood shaft and horn handle carved in the form of a dog, 34in. long, circa 1860. £160

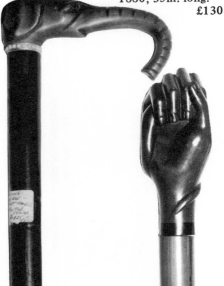

Mid 19th century cane with carved horn handle in the form of an elephant with a collar of turquoise, 35in. long. £90

Mid 19th century cane, the carved wood handle in the form of a hand. entwined with a snake, 35in. long. £86

Victorian corkscrew cane with black horn handle and silver collar, bayonet fitting, 34in. long, circa 1880. £250

A heavy natural growth country walking stick with copper cap on top, 33in. long, circa 1840. £70

(Michael C. German)

WALKING STICKS

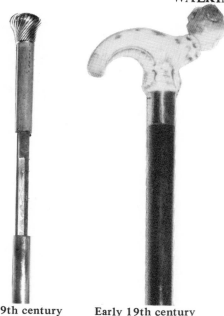

Late 19th century silver mounted sword-stick with etched blade by Swaine, London, 34in. long, circa 1900. £180

Early 19th century Malacca shaft stick with German porcelain handle, 35in. long, circa 1825. £350

English cane with a Malacca shaft and carved wood handle in the form of a dog, 34in. long, circa 1850. £90

Japanese cane with Malacca shaft and good ivory handle carved with heads of rats, circa 1860. £300

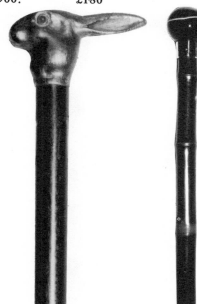

Ebonised shaft cane with a silver gilt handle in the form of a hare's head, 34in. long, dated 1912. £170

Mid 19th century bamboo shaft walking stick with 'tiger's eye' agate ball handle, 34in. long. £100

German stick with Malacca shaft and finely carved ivory handle featuring a seated lion, circa 1840. £400

A Georgian walking stick the exterior wrapped in coloured baleen with space for candlestick, candleholder and spills, 35in. long, circa 1830. £550

(Michael C. German)

WALKING STICKS

An early Victorian telescope walking stick the horn screw-off handle fitted with a compass and presentation silver band, 34in. long, circa 1850. £600

Malacca shaft cane with carved wood handle in the form of a horse's head with gilt collar, circa 1880. £90

Simple country made stick with silver collar, 33in. long, mid 19th century. £25

Bamboo shafted walking stick incorporating a horse measure and spirit level armpiece, 35in. long, circa 1885. £130

Edwardian cane with duck's head handle formed of small jet beads, with silver collar dated 1910, 33in. long. £140

English country made dagger cane, the blade activated by centrifugal force through a brass trap door on top, circa 1850. £160

Walking stick with rosewood shaft and carved ivory handle in the form of a horse's head, 34in. long, circa 1865. £350

Unique English country walking stick carved overall with a foxhunt in full flight, the fox disappearing into the handle to escape the hounds, 35in. long, circa 1870. £180

(Michael C. German)

440

WALL PLAQUES

Wall plaques have never really competed against paintings for wall space but have presented an attractive alternative for interior decoration.

They cover the whole spectrum from cheap pressed brass plaques featuring 'Olde Worlde' scenes for a few pounds, to fine and rare examples by Clarice Cliff from the 1930's which can sell for many thousands of pounds.

The souvenir trade was responsible for many of the three dimensional wooden plaques featuring interior scenes and, Fairground operators produced these as well, together with coloured Plaster of Paris plaques in relief which were offered as prizes on the stalls.

Minton, Imari and Wedgwood plaques are all desirable as are the Goldscheider and Newport pottery masks.

Even the ubiquitous plaster flying ducks have now found their way back into fashion.

A 'Fantasque' circular wall plaque with the Rock of Gibraltar, circa 1931, 33.7cm. diam. (Christie's) £1,350

African copper wall plaque with rural scene, signed Musonga. £8

A Richard Garbe circular bronze plaque, 32.3cm., 1917. £198

A Goldscheider earthenware wall mask of a young woman with turquoise hair, 1920's, 24cm. £143

A large Newport pottery 'bizarre' wall mask, 1930's, 37cm. high. £330

A Goldscheider earthenware wall mask of a young woman with spiralled orange hair, 1920's, 27.5cm. £143

British made 'Olde Inn' scene in pressed brass. £8

Late 16th century German iron plaque of the Entomb-ment, 24.5 x 19cm. (Christie's) £334

'Birds and Rushes' wall plaque in brass. £6

WHISTLES

Whistles have been made since the dawn of time, but they were generally crafted from a reed or other such perishable material and have not survived.

One of the earliest known examples is of mediaeval origin and is carved from the leg bone of a swan.

Any collector today must be quite discerning for there are numerous types of whistles made in a variety of materials including gold, jet, ivory, brass, wood, silver and porcelain. Silver military whistles are sought after, especially early 18th century bosuns' whistles, as are those for the Police or Railway Officials particularly if they sport the insignia of one of the early companies.

Dog whistles is another area for collecting as are the whistles which are incorporated into some other object such as a penknife, rattle, spoon or tape measure.

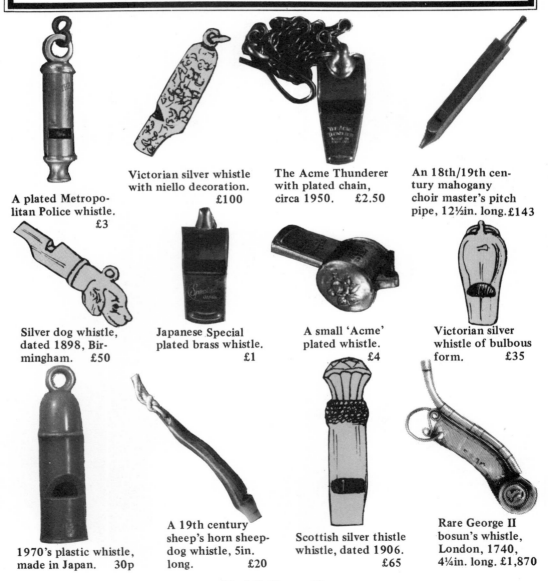

A plated Metropolitan Police whistle. £3

Victorian silver whistle with niello decoration. £100

The Acme Thunderer with plated chain, circa 1950. £2.50

An 18th/19th century mahogany choir master's pitch pipe, 12½in. long. £143

Silver dog whistle, dated 1898, Birmingham. £50

Japanese Special plated brass whistle. £1

A small 'Acme' plated whistle. £4

Victorian silver whistle of bulbous form. £35

1970's plastic whistle, made in Japan. 30p

A 19th century sheep's horn sheepdog whistle, 5in. long. £20

Scottish silver thistle whistle, dated 1906. £65

Rare George II bosun's whistle, London, 1740, 4¼in. long. £1,870

(Paul G. Sheppard)